*New*

# LOW-FAT
# FAVORITES

# New
# LOW-FAT
# FAVORITES

*Fabulous Recipes*
*from the*
*World's Healthiest*
*Cuisines*

## RUTH SPEAR

**LITTLE, BROWN AND COMPANY**

*Boston   New York   Toronto   London*

FIRST EDITION

Permissions for recipes reprinted, adapted or derived from published sources
appear on page xi.

Library of Congress Cataloging-in-Publication Data

Spear, Ruth A.

New low-fat favorites  /  Ruth Spear. — 1st ed.

p.     cm.

Includes index.

1. Cookery, American.   2. Low-fat diet — Recipes.   I. Title.

TX715.S7414  1998                                          97-41880

641.5'638 — dc21

10  9  8  7  6  5  4  3  2  1

M V - N Y

Designed by Barbara Werden

Published simultaneously in Canada by Little, Brown & Company (Canada) Limited

PRINTED IN THE UNITED STATES OF AMERICA

*For my husband, Harvey,*
*who makes every meal an occasion*

# Contents

*Part Two*
# THE RECIPES

# Acknowledgments

I'VE NEVER written a cookbook without a great supporting cast to help make it possible, and this book is no exception.

First I would like to thank Jane Goodman, who tested recipes with total focus and cheerfully shopped, chopped, cooked, stirred, and made valuable suggestions drawn from her good cooking instincts, love of food, and considerable expertise; Sonia Smith, whose enthusiasm in the kitchen often kept me going; and my husband, Harvey Spear, and my daughter, Jessica Spear Tjernberg, my final taste arbiters.

Jennifer Josephy at Little, Brown proved to be the editor of my dreams, and for that and more I give special thanks to my agent, Susan Lescher. Barbara Jatkola polished my book with her dedicated copyediting.

I am deeply grateful to Tina Papoutsakis, M.S., R.D., of the American Health Foundation, who, as nutrition consultant for this book, read the manuscript thoughtfully, made many valuable comments and suggestions, and answered my never-ending questions with the patience and thoroughness of a born teacher. Thanks also are due to the foundation's Dr. Barbara Winters, who brought us together.

I'd like to thank my former editor, Liv Blumer, who did much to enhance this book before she left publishing to take another position; Colleen Kapklein of Warner Books for her suggestions; Bruce Stark, the wizard Computer Tutor who came to my rescue many times, but especially during the dark days of a mysterious virus (the machine, not me); Dun Gifford of Oldways Preservation Trust; Ed Blonz, who took time to give valuable advice; Pada Lucentini, my authority on all things Italian; and last but certainly not least the chefs, food writers, and friends who so kindly shared recipes with me.

# Permissions

The author is grateful for permission to include the following previously copyrighted material:

"Korean Scallion Pancakes with Bean Sprout Salad" adapted from *Pancakes and Waffles* by Elizabeth Alston, published by HarperCollins Publishers. Copyright © 1993 by Elizabeth Alston. Reprinted by permission of the author.

"Yellow Rice and Black Bean Pilaf" adapted from Melanie Bernard, spokesperson of the Steel Packaging Council. Reprinted by permission of the author and the Steel Packaging Council.

"Cauliflower, Anchovies and Capers" adapted from *The Italian Pantry* by Anne Del Conte, published by HarperCollins Publishers. Copyright © 1990 by Anne Del Conte. Reprinted by permission of the author.

"Buttermilk Mashed Potatoes" from *Eating Well Magazine Recipe Rescue Cookbook*. Copyright © 1993 by Eating Well Books. Reprinted by permission of Eating Well.

"Linguini with Tomatoes and Leeks" by Christi Finch, Word of Mouth NYC. Copyright © by Christi Finch. Reprinted by permission of the author.

"Sweet Potato Soup" adapted from *Bold American Food* by Bobby Flay. Copyright © by Bobby Flay. Reprinted by permission of the author.

# Introduction

NUTRITIONALLY SPEAKING, we live in wondrous times. Every other week, it seems, we read about another discovery, insight, or observation that if properly applied may lengthen or enhance our lives. And often enough to make it commonplace, these discoveries have some dietary component. As scientists zero in on finding cures, or at least causes for many of the major diseases that afflict us, the result is a kind of nutritional Age of Enlightenment that I find thrilling and empowering.

My earlier book *Low Fat & Loving It* dealt with the basic guidelines that have emerged from today's nutritional thinking. It gave you a food philosophy and recipes for adapting it to your lifestyle in the easiest and most pleasing ways. By gradually building a repertoire of low-fat dishes you really like (and *only* ones you like), you could replace the fattier and more calorie-dense ones without really missing them.

You loved the recipes and asked for more. You also let me know what you liked (real food, without food analogues or tricky fat substitutes) and what you wanted more of (quick, main-course pasta recipes, nonmeat "centerpieces," more information on vegetable preparation). And although it wasn't a primary goal, you reported a general increase in a sense of well-being, sometimes tinged with mild astonishment, not only from enjoying the way you were eating but also for having dropped a few pounds.

Now I'd like to take you one step further. Today we not only know what eating habits can damage us, but we also have a lot more information about those that can actively keep us healthy. There's a lot to know, a lot of information to digest. Without obsessing about this or that study, what it all boils down to is this: We have more proof than ever before of the importance of a diet in which foods from plant sources predominate. And the greater the variety of these foods in your diet, the greater health insurance you derive, because eating more and varied foods from plant sources not only gives you the fiber and nutrients you need to be healthy, but also replaces a significant portion of your usual calorie- and fat-dense animal foods.

So it's time to expand your food horizons some more. I can assure you now, as I did earlier, that you won't have to give up pleasurable eating for a bland and boring diet. You will continue to balance by trading off a higher-fat item here with a low-fat one there, always drawing on foods that truly please and satisfy you. For maximum health insurance, you do need to have an expanded range of plant foods from which to choose, but you don't have to become a vegetarian unless you want to. Think of this approach as fine-tuning. Above all, think of it as a marvelous, continuing food adventure.

— RUTH SPEAR

# Part One

# FOOD AND HEALTH

# 1
## *What You Need to Know*
## *About Food*

WHEN I WAS growing up, there were a few rather basic things you needed to know about food. It was either good for you or it wasn't. Some foods could make you fat. Or constipate you. Or do the opposite. Too much of something could give you a stomachache. Carrots were good for your eyes. Fish was brain food. Spinach made you strong, at least according to your mother and Popeye (who tossed back cans of it before any physical challenge). Today nutrition is destiny. Among the possibilities: certain foods can lead to heart attacks, raise or lower your risk for or prevent certain cancers, cause or prevent osteoporosis, and in general improve or wreck your health. To confound the picture, there's at least one ancient relative in every family who broke all the rules and lived to be ninety-nine.

And if this isn't confusing enough, many people have the impression that today's nutritional recommendations are always being modified and changed. Butter is bad; margarine is okay. Margarine isn't okay because the hydrogenation process of turning an oil into something hard resembling the high-priced spread creates potentially damaging trans fats and saturated fat. (Eating foods containing saturated fat raises your cholesterol level more than eating foods containing cholesterol.) Back to butter — but not too much. Fish is good; it's low in fat. Fish is bad; it contains mercury and other unspeakable pollutants. Fiber is all; hello, oat bran. Oat bran is a scam; good-bye, oat bran. Hello again; it's good for you, but to make it work, you have to eat a lot each day. Nix shellfish; it's high in cholesterol. Whoops, that's okay here, because it's low in fat, and that's what keeps cholesterol down.

Well, here's what you really need to know. Some broad goals emerging from today's nutritional research make what we must do for health clear.

What we're after is a healthy diet. And a healthy diet isn't all that complicated. The idea is to cut down on fat, particularly saturated fat, and craft a diet you enjoy. But focusing on fat alone, as one nutritionist says, "isn't a stand-alone strategy." Crafting a healthy diet means examining not only what you might eat to excess, but also what you don't eat enough of or at all.

Another mistaken notion concerns "forbidden foods." You *can* eat everything — just not everything all the time, and some things only occasionally and in strictly limited amounts. What you'll find, though, is this: as you gradually build meals around less fatty foods and start eating well-prepared vegetables, tasty grain and bean dishes, succulent fish, and so forth, your taste for the rich, fatty stuff will diminish. Some of the fatty foods you used to love may even make you feel slightly unwell, which may be nature's way of telling you something. And many researchers believe that a diet based on fruits, vegetables, grains, and beans is the one most protective against cancer because it is likely to be not only low in fat but also high in fiber and protective vitamins, minerals, and other non-nutrient dietary components about which you will read more in Chapter 2.

Restructuring your diet takes a bit of thought and a heightened awareness of how you eat (at least in the beginning). You do it by identifying the high-fat foods you now eat, then finding lower-fat foods you really like and adding them gradually to your diet, displacing the fattier and more calorie-dense ones. I am absolutely not talking about nonfat, loaded-with-sugar cookies and the like, but real food. More complex carbohydrates, vegetables, grains, legumes, and fruits; fewer foods, in both quantity and frequency, from animal sources.

Following the guidelines does not mean that you must give up forever a food you love but that you change its importance in your life. I am suggesting not only that you lower your consumption of fat but also that you add to your diet a greater variety of healthful foods of plant origin than you are now eating, prepared in such delicious ways that, in the process, perhaps you will find some new loves. This is not about a diet, but an adventure in eating for pleasure *and* health. Not only do you build a repertoire of foods that truly please and satisfy you, but you trade off an indulgence (should you wish) so that a high-fat food here is balanced by a low-fat food there. By eating more foods from plant sources, you are also getting the fiber and nutrients you need to be healthy. You are eating well in every sense of the word. And to make maximum use of good health guidelines, there are some things you'll want to know.

### How Bad Is Fat?

If fat is so bad, I am asked from time to time, why not just eliminate it altogether? The answer is that fat is a nutrient, and we do need a certain amount.

Just because less is better doesn't mean that none is best of all. Many people have misconstrued the warnings against a high-fat diet as a blanket condemnation of any and all fat.

What we are trying to do is moderate fat intake, not eliminate it. We need some fat in our diet! Of course, fat provides a lot of calories, but it also provides nutrients called essential fatty acids, which the body cannot manufacture itself but which it needs for hormone production and healthy skin. Fat also enables the body to absorb valuable fat-soluble vitamins A, D, E, and K, which we need for good health.

One must be wary of very low fat diets, unless a real expert is holding your hand. Many sources of dietary fat are the very foods we eat as convenient, easy sources of high-quality protein, such as eggs, meat, and cheese. Although most Americans consume more protein than they need, you must keep adequate protein in mind when revamping your diet. This is especially true for women and children, as men tend to be more interested in protein-rich diets than women. In fact, women often consume too little protein, which usually means they aren't getting enough iron either, since the foods that contain high-quality iron are usually protein foods and sources of calcium as well.

When you reduce your fat intake, it's important not to go too far. To maintain a healthful lifestyle, we all need a basic level of fat in our diets. The general recommendation for fat consumption at the moment is a diet in which no more than 30 percent of calories derive from fat, with no more than one-third of those calories from saturated fat.

Many nutrition experts really believe that the most meaningful reduction is a diet in which no more than 20 percent of calories are from fat. A diet at or below this figure can be very challenging, however, especially for women. Even at 20 percent, women need to be careful to choose foods with a very high mineral and vitamin content. This is especially important for women of childbearing age, since mineral and vitamin deficiencies increase the risk of birth defects. The point is you have to be extraordinarily knowledgeable about nutrition to follow an ultra-low-fat diet. Probably the best part about very low fat diets is that most people won't stick to them for long.

Let's be clear that we are not talking about low-fat eating by consuming what one professional calls the "Entenmann's Diet": nonfat cakes, cookies, and nonfat frozen yoghurt. These foods, though almost fat free, are still extremely high in calories due to their sugar content, and because they contain little or no fiber, it is easy to eat too much of them. This amounts to a low-fat diet that is also low in fiber and lower yet in nutrients.

For the long haul, you need a diet that is comfortable, convenient, and pleasant to maintain and that includes generous amounts of a variety of fruits, vegetables, grains, and legumes — in other words, a healthy diet. There are no shortcuts.

## Children and Fat Intake

Parents must be careful not to trim so much fat from a child's diet that it becomes nutritionally unsound. I have heard of young families who get so caught up in low fat that their kids fail to thrive. Experts agree that children under two years of age should not have their fat intake restricted at all because they are growing rapidly and are more active than adults. They need fat for proper growth and development and very low fat diets can lead to growth retardation. In fact, young people can continue to grow until they are seventeen or even twenty years old.

American children, however, eat too much fat in general and especially too much saturated fat — the kind that contributes to clogged arteries, heart disease, and strokes. Health authorities agree that children over the age of two should get no more than 30 percent of their calories from fat of any type, and many experts encourage aiming for 25 percent — provided, of course, that children get adequate calories and nutrients. Even more important than limiting total fat is limiting saturated fat to 10 percent, or even 7 percent, of calories. American children now eat about one-third more than this amount of saturated fat.

## Where We Are Today

It seems that many Americans have gotten the message that our national diet is too fatty and that there is a strong connection between fat consumption (saturated fat in particular), high blood cholesterol, and heart disease. In February 1993 the government's third National Health and Nutrition Examination Survey (NHANES III) was published, which looked at the eating habits of more than thirteen thousand Americans between 1988 and 1991. Compared to the previous study (NHANES II), which collected data from a decade earlier, Americans cut their fat from 36 to 34 percent of calories and slightly lowered saturated fat intake as well.

Although this small but significant step seemed encouraging, the discomfiting flip side was that during the same period, our *total* fat intake (amount in grams) stayed the same, and we're fatter than ever. How can this be? The percentage of calories represented by fat dropped in a relative sense only because we're eating more calories each day — 231 more on average — than we did earlier.

Confusing information about the relative importance of fat and calories may be the reason. At varying times, we have been told to eat more polyun-saturated fat, increase monounsaturates, cut down on total fat, and eat as much fat as we like if it's olive oil. And no-fat foods beckon from every su-permarket aisle, making the average shopper forget all about calories, not to mention good nutrition.

I believe that if you reduce your consumption of fatty foods, especially those from animal sources, and increase your consumption of foods from plant sources (such as vegetables, grains, and fruits), your caloric intake will automatically drop because these foods tend to fill up the stomach long be-fore the calorie count can get too high. With more than nine calories per gram, fat has more than twice the number of calories (four) in a gram of car-bohydrates. A one-and-one-half-ounce bag of potato chips has as many calo-ries as a twelve-ounce baked potato. So it stands to reason that if your diet is predominantly complex carbohydrates (vegetables, grains, and fruits), you will be consuming fewer calories, not to mention getting valuable fiber and other health benefits.

## Reviewing Fat

In *Low Fat & Loving It,* I suggested that switching from butter (a saturated fat) to margarine (a polyunsaturate made from vegetable oil) was not necessarily a meaningful change. A gram of fat contains nine calories regardless of the source. Fat is fat, no matter the source, and if you want to be healthy, you limit intake across the board (although thinking is even relaxing here some-what as the health benefits of olive oil are scrutinized).

What we call "fat" is actually a class of triglyceride molecules called fatty acids — strings of carbon atoms dotted with hydrogen atoms. The amount of hydrogen is what makes the difference. The fat that predominates in butter, lard, and tropical oils is thoroughly "saturated" with hydrogen atoms, whereas the "unsaturated" fat that dominates vegetable oils carries fewer atoms.

The fat in food is classified according to which of the three types of fatty acids — saturated, monounsaturated, or polyunsaturated — predominates, but most foods contain all three in varying amounts. The more saturated fatty acids a fat contains, the harder it is at room temperature, like the fat that edges and marbleizes most meats and lard. Most saturated fats raise serum (blood) cholesterol, especially the "bad" kind — the artery-clogging low-density lipoproteins, or LDLs. Olive oil, canola oil (made from rapeseed, a member of the mustard family), and peanut and walnut oils are monounsat-urated. Soybean, sunflower, and safflower oils are polyunsaturated.

An unsaturated fat can be made firmer, and thus saturated, by a commer-cial process called hydrogenation. Remember this: if the source is vegetable and the product is relatively firm, it's hydrogenated. Thus trans fats are highest in the solid white shortening Crisco (originally created to look like lard for people who didn't want to eat a pork product) and stick margarine (created for consumers who want to fool themselves into believing they're eating butter). Here's the problem. The process of hydrogenation creates trans fatty acids or trans fats, which a study has linked to a higher heart attack risk. Some studies suggest that trans fats may be a more serious risk than saturated fats. There is a growing consensus that these fats increase LDLs, the "bad" kind of cholesterol that just gloms onto arterial walls and is not carried out of the body as are high-density lipoproteins (HDLs), or "good" cholesterol. So even though you're not eating saturated fat, the net result for your arteries may be the same.

Why not just stick to the liquid forms of polyunsaturates, such as corn oil? First, although they have been promoted for years as lowering cholesterol, they lower not just the LDLs, which we don't want, but also the HDLs, which we need. Second, polyunsaturates have been shown to cause mammary tumors in rats.

You can't assume that by not using polyunsaturated oils as a cooking medium you are avoiding them. Hydrogenated vegetable oils abound in packaged foods. That's why it is important to read nutrition labels, which describe the kinds of fat the product contains. Trans fats, however, are not required to be listed, and it is in packaged foods that most trans fats are found.

So that leaves us with monounsaturates. Although they were previously considered to have a neutral effect on serum cholesterol, it is now known that they lower LDLs but do not affect, and even may raise, HDLs, which clear fat out of the system. That is why you hear so much about the benefits of the Mediterranean diet. People living in countries along the Mediterranean, whose diet is based on olive oil, a monounsaturate, have a much lower rate of heart disease.

Okay, you say wearily, olive oil it is. But wait. You can't go hog-wild here either. The calorie content of all oils is the same: almost fourteen grams of fat in a tablespoon. A high-fat diet of any type of fat is going to provide lots of calories, frequently more than we need. This can promote obesity, which is linked with a heightened risk of heart disease and some types of cancer, as well as other ills associated with being overweight. So my message is still the same: get accustomed to moderation and eating more low-fat foods by raising your consumption of vegetables, fruits, and grains, which you need for many other reasons. Be sparing in your use of oil and fat as a cooking medium. You have everything to gain — except weight!

# 2
# *Preventing Illness Starts in the Kitchen*

A GROWING BODY OF evidence indicates that eating fruits and vegetables may help prevent certain degenerative disorders such as cancer and heart disease. It is no secret that those people who eat a largely vegetarian diet not only are long-lived but also do not suffer from many of the diseases that are major killers in this country. Only recently, however, has it been possible to gather laboratory data to help us understand exactly how plant foods work in protecting against chronic diseases.

Studies have shown that eating lots of vegetables and fruits can curb strokes in men and that many plant foods contain substances that may inhibit cancer. At least half a dozen studies in several countries have indicated that vegetables and fruits might protect specifically against breast cancer. It's no wonder that leading government agencies have been recommending that we include ample amounts of these foods in our diets.

The reason is going to sound like old news to you: We need plant foods for the vitamins they contain. Vitamins are necessary as chemical partners for the enzymes involved in metabolism, cell repair, and other vital body processes. Specifically, vitamins E, C, and A, along with beta-carotene plus the plant form of vitamin E, and selenium, have been under intense scientific scrutiny for their role as antioxidants, a class of chemicals that may play a key role in fighting heart disease and cancer.

## Antioxidants

Antioxidants are scavengers of particles known as free radicals, highly reactive molecules in search of a partner. These unstable molecules can damage cell integrity and, by causing injury to genes, lead to cancer. Because they are missing an electron, free radicals tend to bind with other molecules in the body. An excess of free radicals can set off a chemical chain reaction that damages cells and even interferes with their DNA. Although you can't see what free radicals do in your body, you can imagine it by observing what these rogue molecules do elsewhere, as in the rapid browning of an apple. By the same process, free radicals also can initiate the buildup of plaque in arteries. Antioxidants have the ability to "mop up" free radicals and thus prevent the damage they cause.

Free radicals are released naturally as part of your body's chemical processes and are increased by smoking, environmental toxins, and stress. Your body's own defense system contains enzymes that channel these excess free radicals into harmless substances. Although our bodies usually respond automatically to the presence of free radicals by boosting the production of antioxidant enzymes, most of us don't have sufficient reserves of these "defenders" to handle our everyday exposure to toxins and pollutants. That's where antioxidants such as vitamins E and C and beta-carotene come in. Researchers believe that these are the most potent and valuable antioxidant allies, along with lycopene and the trace mineral selenium. Fortunately, we don't have to look very far to find them.

Fruits and vegetables are excellent sources of antioxidants. Vitamins C and E are produced in plants, including edible ones, that need to protect themselves from the oxygen they produce during photosynthesis. In fact, many of the fruits and vegetables we eat are complex chemical storehouses that contain a range of different antioxidants, one of the many compelling reasons to eat a balanced and varied diet.

Antioxidant levels in our bodies may relate to many age-related diseases, such as age-related macular degeneration (AMD), a condition responsible for the loss of central vision and the leading cause of blindness in people over age sixty-five. In one study, those who ate the most carotenoids had a 43 percent lower risk of developing AMD than those who ate the least. Spinach and collard greens, which have high levels of the carotenoids lutein and zeaxanthin, were the vegetables most strongly associated with a reduction in AMD risk.

### Beta-Carotene

Beta-carotene, one of four related compounds called carotenes and a key constituent in many fruits and vegetables, continues to be the focus of major scientific research, both because it is a precursor of vitamin A and because it acts as an antioxidant. Once in the body, beta-carotene is converted into highly active forms of vitamin A, which play an important role in vision. Vitamin A also helps build bones and teeth and maintain skin, hair, gums, mu-

# SOURCES OF BETA-CAROTENE

*Although the amount of the antioxidant beta-carotene one needs to consume for the maximum protective effect against heart disease has not yet been established, experts generally recommend that you consume five to six milligrams a day. This recommendation is for food sources, not supplements. All values are for 3½ ounces of food, uncooked, unless otherwise indicated.*

| | | | |
|---|---|---|---|
| Carrots, 1⅓ carrots | 17 mg | Watercress, 2 cups | 3 mg |
| Sweet potato, ¾ potato | 12 mg | Hubbard squash, 1 cup | 3 mg |
| Pumpkin, 1 cup | 8 mg | Pepper, sweet red, 1 cup | 3 mg |
| Dandelion greens, 2–3 cups | 8 mg | Apricots, 3 fresh | 2 mg |
| Peppers, hot red, 2 peppers | 6 mg | Cantaloupe, ⅔ cup | 2 mg |
| Turnip greens, 2–3 cups | 5 mg | Swiss chard, 2–3 cups | 2 mg |
| Kale, 2–3 cups | 5 mg | Collard greens, 2–3 cups | 2 mg |
| Butternut squash, 1 cup | 5 mg | Romaine lettuce, 2 cups | 2 mg |
| Beet greens, 2–3 cups | 4 mg | Chicory, 2 cups | 2 mg |
| Spinach, 2 cups | 4 mg | Mango, ½ mango | 2 mg |
| Arugula, 2 cups | 4 mg | Broccoli, 1 cup | 1 mg |
| Lamb's lettuce, 2 cups | 4 mg | Brussels sprouts, 1 cup | 1 mg |
| Mustard greens, 2–3 cups | 3 mg | | |

*Source: University of California at Berkeley Wellness Letter* and the National Cancer Institute Beta-Carotene Database.

cous membranes, and nerve cell sheathing. Studies have shown that when this hardworking carotene turns into one vitamin A compound, it fights the free radical damage that causes cancer and heart disease.

Preformed vitamin A is available to us in animal foods such as liver, cheese, butter, and eggs, but these foods are high in cholesterol, saturated fat, or both, and their consumption should be limited. Chalk up another reason to seek out plant foods.

Beta-carotene is found in cruciferous vegetables — deep orange, green, and yellow vegetables and fruits. Carrots and sweet potatoes top the list (see the box above). Pumpkin, also right up there at the top, deserves a more prominent place in our food pantheon than simply as a pie filling. Other good sources of beta-carotene are spinach, kale, chard, peaches, and cantaloupe, as well as dried apricots and winter squash, all of which provide fiber and other important vitamins and minerals as well.

Yet with all these splendid choices, a U.S. Department of Agriculture (USDA) food intake survey shows that, on the average, the foods Americans eat provide only about 1.5 milligrams of beta-carotene a day — or 25 to 30 percent of the amount recommended.

It may take years for scientists to develop final answers to questions about the role of beta-carotene in human health. And sometimes research throws us a curve. Thus far, in three large human studies, researchers have found that beta-carotene supplements produce no apparent benefits to participants. But this has not diminished scientific belief in the value of plant food consumption. Many experts now believe that the observed protection against cancer and other diseases given by foods rich in beta-carotene may arise from other nutrients that these fruits and vegetables contain, either alone or in combination with beta-carotene. Or perhaps supplements simply cannot do what a natural diet rich in these compounds does.

Vitamin supplements do not provide the additional health benefits that are derived from eating a variety of fruits and vegetables. And remember that some of these foods are good sources of other nutrients as well, such as folacin, potassium, and calcium. In fact, according to one large and careful study, vitamin supplements were found to be no guard against diseases and may even do actual harm. Since fruits and vegetables also promote a healthy digestive tract, why not try to develop an eating repertoire of foods you like that are good for you?

## Phytochemicals

In addition to beta-carotene, there are hundreds, perhaps thousands, of little-known compounds found in fruits, vegetables, and grains that could become the vitamins of the future. Called phytochemicals (from the Greek *phyton*, meaning "plant"), they may have some medicinal properties, including the ability to inhibit tumor growth.

They work in different ways. *Sulforaphane*, which belongs to a class of chemicals called *isothyiocyanates*, is thought to protect by jump-starting the body's output of an enzyme that detoxifies carcinogens and helps to flush them from the body. Scientists have found new proof that this compound, isolated from broccoli, blocks the growth of tumors in rats treated with a cancer-causing toxin. Another group of phytochemicals called *indole 3-carbinols* might affect the role of estrogen in the etiology of breast cancer. *Isoflavones*, found in soybeans, may reduce estrogen-related cancers in women. *Limonene*, the most potent of the *coumarins*, found in citrus fruits such as lemons and oranges, produces enzymes that seem to slow tumor growth. (See the box on page 13.)

### Lycopene

Health benefits continue to emerge as scientists examine the lesser-known phytochemicals as well. One little understood carotenoid, lycopene (the nu-

# PHYTOCHEMICALS

*These compounds fight cancer in a number of different ways. This is not a comprehensive list and reflects only some of the phytochemicals more widely studied to date.*

| Phytochemical | Source | Action |
|---|---|---|
| Allyl sulfides | Garlic, onions, chives, leeks | Initiate production of enzymes that may help dispose of potential carcinogens |
| Bioflavenoids | Fruits, oregano, spices, tea, vegetables, wine | Antioxidant action; may reduce cancer risk |
| Capsaicin | Hot peppers | Regulates blood clotting, which may reduce risk of fatal clots in heart disease |
| Genistein | Soy products | Helps block estrogen; may play a role in preventing breast cancer |
| Indoles | Cruciferous vegetables* | Stimulate enzymes that make the hormone estrogen less effective |
| Isothyiocyanates | Dark green vegetables | Trigger the formation of an enzyme that may block carcinogens from damaging a cell's DNA |
| Limonene | Peels of citrus fruits | Initiates production of enzymes that may help dispose of potential carcinogens |
| Lycopene | Tomatoes, some other fruits | A potent antioxidant; may protect against colon, prostate, and bladder cancers |
| Protease inhibitors | Soybeans, dried beans | Suppress production of enzymes in cancer cells, which may slow tumor growth |
| Sulforaphane | Cruciferous vegetables* | Triggers the formation of an enzyme that may block carcinogens from damaging a cell's DNA |

*Bok choy, broccoli, brussels sprouts, cabbage, cauliflower, collards, kale, kohlrabi, mustard greens, rutabagas, turnip greens, turnips.

trient responsible for reddening tomatoes), appears to be one of these. Although studies are preliminary, they are promising. Tomato consumption has been found to be associated with a reduced risk of cancers of the digestive tract, prostate, and breast. Lycopene, the most abundant carotenoid in human blood and tissues, also is an antioxidant, more potent than beta-carotene.

Tomatoes (and tomato products) are the only major dietary source of lycopene, one of five hundred carotenoids found in plants. Watermelon and pink grapefruit are the only other commonly eaten foods known to contain a significant amount of lycopene, though far less than tomatoes. Scientists feel that since lycopene is a fat-soluble substance, tomatoes must be consumed with a little fat, such as vegetable oil or cheese, to effect absorption. Although you will benefit from eating tomatoes raw or cooked, cooking them actually enhances lycopene availability by breaking down fibrous cell walls. So the processed tomato products we so love — ketchup, salsas, canned tomatoes for sauces — are actually good for us.

### Selenium

Until recently feared for its toxicity, selenium, a trace mineral, has at last joined the list of nutrients considered essential for human health. Selenium is important because it works in concert with vitamin E to protect cell membranes from oxidative damage. Selenium also helps regulate various metabolic processes and the utilization of vitamin E.

Needed only in trace amounts, selenium tends to be richest in foods high in protein. The main sources are meats, poultry, fish, cereals, and other grains. Brazil nuts, especially those in their shells, are a super source: two nuts a day can more than meet the daily requirement of selenium (an item that might be of interest to vegetarians who do not eat fish, another excellent source).

The National Academy of Sciences' Food and Nutrition Board recommends a daily dietary intake of seventy micrograms of selenium for adults — about the amount you would get from half a tuna sandwich. A daily intake of between fifty and two hundred micrograms is considered safe and adequate by the board. In the United States and Canada, most people get enough selenium in their food to satisfy current recommendations. Most researchers feel that it is premature to start taking selenium supplements, although investigation into supplements continues. Most experts feel that selenium supplements should not be given to children.

### The Brassicas

Broccoli — a member of the *Brassica* genus, belonging to the cruciferous family of vegetables, which includes cauliflower, brussels sprouts, cabbages, and leafy, slightly bitter greens such as collards and broccoli rabe — is as good for you as it's been touted to be. Broccoli and family all contain sulforaphane, a compound that is not destroyed by cooking or microwaving.

## Soybeans

Soybeans and foods made from them contain all the amino acids that make high-quality protein and are a valuable alternative to meat in Asian and vegetarian diets. Along with fish, vegetables, noodles, and rice, soybean foods are a staple of the Japanese diet, which many experts believe plays a key role in that country's low rate of heart disease. And now there is increasing evidence that soybeans themselves may contain potent substances that can actually help fight heart disease and even certain types of cancer.

Dozens of studies have shown that regular consumption of soy foods can lower blood cholesterol levels. A meta-analysis of thirty-eight studies analyzing the effect of soy protein on cholesterol showed that the consumption of soy protein rather than animal protein significantly decreased serum (blood) concentrations of total cholesterol, artery-clogging LDL cholesterol, and triglycerides. HDL cholesterol was unaffected or slightly increased. These findings may mean that soy could be one of the most potent cholesterol-lowering dietary factors yet discovered.

Besides keeping blood cholesterol down, there is some evidence that the phytoestrogens, or plant estrogens, in soy protein might help ease night sweats, mood swings, and other discomforts of menopause. Preliminary research also suggests that estrogens in soy foods may help prevent bone loss by inhibiting bone resorption — the process by which calcium is pulled from the bones and into the bloodstream. Some researchers have suggested that such evidence may help explain the low rate of osteoporosis in Asian countries, where soy products are a much bigger part of the diet and high-calcium dairy foods are largely absent.

Soybeans also are being investigated for their cancer-preventing effects. One compound, genistein, has an antiestrogenic effect similar to that of tamoxifen, a drug that plays a major role in preventing breast cancer recurrence and may prevent the disease in high-risk women. A large body of epidemiological evidence suggests that people with diets high in soybean content have very low rates of cancers of the breast, prostate, and colon. Studies in China and Japan comparing people eating different amounts of soy support the cancer prevention theory. There is also evidence that soy is rich in compounds that block the development of new blood vessels, without which tumors cannot grow or spread to other sites of the body.

Food products made from soybeans include tofu (bean curd), made from ground cooked soybeans and water; tempeh, a cultured soybean product like tofu but not as bland; and miso, a fermented soybean paste. Soy milk can be used as a milk replacement in blended shakes.

Tofu, an undeniable bland food, has not become a part of our pan-Asian food scene the way, say, sushi has. Even the texture is off-putting to many Americans. It does, however, have the chameleon-like advantage of tasting like whatever it's cooked with, as in Tofu with Watercress (page 190) or Ma Po's Tofu (page 191). If you wish to add soy to your diet, tofu is probably the easiest way to do it. For types of tofu available, see the Appendix.

Miso, a basic flavoring in much of Japanese cooking, is used as a table condiment and in sauces, soups, marinades, dips, and main dishes. It is easily digested and extremely nutritious, rich in B vitamins and protein.

No researcher has come up with an optimum amount of dietary soy, but it is thought that even a relatively small amount — one-half cup of tofu or a glass of soy milk a day — seems to be enough to confer benefits. Following are some easy ways to increase soy intake.

Stir a tablespoon of miso paste into a pilaf.

Use cubed tofu to lend a meaty quality to vegetarian dishes.

Add tofu cubes to stir-fries.

Crumble tofu into a meat loaf mixture.

Mix tofu with peanut butter in a peanut butter and jelly sandwich.

Puree tofu in a blender and add to soups for a creamy texture.

Add 2 tablespoons of soy protein isolate powder (available in health food stores) to smoothies and other blended drinks (see page 279).

Make a creamy salad dressing with miso paste.

Whip soft tofu and combine it with minced chives or scallions as an alternative to cream cheese.

Toss small cubes of firm tofu with chopped chives or scallions and a little lemon juice and use as a garnish for a clear broth.

Use firm or extra-firm tofu instead of meat in chili.

Replace cheese in lasagna and enchiladas with tofu.

Add soy milk to breakfast cereal.

## Garlic

For thousands of years, garlic has been thought to have properties commensurate with its powerful aroma, which include everything from curing the common cold to warding off vampires. An Egyptian papyrus dating to 2500 B.C. lists it as a cure for twenty-two ailments. The Roman naturalist Pliny noted sixty-one uses, including driving away scorpions and disinfecting dog bites. Louis Pasteur first documented that garlic kills bacteria in 1858.

Scientific efforts to separate fact from folklore have turned up some more interesting possibilities. It's already well documented that eating a clove or two of garlic a day can reduce blood pressure. Other studies have indicated that garlic can inhibit blood clots and ease asthma. Researchers are zeroing in on compounds in garlic that can inhibit the growth of tumors in rats.

But garlic's biggest turnoff may not be to vampires but to cholesterol. Preliminary studies hint that garlic seems to inhibit the production of cholesterol in the liver and may help lower LDLs ("bad" cholesterol) and raise HDLs (the "good" kind).

Garlic's pungent aroma comes from the chemical allicin, which research has shown can inhibit the growth of or kill about two dozen kinds of bacteria, including staphylococcus and salmonella. If allicin is destroyed in cooking or processing, the bacteria-fighting capacity is lost.

Medicinal claims notwithstanding, from my point of view garlic is of great value in low-fat cooking for its flavor and ability to enhance the flavor of other ingredients. In this book, garlic is used in many recipes, especially in its roasted form, which renders it sweet and mild, yet concentrates the flavor. If you need further persuading, the bulb is also a good source of vitamin C and contains sulfur compounds and trace minerals such as iron. And one clove of garlic has only four calories!

### Olive Oil

Olive oil has become the oil of choice because of its low saturated fat content and because, as a monounsaturate, it is thought to protect against heart disease by reducing LDLs. This occurs without lowering HDLs, which is a drawback of polyunsaturated oils.

The benefits of olive oil do not end there. A recent survey in Greece revealed that along with eating lots of fruits and vegetables, consuming olive oil seems to lower the risk of breast cancer. The apparently protective effect of olive oil was mainly found among women past menopause, while the protection from fruits and vegetables was found among women of all ages. Dr. Dimitri Trichopoulos, an epidemiologist at Harvard and a coauthor of the study, has said that "American women might actually experience as much as a 50 percent reduction in breast cancer risk" if they consumed more olive oil in place of other fats.

# 3

# *Protein, Calcium, and Sodium: The Nutrients We Are Most Concerned About*

### Protein

PROTEIN IS undeniably a major player in our body's life-support system. It helps maintain fluid balance, make antibodies to fight foreign organisms such as viruses, and move other nutrients into and out of cells to maintain the balance needed to allow impulses to travel along nerve pathways. Among its many roles, protein helps blood to clot, creates scar tissue when needed, makes the visual pigment that allows us to see, and plays a role in creating new cells when old ones die, just to mention a few of the vital functions it helps the body perform.

And amazingly, although it is such a vital workhorse, to ensure an adequate supply, only 10 to 15 percent of one's calories need come from this nutrient. Nevertheless, the American diet is enormously protein-heavy. We are obsessed with it and eat too much of it. Although excess protein is not a danger to health, it doesn't do us any particular good either, especially since protein often travels in bad company: the usual animal sources, such as meat, poultry, and dairy products, are loaded with fat. One big benefit of making an effort to get the major portion of your protein from plant sources is that you will be consuming a lot less fat. It is interesting to note that earlier in this century, when Americans obtained half their protein from animal sources and half from plant foods, they were eating less fat than they are today, when two-thirds of the protein in the average diet comes from animal foods and one-third from plants.

Plant sources of the amino acids that make up protein are just as good as animal sources, but not all are found together in one food, as they are in meat, for example. This is why a varied diet is important. Even a total vegetarian diet, unless poorly planned or concentrating too much on one kind of food, will provide amino acids that complement each other in a way that equals complete protein, as high in quality as that from animal sources.

### How Much Protein Do I Need?

You really don't have to know this, since most of us get more than we need without trying. *The Tufts University Diet and Nutrition Letter** reports that even American vegetarians consume at least 100 grams of protein a day. In case you're curious, however, your recommended daily allowance (RDA) of protein is computed by multiplying your weight by 0.36. Example: My weight hovers around 120. That means 43 grams of protein daily will keep me perking along ($120 \times 0.36 = 43$). Obviously, this requirement pertains to normally healthy adults and does not apply to those with metabolic disorders, children, or pregnant or breast-feeding women, all of whom have special needs that should be monitored by appropriate medical specialists.

I find that my 20 percent fat diet, in which the biggest chunk of calories (say, 55 to 60 percent) comes from a variety of complex carbohydrates, with fat supplying the remainder, automatically takes care of my protein needs. Without making any particular effort to do so, I get more than enough protein from grains, vegetables, fish and shellfish, and a few animal sources such as chicken, skim milk, small amounts of cheese, eggs (mostly egg whites), and very occasionally, meat.

### Complementarity

There are nine essential amino acids that the body is unable to make that therefore must be obtained from the foods we eat. In reducing one's intake of flesh foods and dairy products, and hence the high-quality protein they contain, it is useful to know about complementarity — the several food groups that complement each other to provide complete protein. These groups include beans of any kind; grains, such as wheat, corn, rice, and oats; and legumes, such as peas, lentils, nuts, and seeds. Any two foods from these groups, in combination, provide complete protein. A simple example of complete protein from plant sources is a peanut butter sandwich (legume) on whole wheat bread (grain); rice with beans is another example. These combinations do not have to take place in the same meal as was once thought; the same day or over a two-day period is fine. Supplemented by low-fat dairy products, a diet based on these food groups is a reasonable and healthy way to eat.

Of course, animal sources of protein are often richer in essential vitamins and minerals than plant foods, so when you're constructing a high-plant-

---

* Name recently changed to *The Tufts University Health and Nutrition Letter.*

food, low-animal-food diet, you need to be careful about including foods varied enough to ensure adequate intake of iron, calcium, and zinc. It's eminently doable, as witnessed by the legions of vegetarians who eat dairy products and eggs but no other animal protein.

The real downside of the American protein mania is that when we fill up on the animal sources of the nutrient, we don't leave room for the plant foods — the vegetables, legumes, grains, and fruits that our bodies require for maximum health. So consume protein in moderation — no more than 15 percent of your daily calories. Try to abandon the notion that dinner is incomplete without meat, and investigate the other sources of protein that do not come packaged with fat and yet are filling and utterly satisfying at meals.

There is one small health risk associated with consuming excess protein. Heavy protein excretion can put a strain on our kidneys, and some studies have shown that protein binds with calcium in the body, causing this mineral to be excreted as well and heightening osteoporosis concerns. In fact, osteoporosis is largely a disease of industrialized Western countries, where a large amount of protein from animal sources is routinely consumed. Consider this: New Zealand, where eating meat daily is a religion, has the highest rate of hip fractures in the world. Doesn't that tell you something?

## Calcium

Calcium is not only a building block for our bones, nails, and teeth, but it is also vital to muscle contraction and relaxation, including heart muscles and those in the walls of our blood vessels and intestinal tract.

Government surveys show that most Americans, particularly women, don't meet their calcium needs. In June 1994 a panel of thirty-two experts examined calcium intake in the United States (largely because of concerns about osteoporosis). They concluded that the then-current recommended daily allowance of this important mineral was inadequate for teenagers, men of middle age and younger, and all women, and they recommended increased consumption for these groups. A new set of recommended daily allowances (RDAs) was issued for calcium and has since become obsolete, as new recommendations for each nutrient group, not just calcium, are being issued by the National Academy of Sciences with the intent of optimizing health rather than merely preventing nutritional deficiencies. The latest recommendation for calcium (there eventually will be DRIs for all nutrients) is that adult men and women, nineteen to fifty, consume 1,000 milligrams daily and those fifty-one and older, 1,200 milligrams daily, with an upper limit of 2,500 milligrams a day.

These levels of calcium intake are necessary in part, say the experts, because of the excessive amounts of protein and sodium in the average American diet. Protein and sodium leach calcium from the body, and the calcium is then excreted in urine. In fact, an individual's daily calcium requirement increases in direct proportion to the amount of protein and sodium in his or her diet.

### Osteoporosis

Bone mass plummets after menopause, which can set women up for osteoporosis, a disorder in which the bones, because of their lost density, become brittle and fracture easily. Many women take estrogen replacement therapy after menopause to slow this process. Osteoporosis affects one in two women and, surprisingly, one in five men and can develop in the early forties. It is the second most common skeletal disorder in the world after osteoarthritis.

Osteoporosis can be prevented by getting enough calcium, especially before age thirty, but even in this milk-drinking, dairy-product-loving country, this is not as simple as it would seem. Both men and women start to lose calcium in their thirties, a loss that increases markedly for women during and after menopause. Although the losses cannot be replaced, continued consumption of calcium throughout one's life can prevent even greater loss.

Adequate calcium is as important for young girls as it is for older women, since young girls are building the bone structure that has to get them through life, even though bone mass is continually replaced.

### Sources of Calcium

According to the experts, the ideal way to get calcium in your diet is through food: skim milk, low-fat or nonfat yoghurt, and green leafy vegetables such as broccoli and kale. Dr. Paul Saltman, professor of biology at the University of California–San Diego, says yoghurt is the best source of dietary calcium, with 100 milligrams per cup more than the same amount of milk. What milk does have over yoghurt is vitamin D (the so-called sunshine vitamin, which serves to regulate calcium and phosphate in our bodies). You can get around this, however, by adding yoghurt instead of milk to a breakfast cereal fortified with vitamin D. Yoghurt Cheese (page 260) — yoghurt made double-thick by allowing the whey to drip out — has 25 to 35 milligrams of calcium in one tablespoon.

If you don't get all the calcium you need from your diet, calcium-fortified foods and calcium supplements are helpful in filling the gap so that you can reach your calcium requirement each day.

It should be noted that foods high in dietary fiber, fat, phytic acid (found in wheat bran), and phosphates (found in brown rice) have been found to decrease calcium absorption. So if you are a vegetarian or you eat a lot of high-fiber foods, you may need to increase your overall intake of calcium. The good news, especially for vegetarians, is that the calcium in fortified foods, such as fruit juices and cereals, appears to be absorbed as readily as that in milk.

Which brings us to dairy products. Although these products seem to be an easy way to get enough calcium, milk, cheese, and other dairy products are usually fat-dense. With the advent of low-fat and nonfat dairy products, including nonfat yoghurt, reduced-fat and nonfat sour cream, and skim milk, however, this ceases to be a problem. People who are unable to consume dairy products can use calcium-rich lactose-free products and lactase enzyme pills.

Calcium also is available in leafy green vegetables such as broccoli and Swiss chard, but you would have to eat an unseemly amount daily to get anywhere near the current recommended allowance. Although cooked spinach contains 139 milligrams of calcium per one-half cup, the calcium may not be absorbed at a level high enough to confer benefit. (In one test, it was learned that only 5 percent was absorbed.) That leaves calcium supplements. But the more calcium you take in, the more you can lose if you do not trim your protein and sodium intake, so it is a good idea to reexamine the amount of protein and sodium in your diet.

### Calcium Interaction

Besides protein and sodium, several other substances found in foods can interfere with the body's ability to use calcium. The most common of these are oxalates and phytates. Foods high in oxalates include spinach, rhubarb, beet greens, and almonds. Legumes, such as pinto beans, navy beans, and peas, are high in phytates. The calcium in legumes, for example, is only half as available as the calcium in milk. That doesn't mean you shouldn't eat them, for they have many other benefits, but you shouldn't regard them as a major source of calcium. And to derive the maximum benefit from the calcium-rich foods you do eat, you should not consume these foods at the same time you consume foods high in oxalates and phytates. If you do wish to eat foods from these categories, eat them one hour before or two hours after you eat calcium-rich foods.

### How to Take Calcium

Your body can best handle about 500 milligrams of calcium at any one time, whether from foods or supplements. Therefore, consume your calcium-rich foods and/or supplements in smaller doses throughout the day, preferably with a meal. Because the body requires calcium 24 hours a day, some experts suggest consuming a calcium-rich food such as yoghurt, a hot drink such as cocoa, or a calcium supplement at bedtime to provide a calcium source throughout the night. As a bonus, milk supplies you with tryptophan, which is a precursor of serotonin, a neurotransmitter associated with good sleep.

## Sodium

For many years, there was a great deal of emphasis on salt as the culprit in high blood pressure. Mindful that the chances of developing serious health problems increase as blood pressure increases, attention to salt consumption intensified about a decade ago, when studies showed that low blood pressure levels were found in cultures where salt intake was very low.

Although some people do need to watch their salt intake, such as those suffering from heart failure, kidney or liver dysfunction, or salt-sensitive hypertension, in 1989 a large epidemiological study at the London School of Hygiene and Tropical Medicine found that sodium intake had nothing to do with high blood pressure for most people. In fact, in China, where sodium intake is greater than anywhere else in the world, average blood pressure is a normal 119/71. However, medical authorities do acknowledge that about half of all people with hypertension seem to be sensitive to sodium, and when they reduce its intake, their blood pressure drops. According to the American Heart Association, sodium also holds excess fluid in the body, which puts an added burden on the heart.

Is it prudent, then, to watch salt intake even if you have no medical problems associated with it? Although there is some disagreement over the universal recommendation that everyone limit dietary sodium, every major health authority, including the National Heart, Lung and Blood Institute, the American Heart Association, and the National Academy of Sciences' National Research Council, agrees that all healthy people should cut back on salt to reduce their risk of high blood pressure.

One researcher contends that the amount of salt people prefer in foods is determined by the levels they are exposed to, and there's no question that Americans have a taste for salt. This is probably influenced by our eating habits. As much as 80 percent of the salt we consume comes from processed foods, a particularly American phenomenon. For example, frozen entrées, including breaded meats and fish, usually contain much more sodium than their fresh counterparts, as do canned soups.

We all need a little sodium in our diets to maintain proper fluid balance. The minimum daily requirement of sodium for most adults is about 500 milligrams, a level that can be acquired without thinking about it, since small amounts of the mineral are present in a wide variety of foods, including many vegetables. About 75 percent of our salt supply is added by food manufacturers, with another 15 percent added at the stove or table. The government recommends that the maximum daily salt intake not exceed 2,400 milligrams. The average American consumes more than twice that.

One adverse effect of excess sodium is the leaching of the important nutrient calcium from our bodies. In this context, one should remember that many carbonated beverages are high not only in caffeine but in sodium as well.

### How Not to Be a Salt Freak

I'm always amazed when I see people salt food routinely at the table before even tasting it. How significant is that shake of the saltshaker? Try this: with about as many shaking motions as you would use over a plate of food, shake out some salt over an empty plate, then collect and measure it. If you used about one-eighth of a teaspoon, that's about 250 milligrams of salt that you don't need. If you're used to salting food this way, try halving the amount you use.

Another thing you can do to lower your salt intake is to take the saltshaker off the table. And whenever possible, avoid processed foods and canned soups and foods. They are usually full of salt unless the label specifically states otherwise.

Prepare fresh foods with a wide variety of seasonings that can easily replace salt as a flavor booster, and if you're used to salty foods, try halving the amount of salt you use at the same time. Consider a dash of cayenne pepper; a squeeze of lemon juice; aromatics such as fresh garlic, yellow onions, and red onions; a tablespoon of freshly grated Parmesan cheese, which has only 1.5 grams of fat per tablespoon; and, of course, herbs and spices such as fresh cilantro, marjoram, rosemary, tarragon, basil, cumin, or oregano, as well as fresh or powdered chili peppers or a dash of red pepper flakes or Tabasco. These also will help you to conquer your fat addiction at the same time.

You also might try crushing dried herbs and spices with a mortar and pestle before using them in cooking. Crushing releases their full flavor and aroma. Toasting whole spices such as cumin seeds in an ungreased skillet also enhances their flavor, bringing out the aroma and adding a slight, pleasant smokiness.

Be patient: kicking a salt addiction takes an eight- to twelve-week adjustment period. Fortunately, the taste for salt can be unlearned. You'd be surprised how addictive salt is, but it's an addiction you can break. When your taste buds recover, you'll discover the delightful natural flavors of, say, fresh vegetables, and you'll stop missing salt. You may even end up, as I have, finding salty foods downright unpleasant.

# 4

# *The Best Diet for You from the World's Best Diets*

MOST OF THE evidence we have linking diet to the prevention of chronic diseases comes from epidemiological studies — large-scale surveys of what is eaten by certain world populations and the prevalence of various diseases among them. Based on these studies, we have been encouraged to adopt the dietary patterns of countries such as Japan and China, those of Southeast Asia, and those bordering the Mediterranean Sea.

Of these, much attention has been paid to eating habits in Italy and Greece. In a 1960 study, researchers focused on the island of Crete and found the incidence of death from heart disease to be only one-tenth that in the United States. When compared with northern European countries and the United States, cancer rates, especially for colon and breast cancers, were also much lower, a finding also noted in the rest of Greece, in southern Italy, and in Spain.

These findings, as well as those from an earlier study of Crete, sparked the interest of a small group of nutrition experts, and their insights (especially those of Dr. Ancel Keys, who began his pioneering study of diet and heart disease by looking at what Italians were eating at the start of the 1950s) led to the formulation of the Mediterranean diet. This pattern of eating, developed by leading nutrition authorities and scholars from many countries and institutions, was intended to encourage people everywhere to eat better.

## The Mediterranean Diet

The Mediterranean diet centers on foods from plant sources: fruits, vegetables, and legumes plus breads and other grain-based foods such as pasta, rice, and polenta. People in the Mediterranean eat cheese and some meat, but not a lot. Although this diet features a relatively high fat intake — as much as 40 percent of total calories (the average American fat intake when experts began to try and modify it) — there is a big difference between it and the American diet. Much of the fat consumed in the Mediterranean comes from olive oil, a monounsaturate, in contrast with the saturated fat that predominates in the standard American diet.

The fallout from this study and others like it resulted in a bombardment of diet dos and don'ts that confused the American people as often as it enlightened them. In 1992, in an effort to simplify this massive amount of diet information and advice, the USDA came up with a diet model, in the form of a pyramid, that would express its recommendations for a diet based largely on grains, fruits, and vegetables.

There's nothing magical about the USDA Food Guide Pyramid. It's simply a visual nutrition guide for the general public, a handy way of setting forth the kind of balanced diet experts would have us eat. You can eat a lot of the foods at the bottom of the pyramid, but you should consume foods at the top in small (and presumably less frequent) amounts. At the base of the pyramid, you find bread, cereal, rice, and pasta. Fruits and vegetables come next. Dairy products, meat, fish, poultry, eggs, dry beans, and, oddly, nuts share the next, more limited level. The pyramid peaks with a small amount of fats, oils, and sweets, meant to be used sparingly.

## FOOD GUIDE PYRAMID
A Guide to Daily Food Choices

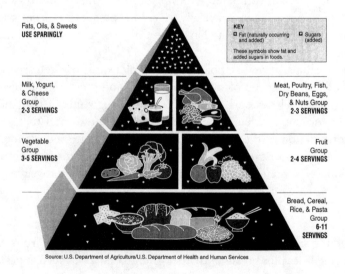

Source: U.S. Department of Agriculture/U.S. Department of Health and Human Services

*Food and Health*

Simply put, the "base" of a healthy diet is bread, cereal, rice, and pasta (six to eleven servings a day), followed by fruits (two to four servings a day) and vegetables (I would include beans here; four to six servings a day). The milk, yoghurt, and cheese group and the meat, poultry, fish, nuts, beans, and eggs group are both accorded two to three servings daily, topped with a sparing use of fats, oils, and sweets. Critics charge that meat and dairy products occupy far too prominent a place on the pyramid (made more confusing by being lumped together with nuts and beans), and that this is a result of pressure from industry groups.

While Americans were digesting this advice (and puzzling over the inclusion of beans, a healthy food, and nuts in the same category as meat), along came a second pyramid graphic, released in 1993 and based on the Mediterranean diet. Many food writers like myself, who liked the idea of being able to tell people simply to eat "low on the pyramid" but had difficulty explaining the positioning of beans, liked this second diet, even though it, too, was not without a weakness. An oil (albeit olive oil, a healthy monounsaturate) was positioned smack in the middle. Other monounsaturates, such as canola or peanut oil, may be substituted, and there is an attendant caveat that "people watching their weight should limit their oil consumption." Vegetables

## THE TRADITIONAL HEALTHY MEDITERRANEAN DIET PYRAMID

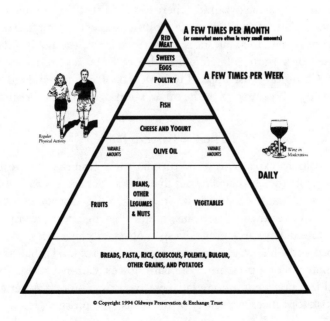

© Copyright 1994 Oldways Preservation & Exchange Trust

and fruits are properly positioned near the base of the pyramid, although some people quibble with the inclusion of nuts with beans and other legumes. Though not unhealthy if eaten in the quantities implied, nuts could theoretically contribute to obesity in susceptible people, since they are extremely high in fat and difficult to resist — a minor problem, to my mind. The Mediterranean diet pyramid also generated some criticism because the olive oil and wine industries had played a leading role in much of the research and in publicizing the findings.

These quibbles aside, what useful information is included in these recommendations? Both guides emphasize the importance of a plant-based diet; feature only small amounts of fish, poultry, and occasionally red meat; and de-emphasize meat, dairy products, and processed foods. The USDA pyramid provides specific amounts of foods to be eaten daily; the Mediterranean pyramid makes weekly and monthly recommendations as well, giving an edge to fish and poultry over red meat. Eggs, given their own niche, are to be eaten a few times a week. Wine or spirits should be consumed in moderation and with meals, and avoided wherever consumption would put an individual or others at risk. Daily exercise is also recommended.

Both diets are generally high in vitamins and minerals, though from an American point of view, the Mediterranean diet could lead to a less-than-optimum amount of calcium, since it offers only cheese and yoghurt daily and omits low-fat or nonfat milk in favor of cheese (usually a concentrated source of animal fat unless the lower-fat kinds are used). Both diets place sweets at the top of the pyramid, where it is clear that they should be kept to a minimum. Although olive oil (a healthy choice) is emphasized in the Mediterranean diet, the amount is not specified. So although this diet seems to be based on a more refined and doable concept, it also has some shortcomings. Common sense applied to both sets of recommendations, rather than slavishly following one or the other, seems to be the best course.

### The Far Eastern Diet

Not surprisingly, experts are now turning their attention to the Far East, where many of the chronic illnesses that plague our society are rare. People in Japan, even with its industrialization, have a life expectancy of seventy-nine years. By contrast, Americans, despite having access to an advanced medical system, have an average life span of seventy-five years.

In Japan and China, the average serum cholesterol level is half that of the United States; blood pressure is similarly lower. Coronary heart disease is one-third less prevalent among Japanese men than among American men, and the risk for cancer, especially of the breast and prostate, is similarly low (although this is beginning to change in areas where a more Western diet is gaining appeal).

In general, the diets of these countries are relatively low in animal products and saturated fat and high in foods from plant sources and the sea, with rice the principal grain. Although specific foods are quite different from those in healthy Western models, apart from the virtual absence of dairy products and the presence of foods derived from soybeans, Asian diets have much in common with the two Western models mentioned here. All are varied diets in which plant foods predominate and those from animal sources form a small part. By keeping these basic concepts in mind, it is not hard to build a diet with variety and taste appeal, composed of foods you really enjoy eating.

## Building a Better Diet

The following plan is based on the best intentions of those diets observed to be the healthiest for the people who consume them. Use this information to help build a diet that works for you. Note that no foods are prohibited but a number are assigned to a "seldom" category. Try to identify the foods you really like that meet the criteria mentioned. Make them part of your meal repertoire so that you look forward to each meal and never feel restricted or deprived.

### The Base of Your Diet

1. Build meals around plant foods, especially fruits and vegetables. Try to get five to nine servings a day, specifically three to five servings of vegetables and four to six servings of fruits, which may include real, not merely flavored, fruit juices. (See the next section.)

2. Eat plenty of whole grain breads and cereals, rice, pasta, and other grains, prepared in tasty ways you find satisfying. Aim for six to eleven servings daily.

3. Round out your diet with two to three servings of dairy foods daily, restricting yourself to skim or 1 percent milk, fat-free cheese, fat-free or low-fat cottage cheese, and nonfat yoghurt.

### The Rest of Your Diet

4. Eat small amounts of fish and poultry and, if you desire, red meat occasionally.

5. Choose low-fat meats and dairy products whenever possible.

6. Eat a wide variety of foods, especially fruits, grains, and vegetables.

7. Some foods should be thought of as belonging in a "seldom" category. Seldom doesn't mean never; it means once in a while. This category includes two-crust pies, pecan pie, cheesecake, cakes with frosting, doughnuts, veg-

etables with hollandaise or béarnaise sauce, fried onion rings, whole-milk products, high-fat cheese, hamburgers, cheeseburgers, grilled cheese sandwiches, sandwiches of fatty luncheon meats (such as corned beef, bologna, or salami), BLTs, hot dogs, and fatty sausages. Other specific food items that belong in this category will vary from person to person. Spareribs? Pepperoni or sausage pizza? Ice cream? You'll know what they are!

## The Five-a-Day Program

As you can see, the most important element, the one that makes all the other healthy eating considerations fall naturally into place, is increasing your consumption of plant foods. This recommendation is endorsed by all our leading health agencies, including the National Cancer Institute, which thought the goal important enough to develop a specific program, the Five-a-Day Program, to promote the consumption of fruits and vegetables.

Initially, many people have difficulty embracing the idea of eating five servings of fruits and vegetables and six to eleven servings of cereals and grains a day. But it really is not so daunting when you consider all the options available to reach this goal and keep in mind that there is a difference between a *serving* and a *portion*. What counts as a serving appears on page 31; however, a reasonable portion of a given fruit or vegetable might easily count as two servings. A dinner portion of spaghetti, for example, may count as two or three servings of pasta. You may meet the goal without even trying! For example, with a glass of juice and a sliced banana in your cereal for breakfast, you already have two of the five servings of fruit. Following are some ways you might achieve this goal.

### Breakfast

Drink a glass of pure fruit juice.
Add sliced bananas or strawberries to your cereal.*
Have a bowl of mixed fruits, such as sliced peaches, melon, and a sprinkling of raspberries or blueberries.
Top French toast or pancakes with sliced fruit or apple butter instead of syrup.

---

*A cup of nonfat yoghurt on your cereal instead of milk is an easy way to get 40 percent of your daily calcium requirement as well.

### Lunch

Have a salad or soup made of vegetables. If you have access to a microwave, you might try a baked sweet potato with one of the many kinds of salsa available in markets: zero fat, filling, and tasty.

Accompany your sandwich with raw vegetables such as cherry tomatoes or zucchini, carrot, sweet red pepper, cucumber, or celery sticks. If you eat at the office or buy a sandwich out, simply carry a plastic bag of the vegetables with you.

Take a whole fruit, such as a plum, nectarine, apple, orange, or tangerine, with you for dessert.

If you make your own sandwiches, add sprouts, cucumber, or tomato slices to your sandwich. Make a savory spread with beans, or use coleslaw made with low-fat mayonnaise, watercress, or arugula instead of or in addition to lettuce.

### Snack

Keep cut raw vegetables in water in the fridge. You're much more likely to eat them if they are already prepared when hunger strikes.

---

## WHAT COUNTS AS A SERVING?

*Fruits:* A whole fruit, such as a medium apple, banana, or orange; half a grapefruit; a melon wedge; ½ cup berries; ½ cup cooked or canned fruit; 1 cup pure fruit juice

*Vegetables:* ½ cup cooked vegetables or beans, ½ cup chopped raw vegetables, 1 cup raw leafy greens such as salad greens or spinach

*Breads, cereals, grains, baked goods:* a slice of bread, ½ hamburger bun or English muffin, a small roll or biscuit, ½ cup cooked cereal, 1 cup cold ready-to-eat cereal, ½ cup cooked rice, ½ cup pasta, 2 waffles, 3 pancakes, 4 crackers (Try to include several servings of whole grain products in this category.)

*Fish, poultry, meat, nuts, eggs:* 2½ to 3 ounces cooked meat, poultry, or seafood; 2½ ounces ham; 3 ounces tuna; 2 slices luncheon meat; 1 hot dog; 1 egg; 2 tablespoons peanut butter; ¼ cup nuts

*Dairy products:* 1 cup milk, yoghurt, ice cream, or frozen yoghurt; 1 ounce cheese; ½ cup cottage cheese

---

Choose a glass of juice — perhaps a different one than you had in the morning. Try low-sodium V-8 or tomato juice spiked with a dash of Worcestershire or hot sauce, horseradish, or lemon.

### Dinner

Choose one or two main courses each week that combine a grain and a vegetable, such as bean chili, risotto, vegetable lasagna, pasta with spicy tomato sauce, cracked-wheat pilaf, or your personal favorites in this category. Have a salad of mixed greens, perhaps with the addition of grated carrot (but watch the dressing).

### More Tips

To make it easier to eat more fruit, cut up fruit for salad to keep in the refrigerator for a snack (making use, if you can, of what's most abundant at the moment). If you have no time to shop for and cut up fruit, look for one of the many grocery stores and supermarkets that now sell prepared fruit salad. You can also buy some salad to eat at the office.

# 5
## *Getting It All Together*

### Starting Out

OUR FATTY American diet not only makes us fat, but it also places us at high risk for a number of deadly diseases. Although the "official" recommendation is a 30 percent fat diet, many experts point out that to be really protective where certain cancers are concerned, a 20 percent fat diet should be the goal. If you're new at this, I suggest starting out with a 30 percent goal, then consider getting it down lower when you see how much good food there is that is satisfying and still low in fat. Remember that low in fat doesn't mean low in flavor. Take your time, look for low-fat foods and recipes you find pleasing, and start adding them to your repertoire. Also make note of the foods you like that are high in fat and therefore in the "sometime" or "seldom" category. Keep them for treats or special occasions.

It may be that after establishing your fat gram allowance based on 30 percent of calories, you will find eating this way so delightful and satisfying that you will begin to slide toward 20 percent fat without a strain. (That is what happened to me.) Either way, you're on your way!

*Please note:* This does *not* mean that each recipe, food, or even meal must be no more than 30 percent fat. It means that of your *total* daily caloric intake, no more than 30 percent should come from fat.

Follow these steps to determine your fat gram budget.

### *Keep a food diary.*

Write down everything you eat for four or five days or a week, including one weekend. Next to each food record the number of calories and fat grams it contains. Use an inexpensive calorie counter, available in most bookstores.

You may not get every item of food, but after a few days you'll have an idea. Remember to note portion size.

### Determine your fat allowance.

This will tell you the maximum number of fat grams you can eat on a daily basis.

Add up the daily caloric totals from your food diary and divide the total by the number of days in your record. That gives you your average daily intake.

Select a fat goal. Do you want to stay with 30 percent or start with the newer recommendation, 20 percent? Accordingly, determine your allowable daily fat calories:

$$\text{The approximate number of calories consumed} \\ \text{daily} \times 0.20 = \text{the daily calories from fat}$$

For example, 1,800 calories $\times$ 0.20 = 360 calories from fat. You should consume no more than this number of calories from fat in a day.

To convert those calories into fat grams, divide by nine, since there are nine calories in a gram of fat. That's your fat budget — the maximum number of fat grams you should eat in a day. The number is not inflexible, but a goal to keep in mind.

Whatever your fat gram goal, your *saturated* fat grams should not exceed 10 percent (or, even better, 7 percent) of your total calories (divided by nine).

## Portion Control

It's very important to control not just what you eat but how much. Tripling the size of a serving can turn a low-fat food into a high-fat one.

A portion of ground beef in a hamburger, which may be six ounces cooked weight in an upscale eatery (albeit lean and broiled), contains thirty-six fat grams. You may have "spent" well over half your daily allowance on one food item — which is how you begin to rethink your eating habits. Ask yourself: Does that make sense? How badly do I want it? Is it worth it? How else could I be satisfied and "spend" fewer calories and fat?

## Dieting

Although this book is meant to point you toward a healthy overall lifestyle rather than a diet-for-weight-loss regimen, I have found, as have many others, that a low-fat lifestyle is bound to result in shedding a few pounds and keeping them off. I'll leave the weight loss goal up to you, but it is true that being overweight can be damaging to your health. It's nice to know that cutting back on fat (especially saturated fat) and eating more vegetables, grains, and fruits not only promotes good health but also creates an optimum climate in which to lose some weight.

Here's how it happens: There are nine calories in a gram of fat, more than twice as many as the four in a gram of carbohydrate. It stands to reason that if you eat a proportionately larger amount of fruits, vegetables, and grains (all carbohydrates), you are going to be eating less fat and hence fewer calories. Eating your customary amount of food, you probably will drop a few pounds. Or you can eat more and still not take in more calories. But not too much more. And what constitutes "more" also must be examined.

In the past decade, Americans have cut their fat intake from 36 percent of average daily calories to 34 percent, but they have nevertheless gained about eight pounds per person. According to a survey of 1,456 youths conducted between 1988 and 1991, one in five teenagers in the United States was overweight. This included 20 percent of boys and 22 percent of girls. In contrast, the percentage of overweight teenagers in the 1970s held steady at about 15 percent for both boys and girls. The increase in the number of overweight teenagers mirrored a similar trend in adults.

You certainly can get fat on a high-fat diet, but you also can become overweight and stay that way on a diet high in carbohydrates. How can this happen? By replacing dietary fat not with complex carbohydrates (plant foods) but with simple carbohydrates (such as starch and sugar). Please note that this does not apply to diabetics, for whom carbohydrates can cause an overproduction of insulin. This is for dieters who mistakenly assume that "nonfat" means "nonfattening." Just because a food is fat free doesn't mean you can eat as much as you want. And that goes for large quantities of pasta as well, even though pasta, in moderation, is an important part of the overall low-fat food picture.

The real goal for the weight conscious is to eat a varied diet made up of a large percentage of plant foods (vegetables and fruits) and grains, especially those that are rich in fiber. This is not hard to do if you eat pasta in moderation, other grains, and most important, as many vegetables and fruits as you can. Of these foods, eat only what you really enjoy. Eating well is one of life's pleasures and contributes to your well-being. There is so much to choose from! As you flip through the recipes in this book, your only problem will be in deciding what to have tonight.

While you are watching the fat grams, I recommend also paying attention to fiber. Besides being healthful for a number of reasons, high-fiber foods are more filling but less likely to lead to overeating than high-fat foods. Count fiber grams as well to see if you can raise your intake from the country's deplorable average of about ten grams a day to the recommended twenty to thirty-five grams a day.

Don't skip meals. Have three meals a day and two (low-fat) snacks. Choose foods without fat-laden sauces. When eating salads and vegetables, ask for sauces on the side. Limit your animal protein intake to a portion the size of a deck of cards and eat animal protein only once a day. Plan to have two vegetarian days a week, with meals built around a hearty soup, well-prepared vegetables, a grain dish, and fruit. Exercise three or four times a week and don't give up. Doing this will virtually guarantee a leaner, healthier you.

## Blowing It

Anyone who has ever been on a diet is familiar with blowing it — eating two helpings of a rich dessert, indulging in a pint of Chocolate Almond Heath Bar when you only meant to take a spoonful or two, or gobbling several handfuls of peanuts or cashews at a party. Then you think, I blew it anyway, so I might as well eat these butter cookies or this bag of corn chips and guacamole dip.

I've encountered few people (except those on rigid low-fat diets for serious heart conditions) who meet their exact fat targets every single day. I know I don't. Eating low fat has become a way of life for me, so I don't think too hard about what to eat if I'm at home. But if I go to a dinner party where chicken pot pie with a creamy filling and a buttery crust is being served, well . . . some days you're over, some days you're under. More often I'm under, so I don't worry about it for a second, although I usually automatically compensate at the next meal. The important thing is not to get a case of the guilts and abandon your goal. Don't waste time thinking about what you ate that was "bad." Think about what you are going to choose to eat the next day, from among the foods you like, that will balance the indulgence. It's no big deal unless you make it one.

*Part Two*

# RECIPES

# 6

# HORS D'OEUVRES AND APPETIZERS

Low-Fat Nachos

Seared Shrimp Marinated in Lemon and Ginger

Mussels on the Half Shell with Salsa Fresca

Babagannoush

Bruschetta of White Beans with Rosemary

Bruschetta of Tomatoes and Basil

Crostini of Figs

Eggplant Caponata

Pita Crisps

Hummus

No-Fat Black Bean Dip

Watercress Dip or Spread

Coriander-Mint Dip

Roasted Garlic with Fresh Thyme and
Goat Cheese

I F I W E R E  A S K E D what category of food is most threatening as far as fat consumption goes, I would be hard-pressed to choose between desserts and hors d'oeuvres, but I would probably choose the latter. The reason is one can usually eat a reasonable portion of dessert after a full meal and stop, but in that long stretch of time between lunch and dinner, one gets hungrier and hungrier. And tidbits that accompany the cocktail hour frequently pack a real wallop of fat — deep-fried morsels, cheesy spreads, guacamole, chips, and the like. You can easily consume your whole fat allowance with one hand while a glass is in the other. Nuts, which I adore, are probably the worst because it's so hard to stop eating them. Raw or lightly blanched vegetables, or crudités, make sense as long as you don't consume a high-fat dip with them, although they can be kind of boring by themselves. Cheese and crackers is temptingly easy but makes no sense calorie- and fat-wise as the opening of a meal.

I've assembled here some drink accompaniments that I like to fix when I'm feeling energetic. Just as often, I put out two kinds of interesting olives and some pistachio nuts and leave it at that. Some of the hors d'oeuvres here can be served as a first course at the table, such as Eggplant Caponata (page 48), Mussels on the Half Shell with Salsa Fresca (page 42), or either of the bruschettas (pages 44, 46).

You are not, of course, limited to the foods in this section. There are many other recipes in this book that will serve admirably, such as the lighter soups and seafood dishes, including Greek-Style Cold Stuffed Mussels (page 133), Seviche of Scallops (page 135) and Warm Shrimp and Bean Salad (page 130). And Liv Blumer, my former editor, is so enamored of the flavor and crunchiness of Roasted Brussels Sprouts (page 200) that she serves them on toothpicks with drinks!

# Low-Fat Nachos

*I adore nachos and eat them shamelessly, considering them a really high-class food snack as opposed to snack food because the ingredients are quite nourishing. If we're out of tortillas, we have been known to make them on tostada chips. My friends and family love them either way. Very easy to make.*

2 flour tortillas
¾ cup thick bottled salsa
8 fresh jalapeño peppers, seeded and
 sliced into thin rings (see Note)

⅔ cup shredded low-fat Monterey
 Jack cheese

Preheat the oven to 425°F. Place a metal baking sheet in the oven to heat.
 Using kitchen shears, cut the tortillas into eighths, making the cuts like the spokes of a wheel. Remove the baking sheet from the oven and lay the wedges on it. Add 2 teaspoons salsa and 2 to 4 jalapeño rings to each wedge and sprinkle with the cheese, dividing it equally among the 16 pieces. Bake for about 8 minutes until the cheese melts.

**Makes 16 pieces**

| PER PIECE | |
| --- | --- |
| CALORIES | 34 |
| FAT | 1 GM |
| SATURATED FAT | 1 GM |
| CHOLESTEROL | 3 MG |
| SODIUM | 165 MG |
| PROTEIN | 2 GM |
| CARBOHYDRATE | 4 GM |

Note: If fresh jalapeños are not available, use sliced jalapeños from a jar, found in the Mexican food section of most supermarkets.

# Seared Shrimp Marinated
# in Lemon and Ginger

*These shrimp make a wonderfully flavorsome hors d'oeuvre when you want to serve something substantial. I also make them when I want to flesh out a lunch of leftover vegetables.*

1 clove garlic
1-inch piece fresh ginger
1 cup coarsely chopped fresh cilantro
¼ cup lemon juice
2 tablespoons reduced-sodium
   Japanese soy sauce

1 teaspoon olive oil
20 large shrimp (about 1 pound),
   peeled and deveined

In a food processor, puree the garlic, ginger, and cilantro. Add the lemon juice, soy sauce, and olive oil. In a shallow, medium bowl, toss the marinade with the shrimp, cover with plastic wrap, and refrigerate for at least 1 hour or up to 1 day.

Heat a nonstick skillet over medium heat. Remove the shrimp from the marinade with tongs and add to the skillet one at a time. Raise the heat to medium-high, taking care not to crowd the shrimp in the pan. Cook for 2 minutes on each side or until all are uniformly pink. Serve warm, with toothpicks.

Makes 4–6 servings

➤ *For a simple but elegant meal, try serving these with Black Bean Salsa (page 186) and a green salad.*

| PER SHRIMP | |
| --- | --- |
| CALORIES | 24 |
| FAT | 1 GM |
| SATURATED FAT | 0 GM |
| CHOLESTEROL | 28 MG |
| SODIUM | 88 MG |
| PROTEIN | 4 GM |
| CARBOHYDRATE | 1 GM |

# Mussels on the Half Shell
# with Salsa Fresca

*These succulent mussels make a nice drink accompaniment that can be prepared ahead. You also can use them in lieu of a first course.*

3 pounds large mussels (about 48), steamed according to Master Recipe (page 132) (cooking liquid reserved)

2 recipes Salsa Fresca (recipe follows)
chopped fresh cilantro for garnish

Pull one shell off each steamed mussel, leaving the mussel itself on the other shell. Use a small, sharp knife to release each mussel from the shell and remove. Rinse all the shells and reserve.

Add 3 tablespoons of the reserved cooking liquid to the salsa. Add the mussels to the salsa, cover, and refrigerate until chilled.

To serve, arrange the shells on a serving plate. Place a mussel on each shell and top with a teaspoon of the salsa. Garnish with a sprinkling of cilantro before serving.

**Makes 8 appetizer or hors d'oeuvre servings, allowing approximately 6 per person.**

➤ *You can tell if a mussel is fresh by pinching it between thumb and forefinger and then trying to spread the shells open. If it closes tightly, it is alive.*

## SALSA FRESCA

2 pounds ripe tomatoes, seeded, lightly juiced, and chopped
½ small onion, finely chopped
1–3 fresh jalapeño or serrano peppers, seeded and minced

¼ cup chopped fresh cilantro leaves
1 tablespoon red wine vinegar (or more to taste)
salt to taste

Combine all the ingredients in a bowl and chill for at least 1 hour before serving.

**Makes about 2 cups**

➤ *Fresh salsa will hold for 2 to 3 hours in the refrigerator but will change flavor and become watery after that.*

| PER SERVING | |
| --- | --- |
| CALORIES | 87 |
| FAT | 2 GM |
| SATURATED FAT | 0 GM |
| CHOLESTEROL | 14 MG |
| SODIUM | 157 MG |
| PROTEIN | 8 GM |
| CARBOHYDRATE | 12 GM |

# Babagannoush

*Not exactly low fat but so flavorsome that a little goes a long way. Play around with the proportions to suit your taste. Broiling the eggplant gives the requisite smoky flavor. Leftovers make a great spread for vegetable sandwiches.*

1 large or 2 small eggplants
2 cloves garlic
1 tablespoon canola oil
3 tablespoons tahini (approximately, depending on size of eggplant) (see Note)
3 tablespoons lemon juice (or to taste)

salt and freshly ground black pepper to taste
¼–½ teaspoon ground cumin (optional)
finely chopped fresh parsley or cilantro for garnish

Preheat the broiler or a charcoal grill.

Pierce the eggplant in several places with a fork and broil or grill for 15 to 20 minutes, turning 2 or 3 times, until the skin blackens and blisters. When cool enough to handle, peel the eggplant and squeeze out excess liquid.

In a food processor, combine the garlic, oil, tahini, and lemon juice. Process until you have a smooth, creamy puree.

Mash the eggplant flesh with a potato masher or fork and add it to the puree. Mix briefly to blend; the mixture should have some texture. Season with salt and pepper, taste, and add more lemon juice if desired. Stir in the cumin (if using). Transfer the puree to a serving bowl and garnish with the chopped parsley or cilantro.

**Makes about 1½ cups, serving 6**

➤ *Serve as a dip with small, warmed triangles of pita bread.*

| PER SERVING | |
| --- | --- |
| CALORIES | 78 |
| FAT | 5 GM |
| SATURATED FAT | 1 GM |
| CHOLESTEROL | 0 MG |
| SODIUM | 13 MG |
| PROTEIN | 2 GM |
| CARBOHYDRATE | 8 GM |

Note: Tahini, a thick paste made of ground sesame seeds, is found in cans in many supermarkets and in Middle Eastern grocery stores.

# Bruschetta of White Beans with Rosemary

*Bruschetta, simply garlic bread with any of an endless number of toppings, is one of the most satisfying snacks I know. But it can be surprisingly high in fat due to the olive oil drizzled on both the toast and the topping. Here, bean liquid is used to keep the fat grams in check.*

2 teaspoons plus 1 tablespoon extra-virgin olive oil

3 cloves garlic, 2 finely chopped, 1 clove garlic cut in half lengthwise

1 teaspoon finely chopped fresh rosemary

1 fifteen-ounce can cannellini beans, drained (liquid reserved)

salt and freshly ground black pepper to taste

6 three-quarter-inch-thick slices firm, chewy Italian bread, such as Tuscan sourdough

1 small ripe tomato, finely diced (optional)

Preheat the oven to 450°F.

Combine the 2 teaspoons olive oil, chopped garlic, rosemary, and 2 tablespoons of the reserved bean liquid in a medium sauté pan and cook over very low heat for 5 minutes. The garlic should color only slightly. Stir in the beans and salt and pepper. Cook for about 10 minutes, adding some of the bean liquid if the mixture begins to dry out. Mash the beans with a fork to create a rough puree.

Grill or lightly toast the bread. Rub one side of each slice with the cut sides of the remaining garlic clove and brush lightly with some of the remaining 1 tablespoon of olive oil.

To serve, spread the bean puree on the grilled bread, sprinkle with the tomato if desired, and grind more pepper on top.

**Serves 6**

➤ *For a hearty first course or light lunch, serve two or three kinds of bruschetta.*

| PER SERVING | |
| --- | --- |
| CALORIES | 320 |
| FAT | 8 GM |
| SATURATED FAT | 1 GM |
| CHOLESTEROL | 0 MG |
| SODIUM | 760 MG |
| PROTEIN | 11 GM |
| CARBOHYDRATE | 51 GM |

# Bruschetta of Tomatoes
# and Basil

*Some good things bear repeating. The recipe for tomato bruschetta in **Low Fat
& Loving It** was quite satisfying until I questioned a restaurateur one day
about a mysterious "extra" that made his bruschetta so good. The secret, I
learned, is simply the wood-roasted flavor the bread acquires from being
toasted in an oven so hot it quickly chars slightly on the edges before it has a
chance to harden. Herewith, a revised recipe for one of the simplest and most
delicious snacks known to man.*

2 medium ripe tomatoes, lightly
    seeded and finely chopped
3 teaspoons olive oil
½ teaspoon coarse salt
freshly ground black pepper to taste
6 fresh basil leaves

6 three-quarter-inch-thick slices firm,
    chewy Italian bread, such as
    Tuscan sourdough
2 large cloves garlic, cut in half
    lengthwise

In a bowl, combine the tomatoes, 2 teaspoons of the olive oil, salt, and liberal grindings of pepper. Tear the basil leaves into small pieces and add. Let
the mixture stand at room temperature for 30 minutes.

Preheat the broiler or grill until very hot. Toast the bread until lightly
browned. Immediately rub one side of each piece with the cut side of a garlic clove. Add the remaining 1 teaspoon olive oil to the tomatoes, spoon the
mixture onto the toasts, and serve immediately.

**Serves 6**

➤ *To lightly seed tomatoes, cut in half vertically (top to bottom) and squeeze
each half gently over the sink to express the "jelly" containing the seeds.*

| PER SERVING | |
| --- | --- |
| CALORIES | 110 |
| FAT | 3 GM |
| SATURATED FAT | 0 GM |
| CHOLESTEROL | 0 MG |
| SODIUM | 289 MG |
| PROTEIN | 3 GM |
| CARBOHYDRATE | 18 GM |

# Crostini of Figs

*I am very fond of prosciutto and figs and find this version, which I was served at a hilltop restaurant near Florence, the best way to enjoy the delectable combination. It makes a lovely first course when ripe figs are available.*

8 one-half-inch-thick slices firm, chewy Italian bread

8 paper-thin slices imported Italian prosciutto (about 2 ounces)

4 medium ripe figs

honey

freshly ground black pepper

Preheat the oven to 400°F.

Place the bread slices on a baking sheet and toast for 15 minutes, turning once, until lightly browned.

While the toast is baking, arrange 2 slices of prosciutto on each of 4 plates and set aside. Peel the figs and mash with a fork. Add a drop or two of honey to sweeten. Spread the fig mixture on the toasts and garnish each plate with 2 crostini. Pass the pepper mill at the table.

Makes 8 crostini, serving 4

➤ *Imported Italian prosciutto is so much better (and less salty) than the domestic kind that it is worth seeking out an Italian salumeria or gourmet food shop that carries it. I always look for the Gallione or San Daniele brand.*

| PER SERVING | |
| --- | --- |
| CALORIES | 178 |
| FAT | 4 GM |
| SATURATED FAT | 1 GM |
| CHOLESTEROL | 12 MG |
| SODIUM | 496 MG |
| PROTEIN | 8 GM |
| CARBOHYDRATE | 30 GM |

# Eggplant Caponata

*This zesty Sicilian dish can be quite oily, since the classic recipe calls for sautéing the eggplant in olive oil, which it soaks up like a sponge. In my version, the dish is baked in a hot oven, requiring much less oil, and is further flavored with sweet peppers. Use as an hors d'oeuvre, with taco chips for scooping; a first course, served on a lettuce leaf and accompanied by breadsticks; or just spooned on crostini. Great on a picnic!*

vegetable cooking spray

2 large eggplants (about 1½ pounds each)

salt to taste

3 tablespoons olive oil

2 medium onions, coarsely chopped (about 1¼ cups)

3–4 tablespoons reduced-sodium defatted chicken stock, preferably homemade (page 274)

4 stalks celery, coarsely chopped

½ cup coarsely chopped sweet red pepper

½ cup coarsely chopped sweet yellow pepper

6 tablespoons tomato paste

½ cup red wine vinegar

1½ tablespoons sugar

½ teaspoon salt (or to taste)

freshly ground black pepper to taste

¼ cup capers, drained, rinsed, and chopped

12–15 pitted black olives, such as Kalamata

3–4 tablespoons chopped fresh parsley

Preheat the oven to 450°F. Lightly spray two 9-by-13-inch baking dishes with vegetable spray.

Wash the eggplants, dry, trim, and without peeling, cut into 1¼-inch cubes. (They will shrink in cooking somewhat.) Layer the cubes, salting each layer, in a large colander set over a dish. Let sit for 30 minutes, then rinse and pat dry in a kitchen towel.

Divide the eggplant between the baking dishes. Add 1 tablespoon of oil to each dish and toss with the cubes. Cover tightly and bake for 30 to 35 minutes or until tender.

While the eggplant is baking, add the remaining 1 tablespoon oil to a heavy nonstick skillet and sauté the onion over medium heat until translucent but not colored, adding some stock as needed. Cook for 3 to 4 minutes. Remove from the pan with a slotted spoon and put in a bowl large enough to hold all the remaining ingredients.

Add the celery and red and yellow peppers to the skillet and cook for 4 to 5 minutes, stirring, until softened but still crisp. Add a little stock if needed to prevent sticking. Add the tomato paste, vinegar, sugar, salt, and pepper. Bring back to a simmer and cook gently for a few minutes. Add the mixture to the bowl.

When the eggplant is done, add it to the bowl along with the capers and olives. Mix well. Taste and adjust the seasoning, adding liberal grindings of pepper if desired. The flavors of caponata need to mellow overnight in the refrigerator, so this dish can be prepared 1 to 3 days in advance and refrigerated. Serve at room temperature, sprinkled with parsley.

**Makes about 2 quarts, serving 8–12**

| PER ¾ CUP | |
| --- | --- |
| CALORIES | 130 |
| FAT | 7 GM |
| SATURATED FAT | 1 GM |
| CHOLESTEROL | 0 MG |
| SODIUM | 459 MG |
| PROTEIN | 2 GM |
| CARBOHYDRATE | 17 GM |

# Pita Crisps

*With virtually no fat to speak of, pita crisps are the ideal accompaniment to a low-fat dip. They also go well with a smooth soup, such as Diane's Zucchini Soup (page 73). It is essential to make them with fresh pita bread so that it will not break or crumble when you separate and cut it.*

4 fresh pita bread pockets
2 large egg whites

½ teaspoon cayenne pepper (optional)

Preheat the oven to 350°F.

Open each pita pocket by inserting the tip of a small, sharp knife and gently cutting it all around to separate it into two rounds. Beat the egg whites lightly, adding cayenne if you wish, and brush on the smooth (outer) side of each round. With kitchen shears, cut each round into 8 triangles, placing the pieces on a baking sheet as you work. Bake for 10 minutes or until crisp, being careful not to let them burn.

When cool, store in a tin if not using immediately. Pita crisps will keep for up to 3 weeks.

**Makes 64 crisps**

| PER SERVING | |
|---|---|
| CALORIES | 24 |
| FAT | 0 GM |
| SATURATED FAT | 0 GM |
| CHOLESTEROL | 0 MG |
| SODIUM | 57 MG |
| PROTEIN | 2 GM |
| CARBOHYDRATE | 8 GM |

# Hummus

*This famous Middle Eastern dish is one of my favorite indulgences. It can be quite high in fat depending on how much tahini (sesame seed paste) and oil are used. This recipe produces a tasty, satisfying version with about half the usual amount of tahini and no additional olive oil. The fat is unsaturated, and you get fiber to boot. (Two tablespoons will give you up to 3 grams of fiber.)*

1 nineteen-ounce can chickpeas or 2
   cups cooked chickpeas
2 tablespoons tahini (see Note)
2–3 tablespoons lemon juice (or more
   to taste)
2 cloves garlic, sliced (or more to taste)

2 tablespoons water (approximately)
½ teaspoon salt (or more to taste)
paprika for garnish
1 tablespoon chopped fresh parsley
   for garnish

Drain the chickpeas. Stir the tahini with its oil until well mixed. Set aside. Put the lemon juice and garlic in a blender or food processor and whirl. Add the chickpeas in several batches and process. Add the tahini and process until well blended and creamy, adding up to 2 tablespoons water to make a smooth, fairly firm dip. Scrape down the sides once or twice if necessary. Add the salt. Taste and correct the seasoning, adding more salt, garlic, or lemon juice if desired. Transfer to a bowl and garnish with a dusting of paprika in the center and the chopped parsley.

**Makes about 1⅔ cups, serving 6–8**

➤ *Serve with warmed pita bread or crackers. I also like hummus on a toasted bagel for breakfast or a snack and find it wonderful as a dip for pepper, carrot, or celery sticks.*

| PER TABLESPOON | |
|---|---|
| CALORIES | 21 |
| FAT | 1 GM |
| SATURATED FAT | 0 GM |
| CHOLESTEROL | 0 MG |
| SODIUM | 67 MG |
| PROTEIN | 1 GM |
| CARBOHYDRATE | 2 GM |

Note: Tahini, or sesame seed paste, is available in jars in Middle Eastern markets and specialty food shops.

# No-Fat Black Bean Dip

*This deceptively simple dip is a vehicle for instant hors d'oeuvres. It's delicious with taco chips, Pita Crisps (page 49), or crudités, and I've even enjoyed it slathered on a toasted bagel.*

1 pound dried black beans

1 carrot, peeled and coarsely chopped (about 1 cup)

1 medium onion, coarsely chopped (about 2 cups)

2 cloves garlic, crushed

1 tablespoon plus 1 teaspoon pure chili powder (see Appendix)

several dashes of cayenne pepper (depending on hotness desired)

2 tablespoons dried oregano

juice of 1 medium lime (or more to taste)

2 dashes of Tabasco

salt and freshly ground black pepper to taste

Rinse the beans and pick over, discarding any that are broken or discolored. Place in a pot and cover with 1 quart water. Soak for 4 hours or overnight.

Drain the beans, return to the pot, and add fresh water to cover by about 2 inches. Add the carrot, onion, garlic, chili powder, cayenne, and oregano.

Bring to a boil and cook at a fairly rapid simmer for 45 to 55 minutes. Add more water if the beans appear dry. After 40 minutes, squeeze a bean from time to time to check for doneness (soft but not mushy).

When the beans are done, remove about 2 cups of cooking liquid and set aside. Drain the beans, transfer half to a food processor, and process to a smooth puree. Use some of the reserved liquid if the puree is too thick. Repeat for the second batch of beans.

Return the puree to the pot or place in a large bowl. Season with the lime juice, Tabasco, and salt and pepper, adding more lime juice if desired.

**Makes about 3½ pints**

➤ *This dip keeps in the refrigerator for up to 5 days. You also can freeze it in small plastic containers for up to 1 month. Or use it hot as an accompaniment to chicken, fish, or vegetables. Alternatively, use it as the base for a bean soup, which you can make by adding chicken or vegetable stock to obtain the consistency you like. Serve sprinkled with chopped fresh cilantro.*

| PER TABLESPOON | |
| --- | --- |
| CALORIES | 16 |
| FAT | 0 GM |
| SATURATED FAT | 0 GM |
| CHOLESTEROL | 0 MG |
| SODIUM | 2 MG |
| PROTEIN | 1 GM |
| CARBOHYDRATE | 3 GM |

# Watercress Dip or Spread

*Use as a dip (the color is beautiful with raw vegetables) or as a spread for sandwiches.*

1 cup Yoghurt Cheese (page 260)
2 cups watercress leaves, stems
  removed
2 cloves garlic, minced

1 tablespoon coarsely chopped onion
2 tablespoons finely chopped fresh
  parsley
½ teaspoon salt (or to taste)

Place the Yoghurt Cheese in the bowl of a food processor. Blanch the watercress in boiling water for 15 seconds. Run cold water over it, drain, press out the water, and add to the cheese. Add the garlic, onion, parsley, and salt and process until the greens are reduced to tiny flecks and the mixture is pale green. Transfer to a bowl, cover, and refrigerate for at least 1 hour before using.

**Makes about 1¼ cups**

| PER 2 TABLESPOONS | |
| --- | --- |
| CALORIES | 36 |
| FAT | 2 GM |
| SATURATED FAT | 1 GM |
| CHOLESTEROL | 7 MG |
| SODIUM | 12 MG |
| PROTEIN | 2 GM |
| CARBOHYDRATE | 3 GM |

# Coriander-Mint Dip

*This is a traditional dip for* **pappadums,** *the tortilla-like Indian flatbread made of lentil flour, frequently served as a snack or drink accompaniment. It also makes a lovely sauce for grilled scallops or a simple grilled fish.*

⅓ cup nonfat yoghurt
¾ cup packed fresh cilantro
    (coriander) leaves
¼ cup packed fresh mint leaves
¼ sweet green pepper, seeded and
    chopped

2 fresh green chili peppers or 1½ fresh
    jalapeño peppers, seeded
1 tablespoon chopped onion
1 quarter-size slice fresh ginger
¾ teaspoon sugar
2 tablespoons water

Put all the ingredients in a food processor or blender and puree until smooth. Cover and refrigerate before serving.

**Makes 1 cup**

PER TABLESPOON

| | |
|---|---|
| CALORIES | 16 |
| FAT | 0 GM |
| SATURATED FAT | 0 GM |
| CHOLESTEROL | 0 MG |
| SODIUM | 12 MG |
| PROTEIN | 1 GM |
| CARBOHYDRATE | 3 GM |

# Roasted Garlic with Fresh Thyme and Goat Cheese

*Garlic becomes surprisingly mellow and sweet when roasted and spread with some goat cheese on lightly toasted slices of sourdough or peasant bread. This is a good example of how to make a small amount of good cheese go a long and satisfying way.*

4 whole plump heads garlic
¾ cup defatted, reduced-sodium
   chicken broth
8–10 springs fresh thyme
salt and freshly ground black pepper
   to taste

1 four- to five-ounce log creamy goat
   cheese, cut into 4 portions
4–6 slices lightly toasted sourdough or
   peasant bread

Preheat the oven to 400°F.

With a sharp knife, cut off and discard the upper third of each garlic head, exposing the cloves. Leave the skin intact below the cut.

Set the garlic heads, cut side up, in a small baking dish just large enough to hold them. Pour the chicken broth over the garlic, place the thyme sprigs on top, and season with salt and pepper. Cover the dish tightly with heavy-duty aluminum foil and bake for 1 hour or until the cloves are soft to the touch and the skin resembles lightly browned parchment.

Serve the garlic with the cooking juices spooned over and pass the goat cheese and bread separately. To eat, break off a piece of bread and spread with a small amount of cheese, then scoop out the roasted garlic from one of the cloves with the tip of a knife and spread it on top.

**Serves 4**

➤ *For what I regard as a major dining event, serve with a salad of gutsy greens and a robust wine such as a Nebbiolo Piedmont or a young Rioja.*

| PER SERVING | |
|---|---|
| CALORIES | 176 |
| FAT | 10 GM |
| SATURATED FAT | 3 GM |
| CHOLESTEROL | 23 MG |
| SODIUM | 265 MG |
| PROTEIN | 9 GM |
| CARBOHYDRATE | 14 GM |

# 7
# SOUPS

Chicken Soup

Chicken Cellophane Noodle Soup

Anne Rosenszweig's Shrimp, Leek, and
Sweet Potato Chowder

Soupe au Pistou

Chickpea Soup with Swiss Chard

Mushroom Barley Soup

Pasta e Fagioli with Chicken

Sweet Potato Soup

Kale and Potato Soup with Red Chili

Potato Watercress Soup

Fresh Roasted Tomato Soup

Diane's Zucchini Soup

Cold Broccoli Soup

THE DUCHESS OF WINDSOR didn't think much of soups. ("Why mire a meal in a swamp?" she is reported to have said.) But I love soups and the sense of well-being they engender — both substantial soups such as Soupe au Pistou (page 62) that can be the main course for family or close friends, and lighter, tasty ones such as Diane's Zucchini Soup (page 73) that start a meal pleasantly and, by filling you up a little, help make it easier not to overeat.

With the exception of reduced-sodium chicken broth, I have little use for canned soups. They are frequently lacking in depth of flavor and oversalted to compensate, and the ingredients all taste the same to me. That's why I always have something delicious and homemade in my freezer for the Sunday evening when a bowl of steaming soup in front of the TV seems like heaven, or the day when I've eaten more lunch than usual and want something light and restorative at dinner. I'm especially fond of chowders, and I wouldn't hesitate to use an ounce or two of well-drained bacon to give the special smoky flavor that is so characteristic of them. A stock, either chicken or vegetable, can be invaluable in adding depth and richness. (See the stock recipes on pages 274 and 272.)

The flavors of soups have a way of deepening and intensifying when their ingredients are allowed to "marry," which adds another advantage — they can be prepared a day or two ahead and just reheated when you need them.

# Chicken Soup

*No kidding, chicken soup really is good for you. A study reported in the medical journal* Chest *says that chicken soup helps clear a stuffy nose. Although it's called Jewish penicillin, just about every culture trots it out in some form when healing is needed. Here's a recipe for the real thing, minus the artery-clogging fat. The amount of each ingredient is quite flexible.*

1 four- to six-pound chicken, quartered, excess fat removed, plus giblets, excluding liver

2½–3 quarts water (or to cover)

1 teaspoon salt (or more to taste)

1 large or 2 small carrots

1 *petrouchka* (Italian parsley root) (see Note)

2 stalks celery with leaves

1 large onion

3 or 4 sprigs fresh parsley, preferably Italian flat-leaf parsley

minced fresh dill for garnish (optional)

Put the chicken, giblets, water, and salt in a tall, straight-sided soup pot. Bring to a boil, reduce the heat, and simmer, skimming off any grayish scum that rises to the surface. When the liquid appears clear, cover and let simmer slowly but steadily for about 45 minutes.

While the chicken simmers, prepare the vegetables. Scrape the carrots and *petrouchka* and cut into 3 or 4 pieces along with the celery. Peel and quarter the onion. Add the carrots, *petrouchka,* celery, onion, and parsley to the pot. Raise the heat briefly to bring back to a simmer and cook for 1 hour more or until the meat begins to fall from the bones. As the soup cooks, add a little more salt if needed.

Remove the chicken and set aside. Remove the vegetables with a slotted spoon, reserving the carrots and discarding the rest. Let the soup cool, then strain through a very fine sieve. To use immediately, remove the fat with a fat-removing ladle or Gravy-Skimmer (see Appendix). Alternatively, chill the broth and skim the fat from the top.

Rinse the original pot and wipe away any scum on the sides. Return the broth to the pot. Remove the meat from the bones, discarding the skin and bones, and add to the pot. Taste and adjust the seasoning. Slice the reserved carrots or put them through a ricer and add to the pot.

Heat the soup well but do not allow it to boil, as it will become cloudy. Serve garnished with the dill if desired.

**Makes about 2½ quarts, serving 8**

▶ *A well-washed and trimmed leek or a peeled celery root is a tasty addition to this soup. If you are fortunate enough to have access to chicken feet, several added at the beginning give the broth great body and flavor. For a one-dish meal, serve over cooked white rice.*

Note: *Petrouchka* is often sold in supermarkets in a package of "soup greens."

| PER SERVING | |
| --- | --- |
| CALORIES | 143 |
| FAT | 3 GM |
| SATURATED FAT | 1 GM |
| CHOLESTEROL | 76 MG |
| SODIUM | 312 MG |
| PROTEIN | 24 GM |
| CARBOHYDRATE | 3 GM |

# Chicken Cellophane Noodle Soup

*This is simply Vietnamese chicken noodle soup. It is fast and easy, and it has a lovely clean taste. It also is surprisingly elegant. It could be made with chicken breasts for a lower-fat version, but I do like the silky dark meat here.*

4 ounces cellophane noodles (see Note)

2 quarts water

2 chicken legs and thighs

2 tablespoons finely chopped fresh ginger

3 tablespoons nuoc mam (Vietnamese fish sauce)

½ teaspoon salt

freshly ground black pepper to taste

1 tablespoon chopped scallion, green part only

2 tablespoons chopped fresh cilantro leaves

Soak the cellophane noodles in warm water for 10 minutes and drain. Cut into 3-inch lengths with kitchen shears and set aside.

Bring the water to a boil in a 4-quart pot and drop in the chicken and ginger. Bring to a boil, reduce the heat to low, cover, and simmer for 25 minutes. Remove from the heat and let sit for 5 minutes.

Remove the chicken from the pot. Remove and discard the skin and bones, shred the meat, and set aside. Strain the broth through a cheesecloth-lined sieve and either chill until the fat can be removed by skimming or remove the fat with a fat-removing ladle or Gravy-Skimmer (see Appendix).

Return the broth to the pot. Add the nuoc mam, salt, and several grindings of pepper. Just before serving, bring the soup to a boil, add the reserved cellophane noodles, and simmer for about 3 minutes.

To serve, remove the noodles from the soup with tongs and divide among 6 individual bowls so that each is half full. Add the shredded chicken but do not stir. Mix together the chopped scallion and cilantro and sprinkle on top. Pour broth over all, add more black pepper if desired, and serve immediately.

**Makes about 2 quarts, serving 6**

➤ *This soup is best served with chopsticks to pick up the slippery noodles, as well as a soupspoon, and in deep bowls rather than the flatter Western-style soup plates.*

| PER SERVING | |
| --- | --- |
| CALORIES | 139 |
| FAT | 2 GM |
| SATURATED FAT | 1 GM |
| CHOLESTEROL | 35 MG |
| SODIUM | 520 MG |
| PROTEIN | 10 GM |
| CARBOHYDRATE | 18 GM |

Note: Cellophane or rice thread noodles, made from the starch of green mung beans, are available in oriental markets and in many supermarkets.

# Anne Rosenszweig's Shrimp, Leek, and Sweet Potato Chowder

*A wonderful way to entertain or feed your family on a cold, raw day. Note how a tiny bit of bacon, which otherwise has no place in a low-fat diet, can be sparingly used to add a haunting smoky flavor to a soup or sauce.*

1 pound raw medium shrimp

**Stock**

1 tablespoon vegetable oil
1 medium onion, finely chopped
1 tablespoon minced fresh red chili
   pepper or ½ teaspoon red pepper
   flakes
1 quart bottled clam juice plus 1 cup
   water
2 tablespoons tomato paste

**Chowder**

2 slices lean bacon, minced

1 small onion, finely chopped
1 stalk celery, finely chopped
1 tablespoon minced garlic
2 medium leeks, trimmed, well
   washed, and diced (about 1½ cups)
3 cups 1 percent milk
1½ cups peeled and diced sweet
   potatoes (2 medium potatoes)
1 tablespoon paprika
½ teaspoon salt (or to taste)
freshly ground black pepper to taste
¼ cup chopped fresh chives

Shell the shrimp and remove their tails, reserving the shells. Cut the shrimp in half and reserve.

To make the stock, heat the oil in a medium saucepan over medium-high heat. Stir in the onion and chili pepper or flakes and sauté until the onion is soft, about 4 minutes. Add the reserved shrimp shells, clam juice and water, and tomato paste. Bring to a boil, reduce the heat, and simmer uncovered for 20 minutes. Strain, discarding the shells and reserving the broth. You should have a little under 1 quart.

To make the chowder, place a large pot over medium heat and add the bacon. Cook until crisp, then scoop out with a slotted spoon and drain on a paper towel or brown paper. To the fat remaining in the pot, add the onion, celery, garlic, and leeks. Cook, stirring occasionally, for 4 to 5 minutes. Add the milk, sweet potatoes, reserved bacon, and shrimp broth. Bring up to the boil, stir, and adjust the heat so that the mixture simmers for 20 minutes. Add the reserved shrimp and cook for 2 minutes or until they just turn pink. Add the paprika, salt, and several good grindings of pepper. Check the seasoning, stir in the chives, and serve.

**Makes about 3 quarts, serving 6**

| PER SERVING | |
| --- | --- |
| CALORIES | 255 |
| FAT | 8 GM |
| SATURATED FAT | 2 GM |
| CHOLESTEROL | 101 MG |
| SODIUM | 786 MG |
| PROTEIN | 20 GM |
| CARBOHYDRATE | 27 GM |

# Soupe au Pistou

*Pistou, a kind of pesto without nuts, gives an earthy depth of flavor to this hearty Provençal vegetable soup of Genoese origin. The quantity of olive oil traditionally required to sauté the vegetables is reduced here by sweating them instead in a small amount of oil. I serve this as a one-dish meal with lots of crusty bread, followed by a green salad and fruit for dessert.*

2 tablespoons olive oil

2 or 3 medium onions, coarsely chopped

2 medium carrots, scraped and thinly sliced

2 or 3 medium potatoes, peeled and cut into ¾-inch chunks

2 medium zucchini, cut into ½-inch dice

½–¾ pound young string beans, trimmed and cut into 2-inch pieces

1 twenty-eight-ounce can Italian plum tomatoes, coarsely chopped (liquid reserved)

4 large cloves garlic, finely chopped

bouquet garni (1 stalk celery, 2 sprigs fresh thyme, 2 sprigs fresh parsley, and 1 bay leaf tied together)

4 quarts boiling water

1 cup broken-up dried vermicelli, spaghettini, or elbow macaroni

1 cup cooked chickpeas or cannellini beans, rinsed and drained

salt and freshly ground black pepper to taste

cayenne pepper

### Pistou

4 large cloves garlic

pinch of salt

2 cups tightly packed fresh basil leaves, washed and dried

6 tablespoons freshly grated Parmesan cheese

3–4 tablespoons olive oil

Put a full kettle of water on to boil. Cut a circle of heavy-duty aluminum foil that will fit inside a large soup pot. Set aside.

Heat the oil in the pot. Add the onion and carrot, stir, and press the foil right down on top of the vegetables. Cook over medium heat, lifting the foil to stir once or twice, until the vegetables are soft and tender and the onion is lightly colored, about 6 to 10 minutes. Remove the foil.

Add the potatoes, zucchini, string beans, tomatoes, garlic, bouquet garni, boiling water, and reserved tomato liquid. Bring to a boil, partially cover, lower the heat to medium, and simmer for 30 minutes. *(May be prepared ahead up to this point. If so, bring back to a simmer before proceeding.)*

Just before serving, add the pasta and chickpeas or beans and cook for 10 minutes more or until the pasta is tender. Remove and discard the bouquet garni. Add the salt and pepper and a dash or two of cayenne, remembering that you will have the additional seasoning of the pistou.

While the soup cooks, prepare the pistou. Put the garlic, salt, and basil in a food processor and process until finely chopped but not liquid. Add the cheese and 2 tablespoons of the oil and process with quick on-off turns until the mixture is thick and a creamy pale green in color. Add 1 or 2 more tablespoons oil while the motor is running. The mixture should be almost of pouring consistency; if it appears too dry, add up to 2 tablespoons of the broth from the soup pot, incorporating it with on-off turns. Scrape the pistou out into a bowl and set aside. For each portion, place 1 tablespoon of pistou in a heated soup bowl, mix into it a small ladleful of broth, then carefully ladle in the balance of the soup.

**Makes 2½–3 quarts, serving 8–10**

➤ *The pistou may be prepared 1 hour ahead. The base, without the cheese, can be done days ahead and frozen. If you have any leftover Parmesan rinds, add them with the potatoes and other vegetables for more flavor. Discard before serving.*

| PER SERVING | |
| --- | --- |
| CALORIES | 233 |
| FAT | 9 GM |
| SATURATED FAT | 2 GM |
| CHOLESTEROL | 3 MG |
| SODIUM | 130 MG |
| PROTEIN | 8 GM |
| CARBOHYDRATE | 33 GM |

# Chickpea Soup with Swiss Chard

*A filling main-course soup that needs only some crusty peasant bread and a salad to follow.*

1 pound dried chickpeas
2 tablespoons olive oil
1 large onion, chopped
2 cloves garlic, minced
7 cups cold water (approximately)
6 fresh sage leaves or 1 teaspoon
    crumbled dried sage

½ pound Swiss chard, washed, cut
    into 3-inch pieces
salt and freshly ground black pepper
    to taste

Place the chickpeas in a colander and pick over, removing any stones or discolored beans. Place in a soup pot, add cold water to cover by 2 inches, and soak for at least 3 hours or overnight. Alternatively, bring to a boil, boil for 5 minutes, remove from the heat, and let soak for 1 hour. Drain the chickpeas.

Heat the olive oil in a saucepan, preferably nonstick. Add the onion and garlic and sauté until soft. Transfer to the pot with the chickpeas and add about 7 cups cold water, adding more if needed to cover. Bring to a boil, reduce the heat, and simmer until the chickpeas are tender but firm, about 1 hour.

Puree half the soup and the sage in a blender and return to the pot. Add the Swiss chard. Season with salt and pepper and cook for 15 minutes more. Serve with more freshly ground pepper on top.

**Makes about 2 quarts, serving 6–8**

➤ *Chickpeas exude a lot of starchy residue and so need to be drained and rinsed after they are boiled for the first time and before combining them with other ingredients.*

| PER SERVING | |
| --- | --- |
| CALORIES | 337 |
| FAT | 8 GM |
| SATURATED FAT | 1 GM |
| CHOLESTEROL | 0 MG |
| SODIUM | 89 MG |
| PROTEIN | 17 GM |
| CARBOHYDRATE | 51 GM |

# Mushroom Barley Soup

*This soup (though not this version) was a mainstay of my grandmother's and my mother's kitchens. Although they did not sauté the vegetables and used water instead of stock, their soup got its flavor from bones and beef flank, which made a tasty but fatty soup. Boiled potatoes were served on the side to make a hearty main-course dish. Here, fresh as well as dried mushrooms and sautéed vegetables do the job. This is best made with fragrant dried Polish mushrooms, although dried Italian* boletus *could be substituted.*

½ ounce dried Polish mushrooms

1 cup hot water

1 tablespoon canola oil

1 tablespoon butter

1 medium onion, finely chopped

1 stalk celery, diced

1 carrot, scraped and cut into ¼-inch dice

½ pound fresh cultivated mushrooms, wiped with a damp paper towel and sliced

5 cups reduced-sodium defatted beef or vegetable stock

½ cup fine or medium pearl barley, well rinsed under cold running water

1 parsnip, scraped, halved lengthwise, and cut into equal-sized 2-inch lengths

sea salt and fresh black pepper

¼ bunch very fresh dill

Put the dried mushrooms in a small bowl and add the hot water. Let soak for about 30 minutes. Then line a sieve with a double layer of cheesecloth, place over a bowl, and pour the mushrooms through, pressing down to extract the liquid. Strain the liquid again if it seems sandy, and reserve. Wash the soaked mushrooms carefully, dry with paper towels, chop coarsely, and set aside.

In a large soup pot, warm the oil and butter over medium heat. Add the onion, celery, and carrot and sauté until the onion is transparent, about 2 to 3 minutes. Add the sliced fresh mushrooms, raise the heat, and cook until the mushrooms begin to soften, about 2 to 3 minutes more. Add the stock, barley, parsnip, the chopped dried mushrooms, and the reserved mushroom liquid and bring to a boil. Cover, reduce the heat to low, and cook gently for 50 to 60 minutes or until the barley is soft and the soup is thickened. Stir occasionally.

Season with salt and pepper. Serve piping hot garnished with fresh dill snipped with a kitchen scissors.

Makes about 2 quarts, serving 8

➤ *For an authentic touch, add a 2-inch piece of* petrouchka *(Italian parsley root) in addition to or in place of the parsnip.*

| PER SERVING | |
| --- | --- |
| CALORIES | 119 |
| FAT | 3 GM |
| SATURATED FAT | 1 GM |
| CHOLESTEROL | 4 MG |
| SODIUM | 430 MG |
| PROTEIN | 5 GM |
| CARBOHYDRATE | 19 GM |

# Pasta e Fagioli with Chicken

*This warming, satisfying one-dish dinner was born one cold winter Sunday when I was trying to figure out how to turn a small amount of leftover chicken into a hearty meal. Made without the chicken, this is an exceptionally tasty version of the classic Italian soup.*

1 medium onion, quartered
1 carrot, scraped and quartered
1 stalk celery
3 tablespoons olive oil
1 teaspoon chopped garlic
2 tablespoons chopped fresh parsley
3–4 canned Italian plum tomatoes, chopped (liquid reserved)
1 twenty-ounce can cannellini beans, drained
2 thirteen-ounce cans reduced-sodium defatted chicken broth, mixed with 1 can of water, or an equal amount

(39 ounces) of homemade broth (page 274)
salt and freshly ground black pepper to taste
2 small dried red chili peppers, broken in half
1–1½ cups cubed cooked chicken (optional)
6 ounces orecchiette, tubetini, or other small dried pasta
2 tablespoons freshly grated Parmesan cheese

Put the onion, carrot, and celery in the bowl of a food processor and process with 5 or 6 pulses or until chopped.

Heat the oil in a soup pot, add the garlic, and cook for 1 minute or until soft. Add the parsley and the chopped vegetables and sauté for about 10 minutes, stirring from time to time. Add the tomatoes and their liquid, lower the heat to medium-low, and cook for 20 minutes.

Add a little more than half of the drained beans and let them cook for 5 minutes, stirring well. Add the broth and water and raise heat slightly.

Put the remaining beans through a food mill and add to the pot. Add the salt and pepper and chili peppers. Check the soup for thickness. If it's too thick, add more broth or water as needed. Add the chicken (if using) and bring to a steady boil. *(May be prepared ahead up to this point. If so, bring back to a boil before proceeding.)*

Add the pasta and cook until the pasta is still quite firm to the bite; it will continue cooking off the heat. Let the soup rest for 20 minutes before serving. If at any point the soup appears too thick because the pasta has absorbed all the liquid (which you want it to do), add another cup of hot broth or water. Just before serving, swirl in the cheese.

**Makes 1½–2¼ quarts, serving 6**

| PER SERVING WITH CHICKEN | | PER SERVING WITHOUT CHICKEN | |
| --- | --- | --- | --- |
| CALORIES | 320 | CALORIES | 272 |
| FAT | 9 GM | FAT | 8 GM |
| SATURATED FAT | 2 GM | SATURATED FAT | 1 GM |
| CHOLESTEROL | 26 MG | CHOLESTEROL | 1 MG |
| SODIUM | 515 MG | SODIUM | 494 MG |
| PROTEIN | 21 GM | PROTEIN | 12 GM |
| CARBOHYDRATE | 37 GM | CARBOHYDRATE | 37 GM |

# Sweet Potato Soup

*Silky and delicious, with an enticing play of sweet and hot and chock-full of beta-carotene, only begins to describe this intensely flavored soup created by brilliant chef Bobby Flay. The original version owes its sensuous texture in part to cream, which I've reduced by three-quarters but couldn't bear to omit entirely. It's really worth it!*

2 teaspoons unsalted butter
1 tablespoon canola oil
1 medium onion, coarsely chopped
2 cloves garlic, finely chopped
4 cups reduced-sodium defatted chicken stock, preferably homemade (page 274)
3 large sweet potatoes (about 2½ pounds), peeled and quartered
⅓ cup plus 1 tablespoon honey
2 tablespoons heavy cream
⅓ cup evaporated skim milk

1 tablespoon pureed canned chipotles in adobo sauce (or more to taste) (see Note)
salt and freshly ground black pepper to taste
finely diced tomato for garnish (optional)
blue corn tortilla chips, crumbled, for garnish (optional)
fresh cilantro leaves for garnish (optional)

In a large preferably nonstick saucepan, melt the butter in the oil over medium heat. Add the onion and garlic and cook slowly, stirring continuously, for 3 to 4 minutes or until they soften without coloring. Raise the heat to high, add the stock and sweet potatoes, and bring to a boil. Lower the heat to medium, partially cover, and simmer for about 25 minutes or until the potatoes are very tender.

Remove from the heat and add the honey, cream, milk, pureed chipotles, and salt and pepper. Let cool for a few minutes, then puree in a food processor in two batches and set aside. *(May be made 2 days ahead up to this point and refrigerated. Reheat before serving.)*

Divide the soup among 8 bowls. If desired, sprinkle with a teaspoon or so of diced tomatoes, a handful of crumbled tortilla chips, and a little cilantro. Serve warm.

Makes about 2 quarts, serving 8

➤ *Canned chipotles in adobo sauce can be found in the Mexican section of some supermarkets and in specialty food stores. Be sure to remove any stems before* pureeing. You can keep the puree in the refrigerator, in a tightly covered glass jar, for at least 1 month and use it to flavor other vegetable purees and soups. If chipotles in adobo sauce are not available, reconstitute dried chipotles and use the same amount, plus a splash of balsamic vinegar.

| PER SERVING | |
| --- | --- |
| CALORIES | 227 |
| FAT | 4 GM |
| SATURATED FAT | 2 GM |
| CHOLESTEROL | 8 MG |
| SODIUM | 378 MG |
| PROTEIN | 5 GM |
| CARBOHYDRATE | 44 GM |

Note: If you are not a lover of incendiary foods, I suggest that you start with 1 tablespoon of the chipotle puree and then add a teaspoon or two more as your taste dictates.

# Kale and Potato Soup with Red Chili

*This version of* **Caldo Verde,** *the traditional soup of Portuguese New Englanders, is just the ticket when you want a satisfying meal, perhaps after indulging too much the night before. It's filling and very low in fat.*

1 bunch kale (about 1 pound)
3 tablespoons virgin olive oil
1 medium onion, chopped
6 cloves garlic, thinly sliced
1 small dried red chili pepper, seeded and chopped, or ½ teaspoon red pepper flakes
1 bay leaf
1 teaspoon salt (or to taste)
4 medium potatoes (about 1½ pounds), peeled and cut into ½-inch dice
7 cups water or vegetable stock, preferably homemade (page 272)
freshly ground black pepper to taste
6 slices slightly stale French or Italian bread

With a sharp knife, cut off and discard the lower stems of the kale. Cut the ruffled leaves off their ribs, which are very tough. (Small leaves can be used whole, rib and all.) Wash the leaves well in two changes of water, stack three or four leaves at a time, and cut into ½-inch shreds. Set aside.

Heat the olive oil in a soup pot. Add the onion, garlic, chili, bay leaf, and salt and cook over medium-high heat for 3 to 4 minutes, stirring frequently. Add the potatoes and 1 cup of the water or stock. Stir together, cover, and cook slowly for 5 minutes.

Add the kale (which will shortly reduce to one-fourth its volume), cover, and steam until wilted, stirring occasionally. Add the remaining 6 cups of water or stock, bring to a boil, cover, and reduce the heat. Simmer slowly until the potatoes are quite soft, about 30 to 40 minutes.

Use the back of a wooden spoon to break up the potatoes by pressing them against the sides of the pot. Add more salt if needed and add a generous grinding of pepper. Let the soup sit for an hour or so before serving to allow the flavors to mellow. To serve, reheat without boiling, place a slice or two of bread in each soup plate, and pour the hot soup over the bread.

**Makes 1½–2 quarts, serving 4–6**

| PER SERVING | |
| --- | --- |
| CALORIES | 241 |
| FAT | 10 GM |
| SATURATED FAT | 1 GM |
| CHOLESTEROL | 0 MG |
| SODIUM | 622 MG |
| PROTEIN | 6 GM |
| CARBOHYDRATE | 35 GM |

# Potato Watercress Soup

*This contemporary reading of a favorite French classic is one of the most soothing soups I know, high on my list of comfort foods. It also makes a lovely first course for any meal.*

1 bunch very fresh watercress
4 medium potatoes (about 1½ pounds), peeled and halved
2 cups reduced-sodium defatted chicken broth, preferably homemade (page 274)

1 medium onion, halved
salt and freshly ground black pepper to taste
dash of cayenne pepper (optional)
2 teaspoons butter
1 cup low-fat buttermilk

Wash the watercress, remove the stems, and set aside a few small sprigs for garnish.

Parboil the potatoes for 10 minutes. Reserve 1 cup of potato water. Cube the potatoes and return to the pot with the potato water and chicken broth. Add the onion, put the watercress on top, and bring to a simmer. Cover and simmer for 8 to 10 minutes.

Puree in a food processor or blender until the watercress is reduced to tiny green flecks. (Depending on your processor's capacity, this may have to be done in two batches.) Return the puree to the pot, season with salt and pepper, and add the cayenne (if using).

In a small saucepan, melt the butter over low heat and cook until light brown. Stir in the buttermilk and heat until just warm. Do not overheat, or the mixture will curdle.

Add the buttermilk mixture to the pot and heat but do not boil. Correct the seasoning and garnish each serving with a small sprig of watercress.

**Makes about 1¾ quarts, serving 4–6**

➤ *This soup may be made well in advance and reheated.*

| PER SERVING | |
|---|---|
| CALORIES | 136 |
| FAT | 2 GM |
| SATURATED FAT | 1 GM |
| CHOLESTEROL | 5 MG |
| SODIUM | 353 MG |
| PROTEIN | 6 GM |
| CARBOHYDRATE | 25 GM |

# Fresh Roasted Tomato Soup

*Don't be put off by the large quantity of tomatoes in this recipe. When summer's crop is at its peak, you can have, for very little additional work, some glorious soup now and some to freeze for the inestimable joy of brightening a January day with a taste of summer. The roasting intensifies the tomato flavor and makes peeling very easy.*

9 pounds ripe tomatoes
2 tablespoons butter
1 tablespoon olive oil
2 cups chopped onion
10 cloves garlic, minced
salt and freshly ground black pepper
    to taste

dash of cayenne pepper
½ cup chopped fresh basil leaves, 8
    sprigs fresh thyme, or 1 tablespoon
    dried thyme

Preheat the oven to 350°F.

Wash the tomatoes, cut out the cores and any brown spots, and with the tip of a sharp knife slash a shallow X on the top of each one. Place them, core side down, on a baking sheet or in a shallow glass baking dish (you may need two) and roast for 20 to 30 minutes or until the tomatoes appear soft and the skin has begun to curl back.

Let the tomatoes sit until cool enough to handle. Pull off the skins (they will come away easily), then give each tomato a brief squeeze, holding it upright over the sink to pop out the seeds. Coarsely chop the tomatoes, placing them in a colander set over a bowl as you work. Add to the bowl any juice that collected in the baking sheet(s).

Heat the butter and olive oil in a large, deep nonreactive pot. Add the onions and garlic and sauté until translucent. Add the tomatoes by the handful, reserving the juice. Add the salt, liberal grindings of pepper, the cayenne, and the basil or thyme. Partially cover and cook for 15 minutes. Remove the thyme sprigs (if used).

The soup may be served as is or pureed. If it appears too thick, use the reserved tomato juice to thin the soup to a consistency you like. Correct the seasoning.

**Makes about 2½ quarts, serving 10**

*Recipes*

➤ *I splurge with the butter in this soup because it adds such an incredible depth of flavor. You may omit it if you wish and increase the olive oil by 1 tablespoon. Since seasonings lose strength in the freezer, plan to taste and season again any portion of this soup that you freeze.*

VARIATION:

*Fresh Corn and Tomato Soup:* During the last 5 minutes of cooking, add fresh corn cut from the cob, allowing 1 ear for every 2 persons. Do not puree.

| PER SERVING | |
| --- | --- |
| CALORIES | 129 |
| FAT | 5 GM |
| SATURATED FAT | 2 GM |
| CHOLESTEROL | 6 MG |
| SODIUM | 59 MG |
| PROTEIN | 4 GM |
| CARBOHYDRATE | 22 GM |

# Diane's Zucchini Soup

*My friend Diane Aronian is a talented and creative cook who describes herself as liking "frugal fare: simple foods with maximum taste and the fewest calories." This easy, delicious soup, which "simply evolved," is a perfect example of her philosophy. The lemon and cilantro are perhaps traceable to her Persian background.*

4 teaspoons olive oil

1½ cups chopped onion (about 2 medium onions)

3 cups defatted reduced-sodium chicken broth

4 medium firm, glossy zucchini, washed, sliced ¼ inch thick

2 tablespoons lemon juice (or more to taste)

salt and freshly ground black pepper to taste

1 cup chopped fresh cilantro

several fresh cilantro leaves for garnish

Heat the olive oil in a heavy soup pot, add the onion, and cook, stirring, until softened but not brown. If the onion begins to stick, add a spoonful or two of chicken broth. Add the zucchini and remaining broth, bring to a simmer, and cook for about 10 to 15 minutes or until the zucchini is buttery and soft.

Remove from the heat and add the lemon juice and salt and pepper. Puree in a food processor or blender in several batches. Add the chopped cilantro and pulse several times to blend. Adjust the seasoning, adding more lemon juice or salt and pepper if needed. Serve hot, garnished with 1 or 2 cilantro leaves.

Makes about 1½ quarts, serving 4

➤ *This soup may be served at room temperature. If you prepare it ahead, you may gently reheat it in the microwave or on the stove top, but do not allow it to boil.*

| PER SERVING | |
| --- | --- |
| CALORIES | 102 |
| FAT | 5 GM |
| SATURATED FAT | 1 GM |
| CHOLESTEROL | 0 MG |
| SODIUM | 493 MG |
| PROTEIN | 5 GM |
| CARBOHYDRATE | 12 GM |

# Cold Broccoli Soup

*When you're tired of broccoli every other way, try this zero-fat soup. It's pretty and flavorful and makes a delightful first course in warm weather.*

1½ pounds broccoli
4 cups defatted reduced-sodium
    chicken broth
3 stalks celery with leaves, stripped of
    strings and each cut into 3 or 4
    pieces
1 large onion, chopped (about 1 cup)
2 carrots, scraped and sliced

5 sprigs fresh parsley
salt to taste
1 tablespoon cornstarch
¼ cup water
1 cup evaporated skim milk
freshly ground black pepper to taste
chopped fresh chives for garnish
    (optional)

Separate the florets from the broccoli stems. Peel any large stalks (slender stems do not need peeling) and cut them into 1-inch pieces. Divide the florets into two piles.

Put one pile of florets and the stems into a 5-quart soup pot and add the chicken broth, celery, onion, carrot, parsley, and salt. Bring to a boil, lower the heat, and simmer for 10 minutes.

Bring 2 cups salted water to a boil in another pot. Have a bowl of ice water ready. Drop the reserved florets into the boiling water and cook for 3 minutes. Drain immediately and plunge into the ice water to stop the cooking and set the color.

Put the cornstarch in a blender or food processor, add the water, and whirl until smooth. Add 3 or 4 ladles of hot broth and blend again. Pour back into the soup pot and cook for 5 minutes over medium heat.

Let the soup cool slightly, then puree in a blender or food processor in two batches. Add the milk and season with salt and pepper. Refrigerate and correct the seasoning after chilling.

To serve, ladle into individual soup bowls and garnish each serving with a broccoli floret or two and a sprinkling of chives if desired.

**Makes 2 quarts, serving 8**

| PER SERVING | |
| --- | --- |
| CALORIES | 70 |
| FAT | 0 GM |
| SATURATED FAT | 0 GM |
| CHOLESTEROL | 1 MG |
| SODIUM | 393 MG |
| PROTEIN | 6 GM |
| CARBOHYDRATE | 12 GM |

# 8
# SALADS AND DRESSINGS

Beet, Potato, White Bean, Arugula, and
Red Onion Salad

Roasted Pepper, Mesclun, and
Grilled Chicken Salad

Orzo Salad with Grilled Shiitake Mushrooms, Asparagus, and
Sun-Dried Tomatoes

Tuna and Carrot Salad

"Israeli" Salad

Swedish Cucumber Salad

Fresh Corn and Basil Salad

French Potato Salad

Dale's Summer Slaw

Saloon Slaw

Jicama Relish

Spinach Salad

Sesame Rice Vinegar Dressing

Rosa's Garlic Dressing

Lemon Mustard Vinaigrette

Miso Dressing

S ALADS ARE AN INDISPENSABLE PART of contemporary eating. They can range from a few lettuce leaves moistened with dressing to filling compositions of beans, grains, vegetables, or seafood that constitute an entire meal. A small amount of leftover chicken that by itself would barely feed one person can be combined with other harmonious ingredients to feed four. Roasted Pepper, Mesclun, and Grilled Chicken Salad (page 80) is a good example. A "composed" salad like this can be a light but satisfying lunch or can be served as one course of a meal. And when unexpected diners turn up, you can always flesh out the simplest meal by adding vegetable salads to the menu to broaden the plate or as a showcased extra course.

There is one caveat, however. Although salads carry the connotation of healthy eating, the dressing you select can make the difference between a high-fat food and one that is nutritionally correct. A few tablespoons of classic vinaigrette, with its three parts oil to one part vinegar ratio, can turn what seems like a light meal into one that uses up almost your entire fat allowance for the day. In fact, one study revealed that the average woman between the ages of nineteen and fifty gets more of her fat from salad dressings than from any other single food!

This doesn't mean one should give up salads or, worse, eat them with a sugar- and additive-loaded bottled dressing. Rather, attention must be paid to the fat content of a satisfying dressing. I use mostly recastings of the traditional vinegar and oil formula, extended with another flavorful liquid. Chicken stock can be used to replace some of the oil and is perfect for tender greens. Mirin (Japanese rice wine), vegetable juice, water, even tea can be used similarly. I save the water from soaking sun-dried tomatoes, which has a lovely taste, for just this purpose. A crushed clove of garlic left to steep in a jar of dressing can dramatically raise the dressing's satisfaction quotient. Favorite herbs, mustard, or honey also can be used to add bright and harmonious notes to dressings so that you don't miss the oil. Balsamic vinegar is so tasty that serious dieters often use it alone, or mixed with Dijon mustard, to avoid fat entirely. Sesame oil as part of the recipe's oil requirement also lends a satisfying punch.

If you do use bottled dressings, look for those that have no more than three grams of fat per serving, which is usually two tablespoons.

# Beet, Potato, White Bean, Arugula, and Red Onion Salad

*Chef Mark Strausman devised this appealing shades-of-pink salad as a first course, but I found its simple goodness so filling that I have returned to his New York City restaurant, Campagna, many times to eat it as my main course. In my adaptation, the fat has been lowered.*

1 cup dried white beans, preferably Great Northern, or 1 sixteen-ounce can cooked beans, drained
2 large or 3 medium beets (about 1 pound)
salt to taste
8 small new potatoes (about 1–1¼ pounds)

3 small bunches arugula
1 small red onion, halved and sliced paper thin (about ¾ cup)
2 tablespoons red wine vinegar
freshly ground black pepper to taste
3 tablespoons extra-virgin olive oil

If you're using dried beans, soak the beans overnight in cold water to cover. Drain, place in a heavy pot with cold water to cover by several inches, bring to a slow simmer, cover, and cook slowly until the beans are tender but hold their shape, about 40 minutes. Drain in a colander, gently rinse with cold water, and dry on a clean kitchen towel.

Trim the beets, leaving 1 to 2 inches of stem attached. Place in a medium saucepan, cover with cold water, add the salt, and bring to a boil. Reduce the heat and simmer until tender. (The cooking time will vary according to the size of the beets. Start testing with the tip of a small knife after 40 minutes.) Drain, cover with warm water, and let stand until cool enough to handle, then slip off the skins.

At the same time, put the potatoes in another saucepan, add cold salted water to cover, and bring to a boil. Cover and cook until tender, about 25 to 30 minutes. Drain the beets and potatoes separately and set aside to cool.

Remove coarse stems from the arugula and wash and dry the leaves. You should have about 2 quarts of leaves. Set aside.

Peel the potatoes and cut into ½- to ¾-inch cubes. Do the same with the beets. Place both in a large mixing bowl with the arugula, beans, and onion.

Put the vinegar in a small bowl. Whisk in ½ teaspoon salt (or to taste) and several grindings of black pepper. Add the olive oil and whisk to blend. Add the vinaigrette to the large bowl and toss thoroughly. Check the seasoning and serve immediately.

**Serves 6 as a first course, 4 as a luncheon dish**

| PER SERVING | |
| --- | --- |
| CALORIES | 265 |
| FAT | 8 GM |
| SATURATED FAT | 1 GM |
| CHOLESTEROL | 0 MG |
| SODIUM | 239 MG |
| PROTEIN | 10 GM |
| CARBOHYDRATE | 42 GM |

# Roasted Pepper, Mesclun, and Grilled Chicken Salad

*All of the elements of this attractive and delicious main-course luncheon salad can be prepared ahead for last-minute assembly. Serve with plenty of crusty peasant bread.*

1 sweet red pepper

1 sweet yellow pepper

2 tablespoons balsamic vinegar

½ teaspoon salt

freshly ground black pepper to taste

3 tablespoons extra-virgin olive oil

1 shallot, minced, or 1 clove garlic, crushed

1 teaspoon *herbes de Provence*

1 bunch arugula, stemmed

2 ounces mesclun (see Note)

1 small head frisée or curly endive

1 four-ounce boneless chicken breast, grilled and sliced diagonally into ½-inch strips, or an equal amount of cooked white-meat chicken, torn into strips

1 large ripe tomato, seeded, juiced, and chopped, for garnish

Roast the red and yellow peppers on top of the stove or under the broiler, according to the directions on page 207. Place in a brown paper bag to steam for about 10 minutes, then peel, seed, and stem. Cut into ¾-inch strips and set aside.

In a glass jar or small bowl, combine the vinegar, salt, and pepper. Add the olive oil, shallot or garlic, and *herbes de Provence*. Cover tightly and shake vigorously until the dressing thickens. Set aside. *(May be prepared ahead up to this point.)*

Place the salad greens in an attractive shallow salad bowl, add 2 tablespoons of the dressing, and toss. Add the pepper strips and chicken. Garnish with the chopped tomato. Drizzle the balance of the dressing over all.

**Serves 4 as a luncheon dish**

| PER SERVING | |
| --- | --- |
| CALORIES | 170 |
| FAT | 11 GM |
| SATURATED FAT | 2 GM |
| CHOLESTEROL | 24 MG |
| SODIUM | 317 MG |
| PROTEIN | 11 GM |
| CARBOHYDRATE | 7 GM |

Note: If you cannot find mesclun, a ready-made mixture of a variety of small salad greens, substitute mâche (lamb's lettuce); other tender, soft greens such as Bibb, miniature curly red (Lola Rossa), or oakleaf lettuce; or a mixture of these.

# Orzo Salad with Grilled Shiitake Mushrooms, Asparagus, and Sun-Dried Tomatoes

*If you don't know orzo, the versatile rice-shaped pasta, you should. It's particularly nice in a salad, like this popular one, which East Hampton caterer Michelle Florea graciously shared with me. It makes a great cold lunch.*

½ cup dry-packed sun-dried tomatoes
¼ pound fresh shiitake mushrooms
    (about 8 mushrooms)
1 tablespoon olive oil
½ pound thin asparagus (about 8
    spears)
1 teaspoon salt
½ pound orzo

### Dressing

⅓ cup vegetable stock, preferably
    homemade (page 272)

1 teaspoon salt
1 tablespoon olive oil
2 teaspoons balsamic vinegar
1 tablespoon sherry wine vinegar
juice of 1 large orange
grated zest of 1 orange
¼ cup chopped fresh basil (or more to
    taste)

Soak the sun-dried tomatoes in a small bowl of hot water for 5 minutes. Drain, chop coarsely, and set aside.

Remove and discard the stems of the mushrooms. Wipe the caps with a damp paper towel and cut into ¾-inch slices. Brush the olive oil over the bottom of a heavy nonstick skillet, place over medium heat, add the mushrooms, and stir-fry until they give up their juices. If they seem to be browning too fast, lower the heat. Set aside.

Break off and discard the coarse lower stems of the asparagus and cut the remainder on the diagonal into 3 or 4 pieces. Bring a pot of water to a boil, add ½ teaspoon salt, and drop in the asparagus. Return to a boil and cook for 4 minutes. Drain, run cold water over the asparagus, and set aside.

Bring 2 quarts of water to a rolling boil in a large pot, add the remaining salt and the orzo. When the water returns to a boil, lower the heat to medium. Cook for 8 to 10 minutes or until just tender. Drain in a colander and refresh in cold water.

To make the dressing, in a large bowl mix together the vegetable stock, salt, olive oil, balsamic vinegar, sherry wine vinegar, orange juice, and zest. Add the orzo and mix well. Then add the mushrooms, asparagus, sun-dried tomatoes, and basil and toss lightly. Serve at room temperature.

**Serves 6**

| PER SERVING | |
| --- | --- |
| CALORIES | 224 |
| FAT | 5 GM |
| SATURATED FAT | 1 GM |
| CHOLESTEROL | 0 MG |
| SODIUM | 798 MG |
| PROTEIN | 8 GM |
| CARBOHYDRATE | 37 GM |

# Tuna and Carrot Salad

*A tuna salad sandwich is probably one of America's favorite lunches. Although it seems healthier than meat or cheese, it can deliver a big wallop of fat because of the mayonnaise it contains. Tuna salads available in delis are even worse, and if they are low fat, they are usually dry and tasteless. This version covers all the bases — low in fat, a little different, and very tasty. The carrot adds moisture and an elusive sweet note.*

1 six-ounce can light tuna in water, preferably reduced sodium

1 stalk celery, chopped

1 hard-boiled egg white, chopped

1 tablespoon minced onion

1 small carrot, scraped and grated on finer broad side of box grater

1 heaping tablespoon sweet pickle relish

1 tablespoon snipped fresh dill (optional)

3 tablespoons nonfat mayonnaise

freshly ground black pepper to taste

Drain the tuna and put it in a mixing bowl. Add the celery, egg white, onion, carrot, relish, and dill (if using). Mix lightly but well with a fork. Add the mayonnaise and blend gently but thoroughly. Season with pepper.

**Makes enough for 4 or 5 sandwiches**

➤ *Thin slices of Kirby cucumber, which you can eat with the skin on, are a nice addition to a sandwich made with this salad and add fiber as well.*

| PER SERVING | |
| --- | --- |
| CALORIES | 76 |
| FAT | 0 GM |
| SATURATED FAT | 0 GM |
| CHOLESTEROL | 16 MG |
| SODIUM | 161 MG |
| PROTEIN | 12 GM |
| CARBOHYDRATE | 5 GM |

# "Israeli" Salad

*This healthy first-course or main-course salad, accompaniment, or snack eaten at breakfast, lunch, or dinner is found everywhere in Israel. Called "Turkish salad" by the Israelis and "Israeli salad" by visitors, it is a forgiving assemblage. You put in what you like, in the amounts that please you. This recipe comes from an Israeli friend, Erna De-Shalit.*

1 tablespoon olive oil
juice of ½ small lemon
salt and freshly ground black pepper
    to taste
1 scallion, white and green parts,
    sliced, or ⅓ cup minced red onion
1 medium ripe tomato, diced

1 Kirby cucumber or ½ regular
    cucumber, peeled and diced
⅓ sweet green, red, or yellow pepper,
    seeded and diced
3 or 4 radishes, diced (optional)
2 tablespoons chopped fresh parsley

In a salad bowl, combine the olive oil, lemon juice, and salt and pepper. Stir in the scallion or onion, tomato, cucumber, sweet pepper, and radishes (if using). Sprinkle with parsley just before serving.

**Serves 3 or 4**

➤ *For a more substantial salad, Erna adds a chopped salad green, such as romaine lettuce or arugula. I also like the kick of half a small fresh jalapeño, seeded and minced.*

| PER SERVING | |
|---|---|
| CALORIES | 43 |
| FAT | 3 GM |
| SATURATED FAT | 0 GM |
| CHOLESTEROL | 0 MG |
| SODIUM | 6 MG |
| PROTEIN | 1 GM |
| CARBOHYDRATE | 3 GM |

# Swedish Cucumber Salad

*Some version of cucumber salad appears almost everywhere in Sweden — as part of a smorgasbord or simply as an accompaniment to fish, along with the Swedes' wonderful boiled waxy potatoes. I like this version because it doesn't require the usual preliminary salting to wilt the cucumbers. Serve with any simple, nonsauced whitefish or poached salmon, or as a garnish for smoked salmon when served as a first course.*

4 medium cucumbers (about 1¾ pounds)

6 tablespoons white vinegar

¼ cup sugar

¾ cup water

salt and freshly ground white pepper to taste

2 tablespoons snipped fresh dill (see Note)

Peel the cucumbers, cut in half, and then cut in half again lengthwise. Scrape out the seeds with a teaspoon and cut off the rounded ends. Cut crosswise into slices so thin that they are almost transparent. (A mandoline or the 1-millimeter slicing disk of a food processor will do this quickly and nicely.) There should be about 5 cups. Put the slices in a bowl.

In a small saucepan, combine the vinegar, sugar, water, and salt and pepper and bring to a simmer. Stir over medium heat until the sugar dissolves, about 2 minutes. Pour over the cucumbers and let cool, about 15 minutes. Strew with the dill, toss to blend, and chill for 2 to 3 hours. Just before serving, drain away nearly all the liquid.

**Serves 4**

| PER SERVING | |
|---|---|
| CALORIES | 100 |
| FAT | 0 GM |
| SATURATED FAT | 0 GM |
| CHOLESTEROL | 0 MG |
| SODIUM | 11 MG |
| PROTEIN | 1 GM |
| CARBOHYDRATE | 25 GM |

Note: Snip delicate fresh dill with kitchen shears, which releases the flavor but keeps it fresh and feathery, rather than chopping it, which tends to bruise it.

# Fresh Corn and Basil Salad

*The marriage of basil and tomatoes is well known; lesser known is the simple magic of pairing basil with fresh corn. This salad couldn't be simpler to put together, and the recipe can easily be doubled or tripled.*

3 or 4 ears fresh corn

⅓ cup chopped red onion

5 fresh basil leaves, chopped

freshly ground black pepper to taste

2 tablespoons cider vinegar

½ teaspoon salt (or more to taste)

3 tablespoons canola oil

Bring a pot of water to a boil. (Do not add salt; it toughens the kernels.) Husk the corn, making sure to remove all the silk, and drop the ears into the water. When the water returns to a boil, cover and cook for 2 minutes. Turn off the heat and let sit for 3 minutes more. Have a bowl of ice water ready and plunge the ears into it to stop further cooking and facilitate handling.

With a sharp knife, cut off the corn kernels and place them in a bowl. You should have about 3½ to 4 cups of kernels. Add the onion, basil, and liberal grindings of black pepper and mix gently with a wooden spoon.

In a small bowl, combine the vinegar, salt, and oil. Pour over the corn and mix well. Adjust the seasoning. Refrigerate for 1 hour before serving.

Makes about 4 cups, serving 6–8

➤ *You can make this with either yellow or white corn, but the yellow suits the dish better and is more colorful. In a pinch, you could even use flash-frozen corn, which is not as sweet as fresh but is still quite good.*

| PER SERVING | |
| --- | --- |
| CALORIES | 89 |
| FAT | 6 GM |
| SATURATED FAT | 0 GM |
| CHOLESTEROL | 0 MG |
| SODIUM | 163 MG |
| PROTEIN | 1 GM |
| CARBOHYDRATE | 8 GM |

# French Potato Salad

*The microwave oven makes this dish a breeze, though you can boil the potatoes if you wish. More elegant than conventional potato salad made with mayonnaise, it goes with any food that is not sauced. It's especially satisfying with Soy-Roasted Chicken (page 144) or thin slices of cold turkey, veal, or pork loin.*

2 pounds new potatoes, scrubbed and sliced ¼ inch thick

½ cup defatted reduced-sodium chicken broth

½ cup Lemon Mustard Vinaigrette (page 93)

2 tablespoons minced shallot

2 tablespoons chopped fresh parsley, a mixture of chopped fresh parsley and chervil, or snipped fresh chives

Combine the potatoes and half the broth in a 2-quart microwave-safe dish, cover, and microwave on high for 5 minutes. Toss thoroughly with a rubber spatula, cover, and microwave for 3 to 5 minutes more or until the potatoes are just tender. (Alternatively, you can cover the potatoes with cold water and boil until just tender.)

While the potatoes are warm, pour the remaining stock over them and toss gently with the spatula. Let sit for a few minutes while the potatoes absorb the broth. In a small bowl, combine the vinaigrette, shallot, and half the herbs and pour over the potatoes. Toss lightly with a wooden spoon and garnish with the remaining herbs. Let sit for a while at room temperature to develop the flavor.

**Serves 6**

| PER SERVING | |
|---|---|
| CALORIES | 194 |
| FAT | 8 GM |
| SATURATED FAT | 1 GM |
| CHOLESTEROL | 0 MG |
| SODIUM | 113 MG |
| PROTEIN | 3 GM |
| CARBOHYDRATE | 29 GM |

# Dale's Summer Slaw

*This fresh, crunchy salad comes from an old friend, Dale Loy, a fearless cook who frequently gives dinner parties for seventy-five or more at the drop of a hat. It's one of her large-crowd standbys — easy and delicious, and not a drop of fat!*

1 small head red cabbage (about 2 pounds)
2 large Granny Smith apples
2 bunches (6–8) scallions
1-inch piece fresh ginger

½ cup rice wine vinegar
1½ teaspoons sugar
salt to taste
½ cup chopped fresh cilantro
freshly ground black pepper to taste

Remove and discard any coarse outer leaves from the cabbage. Cut into quarters and shred finely either by hand using a slaw shredder or with the thin (1-millimeter) slicing disk of a food processor. Place in a large mixing bowl. (You should have about 8 cups.)

Core the apples and cut into quarters. Cut on the diagonal into fine slivers. (You should have about 4 cups.) Add to the cabbage.

Trim the scallions and slice the white and part of the green finely on the diagonal. Add to the bowl. Toss well with your hands for even distribution.

Grate the ginger, add to the slaw, and toss with two forks. In a small bowl, combine the vinegar, sugar, and salt and stir until the sugar and salt dissolve completely. Pour over the slaw and toss well with the forks. Add the cilantro and toss again. Add black pepper to taste. Refrigerate for at least 2 hours before serving.

**Serves 8–10**

| PER SERVING | |
| --- | --- |
| CALORIES | 52 |
| FAT | 0 GM |
| SATURATED FAT | 0 GM |
| CHOLESTEROL | 0 MG |
| SODIUM | 13 MG |
| PROTEIN | 2 GM |
| CARBOHYDRATE | 13 GM |

# Saloon Slaw

*Besides being a delightful way to add the powerful nutrient punch of cabbage to your diet, coleslaw makes the most ordinary sandwich satisfying when served on the side and can be used instead of mayonnaise in the sandwich itself. Previously, to keep the fat down, I dressed slaw with a mixture of yoghurt and mayo, but that tended to be watery. This colorful, low-fat version is anything but. Don't be put off by the large amount of sugar in the dressing.*

3 tablespoons Dijon mustard

3–4 tablespoons sugar

2 tablespoons sweet pickle relish

2 tablespoons reduced-fat mayonnaise

3 tablespoons cider vinegar

salt to taste

¼ cup skim milk (approximately)

1 small head green cabbage

1 small onion

2 carrots, peeled

½ sweet green pepper

2 teaspoons celery seed (optional)

freshly ground black pepper to taste

In a small bowl, combine the mustard, sugar, relish, mayonnaise, vinegar, and salt. Thin to a pleasing consistency with the milk. Set aside.

Cut the cabbage into quarters, trim off any coarse outer leaves, and remove the core. Shred, using a slaw shredder or the shredding disk of a food processor, and place in a large bowl. (You should have about 6 cups.) Grate the onion (or chop finely in the food processor with the steel blade) and add to the cabbage. Grate the carrots and green pepper. (Grate the pepper by hand on a box grater; it gets too mushy in the food processor.) Add to the cabbage and mix thoroughly with your hands or toss with two forks. Add the celery seed (if using) and toss again. Add the dressing and black pepper and toss once more. Refrigerate for several hours before serving.

**Makes about 1½ quarts, serving 6–8**

➤ *If you wish, you can make this slaw with a mixture of red and green cabbage.*

| PER SERVING | |
|---|---|
| CALORIES | 83 |
| FAT | 1 GM |
| SATURATED FAT | 0 GM |
| CHOLESTEROL | 0 MG |
| SODIUM | 218 MG |
| PROTEIN | 2 GM |
| CARBOHYDRATE | 17 GM |

# Jicama Relish

*Sweet and nutty with a texture similar to that of a water chestnut, the Mexican tuber jicama makes a simple, crunchy relish that is a pleasant accompaniment to any sandwich.*

1 medium jicama (¾–1 pound)
2 tablespoons lime juice
2 teaspoons sugar

salt to taste (optional)
2 teaspoons powdered ancho or other hot red chili

Just before using, peel the tough outer skin from the jicama with a potato peeler. Using a slicing or julienne disk of a food processor (the 3-millimeter-square julienne disk is particularly good for this), cut into strips about 2 by ⅛ by ⅛ inch. Place in a bowl and toss with the lime juice, sugar, and salt (if using). Sprinkle with the powdered chilies and toss again. Refrigerate for about 1 hour, then remove from the refrigerator and serve at room temperature.

Makes about 4 cups

➤ *Be sure to use powdered red chili peppers, not chili powder (a Tex-Mex blend of spices). If not available, use a small amount of fresh, good-quality cayenne pepper.*

| PER ½ CUP | |
|---|---|
| CALORIES | 26 |
| FAT | 0 GM |
| SATURATED FAT | 0 GM |
| CHOLESTEROL | 0 MG |
| SODIUM | 10 MG |
| PROTEIN | 1 GM |
| CARBOHYDRATE | 6 GM |

# Spinach Salad

*Here's a salad that is pretty enough to serve to guests for lunch but is healthfully low in fat and high in fiber. You can vary the garnish according to availability.*

10 ounces fresh spinach, stems removed

½ sweet red or yellow pepper, seeded and cut into thin strips

8 mushrooms, sliced

1 cup cooked corn kernels, fresh or canned

3 hard-boiled egg whites, cut into eighths

½ cup Sesame Rice Vinegar Dressing (recipe follows)

1 handful alfalfa sprouts

whole wheat garlic croutons (page 270)

In a large bowl, combine the spinach, pepper, mushrooms, corn, and hard-boiled egg whites. Toss lightly. Add the dressing and toss again. Divide among 4 plates, top each with a small tangle of sprouts and a scattering of croutons, and serve.

Serves 4

➤ *For a heartier luncheon salad, add 1 cup bite-size pieces of roasted or poached chicken breast.*

| PER SERVING, INCLUDING DRESSING | |
|---|---|
| CALORIES | 224 |
| FAT | 15 GM |
| SATURATED FAT | 2 GM |
| CHOLESTEROL | 0 MG |
| SODIUM | 1,290 MG |
| PROTEIN | 8 GM |
| CARBOHYDRATE | 19 GM |

# Sesame Rice Vinegar Dressing

2 tablespoons dark sesame oil
¼ cup rice wine vinegar

¼ cup low-sodium soy sauce
2 tablespoons water

Combine all the ingredients in a jar, cover tightly, and shake to blend.

**Makes ¾ cup**

| PER 3 TABLESPOONS | |
| --- | --- |
| CALORIES | 72 |
| FAT | 7 GM |
| SATURATED FAT | 1 GM |
| CHOLESTEROL | 0 MG |
| SODIUM | 600 MG |
| PROTEIN | 1 GM |
| CARBOHYDRATE | 2 GM |

# Rosa's Garlic Dressing

*This is the salad dressing we use more than any other. It was developed by our former housekeeper, Rosa Caldas, who is no slouch at reducing fat while keeping the flavor in cooking. The recipe makes nearly 1 cup and is ideal for any green salad. It keeps well and is a great time-saver.*

2 tablespoons lemon juice
2 tablespoons balsamic vinegar
1½ teaspoons Dijon mustard
½ teaspoon salt

freshly ground black pepper to taste
6 tablespoons extra-virgin olive oil
2 tablespoons water
2 cloves garlic

Combine the lemon juice and vinegar in a small bowl. Whisk in the mustard, salt, and pepper. Add the olive oil and whisk to blend. Add the water and whisk again. Crush the garlic and add. Let dressing steep for at least 30 minutes. Remove the garlic before serving. Leftover dressing may be refrigerated in a tightly covered jar for up to 10 days.

**Makes 14 tablespoons**

| PER TABLESPOON | |
| --- | --- |
| CALORIES | 53 |
| FAT | 4 GM |
| SATURATED FAT | 1 GM |
| CHOLESTEROL | 0 MG |
| SODIUM | 92 MG |
| PROTEIN | 0 GM |
| CARBOHYDRATE | 0 GM |

# Lemon Mustard Vinaigrette

*Chicken stock replaces a good deal of the oil in this dressing, resulting in a classic taste that's ideal for soft lettuces of all kinds.*

2 tablespoons lemon juice
2 tablespoons defatted reduced-
   sodium chicken stock
1 teaspoon Dijon mustard

salt and freshly ground black pepper
   to taste
2 tablespoons extra-virgin olive oil

In a small bowl, combine the lemon juice and chicken stock. Add the mustard and salt and pepper and whisk. Add the olive oil and whisk until smooth.

**Makes about ⅓ cup**

VARIATIONS:

*Classic Vinaigrette:* Substitute red wine vinegar for the lemon juice.
*Garlic Vinaigrette:* Crush a large garlic clove, drop into either of the dressings, and let steep for at least 30 minutes.

PER TABLESPOON

| | |
|---|---|
| CALORIES | 51 |
| FAT | 6 GM |
| SATURATED FAT | 1 GM |
| CHOLESTEROL | 0 MG |
| SODIUM | 40 MG |
| PROTEIN | 0 GM |
| CARBOHYDRATE | 1 GM |

# Miso Dressing

*Fans of creamy salad dressings will feel right at home with this healthful dressing made with miso paste. It's especially delicious on a luncheon salad of shredded carrots, chickpeas or beans, sprouts, and lettuce.*

3 tablespoons white miso paste,
   preferably Cold Mountain
3 tablespoons canola oil
¼ cup rice wine vinegar

1 teaspoon honey
1 teaspoon dry mustard
½ teaspoon minced onion

Place all the ingredients in a jar, cover tightly, and shake vigorously. Keep refrigerated.

**Makes about ¾ cup**

➤ *Miso paste is available in health food stores and oriental markets.*

PER TABLESPOON

| | |
|---|---|
| CALORIES | 46 |
| FAT | 4 GM |
| SATURATED FAT | 0 GM |
| CHOLESTEROL | 0 MG |
| SODIUM | 171 MG |
| PROTEIN | 1 GM |
| CARBOHYDRATE | 2 GM |

# 9

# PASTA

Quick Tomato Sauce

Penne all'Arrabbiata

Penne with Tomato and Sweet Pepper Sauce

Spaghetti with Fresh and Sun-Dried Tomato Sauce

Spaghetti with Eggplant and Tomato Sauce

Linguini with Leeks and Tomatoes

Pesto Sauce

Pasta with Pesto Sauce, Genoese Style

Linguini with Tomatoes, Anchovies,
Basil, and Mozzarella

Orecchiette with Broccoli, Chickpeas,
Onions, and Tomatoes

Fettuccine with Shrimp and Spicy Tomato Sauce

NOT BEING ITALIAN, the word *pasta* was not part of my generation's vocabulary when we were young. We knew spaghetti with meatballs or meat sauce and lasagna, but that was about it. I never even realized the noodles in my mother's chicken soup were pasta!

Today pasta, in its myriad forms, is recognized as a nourishing food that can be prepared so quickly and easily and in so many satisfying ways that it often displaces meat as a main course. I don't know anyone who doesn't love it, and unless you have an insulin problem, pasta is a healthy food that plays an important role in a low-fat lifestyle. In fact, when I canvassed some readers to see what they would like to see in this book, the answer invariably was "new pasta recipes."

Stores everywhere now carry high-quality imported pasta made with durum (hard) wheat or semolina (a more coarsely milled durum). Some names to look for are Delverde, Martelli, Barilla (which makes a very good whole wheat pasta in a variety of shapes), and De Cecco as well as Pasta La Bella, an exceptionally good domestic durum wheat pasta. When you're shopping for pasta to eat that night, try fresh egg pasta. If you've eaten only dried pasta, the way fresh pasta holds a sauce will be a revelation. However, fresh pasta must be refrigerated and used within several days. It can be kept in the freezer, but it will lose its texture and flavor if it's frozen for too long.

Be mindful that many classic pasta recipes still have a disproportionately high fat content due to the olive oil, butter, cream, and cheese usually called for. Avoid dishes bathed in four cheeses or dripping with melted butter. Try reworking a favorite recipe to lower the fat content. For example, the original version of my family's favorite, Linguini with Tomatoes, Anchovies, Basil, and Mozzarella (page 106), called for six tablespoons of oil and six ounces of whole-milk mozzarella, which adds up to about thirty grams of fat per serving. I found that I could make this dish in a good-quality nonstick pan with just one tablespoon of oil. This, together with a reduced-fat cheese, turned it into a wonderful low-fat dish without sacrificing flavor. Each serving has only eight grams of fat and one-third fewer calories.

An intensely flavored tomato sauce is another secret to a good, satisfying pasta dish. It can be made with a moderate amount of oil bolstered by spices, as in Penne all'Arrabbiata (page 98). Freshly grated imported Parmesan cheese packs a lot of flavor into a small amount and makes any pasta luxurious. Don't insult your pasta or your palate with pre-grated Parmesan from a jar. It tastes like soapy sawdust.

You can apply these principles to many of your current recipes, but I also urge you to try some of the wonderful ones in this section. With a variety of pastas on hand and at least one good homemade sauce in your freezer, you'll never be without a quick, healthy dinner!

# Quick Tomato Sauce

*The usefulness of a simple "filetto di pomodoro" with its satisfying depth of flavor and color, needs no promoting. It plays a role in countless dishes and makes any pasta a nourishing low-fat dinner on its own.*

1 twenty-eight-ounce can Italian plum
    tomatoes
3 or 4 cloves garlic
1 large shallot
½ teaspoon sugar
2 tablespoons vegetable or reduced-
    sodium defatted chicken stock,
    preferably homemade (pages 272,
    274)

salt and freshly ground black pepper
    to taste
¼ cup fresh basil leaves
1 tablespoon extra-virgin olive oil

Place the tomatoes in a strainer and let them drain for a few minutes.

Finely chop the garlic and the shallot. Place them in a nonreactive or non-stick skillet. Add the sugar and stock, cover the pan, and cook gently over medium-low heat until the onion is soft and the stock has evaporated, about 2 minutes. Add the tomatoes, breaking them up with your fingers as you do. Season with salt and pepper and bring to a boil. Lower the heat slightly and simmer for 5 minutes. Add the basil and olive oil and cook for 2 minutes more. This sauce can be refrigerated for up to 1 week or frozen for up to 1 month.

Makes 1¾ cups, serving 4

➤ *If fresh basil is unavailable, use 2 tablespoons chopped fresh Italian flat-leaf parsley. Do not used dried basil, which bears more resemblance to grass than to the fragrant fresh leaf.*

| PER SERVING | |
| --- | --- |
| CALORIES | 81 |
| FAT | 4 GM |
| SATURATED FAT | 1 GM |
| CHOLESTEROL | 0 MG |
| SODIUM | 332 MG |
| PROTEIN | 2 GM |
| CARBOHYDRATE | 11 GM |

# Penne all'Arrabbiata

*This name translates as "angry pasta," meaning pasta in a tomato sauce made hot and spicy with chile peppers and garlic. The sauce is fast, easy, and extremely versatile, and it can be made ahead. Adjust the hotness by using more or less pepper flakes.*

1 twenty-eight-ounce can Italian plum tomatoes, drained (liquid reserved)

2 tablespoons extra-virgin olive oil

½ teaspoon red pepper flakes (or to taste)

3 cloves garlic

salt to taste

1 pound imported penne rigate

12 fresh basil leaves, torn into ½-inch pieces (optional)

2 tablespoons freshly grated Pecorino Romano cheese

Make a coarse tomato puree by putting the tomatoes through a food mill or pulsing in a food processor just until they are broken up but not totally smooth.

Heat the olive oil in a skillet over medium heat. Add the pepper flakes. As soon as they begin to release their color, add the tomato puree. Stir to mix well. Put the garlic through a press directly into the sauce, then add the salt. Simmer over medium-high heat, stirring occasionally, until the tomatoes begin to thicken into a sauce, about 15 minutes. Remove from the heat and set aside. *(May be prepared ahead up to this point and refrigerated. Remove from the refrigerator and let come to room temperature before proceeding.)*

Bring 4 quarts of water to a boil in a large saucepan or pot. Add 1 tablespoon salt and the penne, stirring well. A few minutes before the pasta is done, place the sauce over medium heat and add the basil leaves (if using). When the pasta is al dente, drain and toss with the sauce in the skillet, turning off the heat. Stir in the grated cheese. Adjust the seasoning and serve at once.

Makes about 2 cups sauce, serving 4

➤ *The sauce can be used with any shellfish, such as shrimp, lobster, or mussels. You can also bake any filleted fish in it; for textural interest, top with Toasted Bread Crumbs (page 271) before serving.*

| PER SERVING | |
| --- | --- |
| CALORIES | 535 |
| FAT | 10 GM |
| SATURATED FAT | 2 GM |
| CHOLESTEROL | 3 MG |
| SODIUM | 377 MG |
| PROTEIN | 17 GM |
| CARBOHYDRATE | 94 GM |

# Penne with Tomato and Sweet Pepper Sauce

1 small sweet red pepper, halved and seeded

1 small sweet yellow pepper, halved and seeded

1 tablespoon fruity olive oil, preferably extra-virgin

1 medium onion, finely sliced

2 large cloves garlic, finely chopped

scant ¼ teaspoon red pepper flakes (or to taste)

1 twenty-eight-ounce can Italian plum tomatoes, drained

1 teaspoon sugar

½ teaspoon salt (or to taste)

¼ cup (approximately) defatted reduced-sodium chicken stock

freshly ground black pepper to taste

1 pound penne or other hollow pasta

¼ cup shredded fresh basil leaves

freshly grated Parmesan cheese

Cut the red and yellow peppers into ½-inch-wide strips, dice, and set aside.

Heat the olive oil in a large skillet over medium-low heat and add the onion. Cook, stirring, until soft and slightly caramelized, about 8 minutes. Add the garlic and red pepper flakes and cook, stirring, for about 1 minute to release their fragrance. Add the diced peppers and the tomatoes, breaking them up with your fingers as you do. Add the sugar and salt. Cover and adjust the heat so that the mixture just simmers. Cook, stirring occasionally, until the vegetables are soft, about 15 minutes.

Transfer to a food processor and puree, adding chicken stock as needed to make a smooth sauce that still has some texture. Return the sauce to the skillet. Add black pepper. Keep warm or reheat gently at serving time.

In a large pot of boiling salted water, cook the penne al dente, about 8 to 10 minutes. Drain and divide among 4 warm serving plates. Top with sauce and a sprinkling of basil and serve at once. Pass the Parmesan at the table.

Serves 4

| PER SERVING | |
|---|---|
| CALORIES | 351 |
| FAT | 4 GM |
| SATURATED FAT | 1 GM |
| CHOLESTEROL | 0 MG |
| SODIUM | 432 MG |
| PROTEIN | 12 GM |
| CARBOHYDRATE | 67 GM |

# Spaghetti with Fresh and Sun-Dried Tomato Sauce

1 tablespoon olive oil
4 large cloves garlic, chopped
1 small onion, chopped
1 twenty-eight-ounce can Italian plum
   tomatoes
1 cup sun-dried tomatoes, soaked in
   hot water for 30 minutes, drained,
   and chopped
¼ cup white wine

1 small dried red chili pepper,
   crumbled (optional)
freshly ground black pepper to taste
salt to taste (optional)
¾ pound spaghetti
chopped fresh Italian flat-leaf parsley
   for garnish
freshly grated Parmesan cheese

Heat the oil in a large nonstick skillet over medium-high heat, add the garlic and onion, and cook for 2 minutes or until softened but not brown. Add the plum tomatoes, crushing them against the side of the pan with a wooden spoon. Add the sun-dried tomatoes, wine, chili pepper (if using), and liberal grindings of black pepper. Adjust the heat to medium-low so that the liquid just bubbles softly and cook, uncovered, for 20 minutes or until slightly thickened. Taste for seasoning and add a tad of salt if needed.

In a large pot of boiling salted water, cook the spaghetti al dente. Drain well, divide among 4 bowls, add sauce, and garnish with the parsley. Alternatively, you can add the drained pasta to the sauce in the skillet, toss, and transfer to a warm serving bowl or serve right from the skillet. Pass the cheese at the table.

**Serves 4 as a first course**

| PER SERVING | |
| --- | --- |
| CALORIES | 475 |
| FAT | 5 GM |
| SATURATED FAT | 1 GM |
| CHOLESTEROL | 0 MG |
| SODIUM | 352 MG |
| PROTEIN | 17 GM |
| CARBOHYDRATE | 89 GM |

# Spaghetti with Eggplant and Tomato Sauce

*In Sicily, where this dish originated, eggplant is usually fried, which is hardly healthy. Since I learned how flavorsome it can be when baked, requiring vastly less oil, this hearty, delicious, easy dish adapted from Martha Rose Shulman has become one of my favorite weekend standbys. I make the sauce ahead and get salad greens ready, and dinner is a snap.*

1 medium eggplant (about 1 pound)

1 teaspoon salt

vegetable cooking spray

2 tablespoons olive oil

4 cloves garlic, minced (or more to taste)

1 small onion, minced

2 twenty-eight-ounce cans Italian plum tomatoes, drained and chopped

3 tablespoons tomato paste

pinch of sugar (optional)

2–3 teaspoons chopped fresh basil or 2 tablespoons chopped fresh parsley

salt and freshly ground black pepper to taste

¾ pound spaghetti or spaghettini

¼ cup freshly grated Parmesan cheese

Preheat the oven to 450°F.

Wash eggplant and without peeling, cut into one-inch cubes, sprinkle with the 1 teaspoon salt, and let sit in a colander for 30 minutes. Rinse and pat dry in a kitchen towel.

Spray a 9-by-13-inch baking dish with oil, add the eggplant, and toss with 1 tablespoon of the oil. Cover tightly and bake for 30 to 35 minutes or until tender.

Meanwhile, make the tomato sauce. Sauté the garlic and onion in the remaining 1 tablespoon oil over low heat. Cook for about 9 minutes or until the onion turns golden. Add the tomatoes and tomato paste. If the sauce tastes too acidic, add the sugar. Simmer over medium heat, stirring often, for 40 to 55 minutes or until thickened. Stir in the baked eggplant and basil or parsley. Season with salt and pepper. Heat through.

In a large pot of boiling salted water, cook the spaghetti al dente. Drain and toss with the sauce. Pass the Parmesan at the table.

**Serves 4 generously**

➤ *I never peel eggplant if I can help it because I find the color contrast appealing. If you don't like the skin or if your eggplant is large and likely to be fibrous, by all means peel it. I've made this dish both ways, and both are equally delicious.*

| PER SERVING | |
| --- | --- |
| CALORIES | 197 |
| FAT | 8 GM |
| SATURATED FAT | 2 GM |
| CHOLESTEROL | 3 MG |
| SODIUM | 913 MG |
| PROTEIN | 7 GM |
| CARBOHYDRATE | 29 GM |

# Linguini with Leeks and Tomatoes

*I frequently find myself craving this dish, which comes from Word of Mouth, a delightful shop with some of Manhattan's best prepared foods. Christi Finch, the owner, kindly shared her recipe, from which this is adapted. It's easy to make, very flavorful, and low in calories and fat.*

8 or 9 leeks (about 2¾ pounds)

2 tablespoons olive oil

⅓ cup vegetable or defatted reduced-sodium chicken stock

1 thirty-five-ounce can Italian plum tomatoes, drained and coarsely chopped

¾ cup tomato puree (see Note)

2 large cloves garlic, minced

salt to taste

1 tablespoon sugar (optional)

freshly ground black pepper to taste

1 pound fine dried linguini or angel-hair pasta

Trim off the roots and most of the coarse dark green tops of the leeks so that they are about 7 to 8 inches long. Cut into ½-inch-thick slices and wash very well in a colander. Drain and press with your hands to get out as much water as possible. You should have 5 to 6 cups sliced leeks.

Heat the oil in a large nonstick skillet, add the leeks, and sauté for 5 minutes over medium-high heat, but do not let them brown. Add the stock, lower heat slightly, and continue sautéing for 10 minutes more.

Add the tomatoes, tomato puree, garlic, and salt and cook for about 20 minutes or until the leeks are very tender and the sauce is thick. Taste about halfway through, and if the sauce seems too acidic, add the sugar. Season with several grindings of pepper.

In a pot of boiling salted water, cook the pasta al dente. Drain well and combine with the sauce in a warm serving bowl. Toss well to coat the pasta with the sauce. Serve immediately.

**Serves 4 or 5**

| PER SERVING | |
| --- | --- |
| CALORIES | 650 |
| FAT | 10 GM |
| SATURATED FAT | 1 GM |
| CHOLESTEROL | 0 MG |
| SODIUM | 680 MG |
| PROTEIN | 20 GM |
| CARBOHYDRATE | 123 GM |

Note: Tomato puree is available in cans, but usually in a size larger than you'll need here. It does make a lovely thick sauce, however, so I freeze the rest of the puree in small containers for use in other sauces. You also can use an 8-ounce can of tomato sauce, but the sauce will not be as thick.

# Pesto Sauce

*Pesto is one of the stellar creations of the Italian kitchen, and a relatively small amount adds a stunning depth of flavor to soups, sauces, and foods of all sorts. Traditionally, it is made with a lot of olive oil, pine nuts (sometimes walnuts), and butter and cheese added at the end, which makes for a divine flavor but oodles of fat. This recipe eliminates the butter and uses less olive oil, but it is still high in fat. Use it as a condiment, indulge in it occasionally, and enjoy it heartily as a sauce for pasta or vegetables, thinning it with an equal amount of pasta cooking water.*

2 cups packed fresh basil leaves
1 small handful (about ¼ cup) fresh
    parsley sprigs, leaves only
3 large cloves garlic, chopped
2 tablespoons pine nuts
⅓ cup extra-virgin olive oil

2 tablespoons freshly grated
    Parmesan cheese
½ teaspoon salt (or to taste)
freshly ground black pepper to taste
1 cup pasta cooking water
    (approximately)

Put the basil, parsley, garlic, and pine nuts in the bowl of a food processor. Pulse two or three times. Add the olive oil and process until the basil is pureed and the sauce is fairly smooth, scraping down the sides as needed. Do not overprocess. Stir in the cheese with a spatula and season with the salt and pepper. Transfer to a bowl or a container with a tight-fitting lid and refrigerate. Just before using, blend in an equal amount of pasta cooking water.

**Makes 2 cups, serving 6**

➤ *Pesto sauce base freezes very well and can be kept for up to 1 year. The parsley helps keep the color bright green. If you make it for the freezer, omit the cheese and pepper and add after defrosting.*

| PER SERVING | |
| --- | --- |
| CALORIES | 157 |
| FAT | 15 GM |
| SATURATED FAT | 2 GM |
| CHOLESTEROL | 2 MG |
| SODIUM | 225 MG |
| PROTEIN | 3 GM |
| CARBOHYDRATE | 7 GM |

# Pasta with Pesto Sauce, Genoese Style

*I love the Ligurian way of cooking a potato with the pasta and adding it, sliced, at the bottom of each person's dish. Sometimes cooked green beans are added as well. This is a very filling dish, definitely a main course.*

⅔ cup Pesto Sauce without added water (see preceding recipe)

2 tablespoons freshly grated Parmesan cheese

1 pound imported dried linguini or tagliatelle

1 medium potato, peeled, halved, and sliced ½ inch thick

freshly grated Parmesan cheese (optional)

Put a large pot of salted water on to boil. Put the Pesto Sauce in a small bowl, mix in the 2 tablespoons cheese, and set aside.

When the water boils, add the pasta and potato and cook the pasta al dente, about 10 to 12 minutes. Just before the pasta is finished, scoop out about ⅔ cup of the pasta cooking water and set aside.

Drain the pasta and set aside the potato. Before saucing the pasta, add enough reserved water to the pesto to make it the consistency you like. Divide the potato slices among 4 bowls, add the pasta, and top with the sauce. Pass additional cheese at the table if desired.

Serves 4

Add ½ pound young, tender string beans, trimmed, to the pasta after it has cooked for 6 minutes. You may require some additional Pesto Sauce.

| PER SERVING | |
| --- | --- |
| CALORIES | 517 |
| FAT | 8 GM |
| SATURATED FAT | 2 GM |
| CHOLESTEROL | 3 MG |
| SODIUM | 142 MG |
| PROTEIN | 17 GM |
| CARBOHYDRATE | 93 GM |

# Linguini with Tomatoes, Anchovies, Basil, and Mozzarella

*This pasta dish is not only delicious and filling, but it has special appeal because it is so attractive. My family has voted it their favorite and never seems to tire of it.*

1 tablespoon fruity olive oil

½ cup finely chopped onion (1 medium onion)

1 thirty-five-ounce can Italian plum tomatoes, drained (liquid reserved) and chopped

4 large cloves garlic, minced

½ cup minced fresh parsley

½ cup shredded fresh basil leaves (optional)

1 teaspoon dried oregano

salt and freshly ground black pepper to taste

1 two-ounce can flat anchovy fillets, drained and minced

2 tablespoons capers, drained

12 ounces fresh or dried linguini

6 ounces reduced-fat mozzarella cheese, cut into ½-inch dice

Heat the oil in a heavy 10½-inch nonstick skillet, add the onion, and sauté over high heat. After 1 minute, add 2 tablespoons of the tomato liquid, the garlic, and ¼ cup of the parsley and continue sautéing over low heat for 2 to 3 minutes.

Add the tomatoes, basil, oregano, and salt and pepper. Partially cover and cook over medium heat until the sauce is slightly reduced and most of the tomato liquid has evaporated, about 10 to 12 minutes. *(May be prepared ahead to this point. If so, reheat gently at serving time while pasta is cooking.)*

Add the anchovies and capers and keep the sauce warm over a very low flame while the pasta cooks.

Bring 3 to 4 quarts water to a boil, add the linguini, and cook over high heat until barely tender. Drain well and add to the skillet. Remove from heat, toss with the sauce, add the mozzarella, and toss again lightly. Cover and place over low heat again for 2 minutes; the cheese should be barely melted and still retain its shape. Then remove from heat, sprinkle with the remaining ¼ cup parsley, and serve immediately, right from the skillet.

**Serves 6 as a first course, 4 as a main course**

➤ *For a really filling meal, I often serve a side of blanched broccoli with this pasta.*

| PER SERVING | |
| --- | --- |
| CALORIES | 305 |
| FAT | 8 GM |
| SATURATED FAT | 3 GM |
| CHOLESTEROL | 80 MG |
| SODIUM | 877 MG |
| PROTEIN | 18 GM |
| CARBOHYDRATE | 42 GM |

# Orecchiette with Broccoli, Chickpeas, Onions, and Tomatoes

*An attractive, easy-to-prepare, hearty main dish with the healthy bonus of broccoli. Although this deliciously filling pasta can be made with canned chickpeas, it has more "tooth" when you use dried. Vegetarians love this!*

1½ cups canned chickpeas, drained and rinsed, or ¾ cup dried

1 tablespoon plus 2 teaspoons fruity olive oil

2 teaspoons salt (optional)

1 large head broccoli, cut into small florets (about 3 cups)

½ pound orecchiette or rigatoni

1 cup diced red onion

¼ cup vegetable or defatted, reduced-sodium chicken stock, preferably homemade (pages 272, 274)

2 tablespoons finely minced garlic

1 thirty-five-ounce can imported Italian plum tomatoes, drained and chopped

salt and freshly ground black pepper to taste

½ cup freshly grated Parmesan cheese (optional)

If you are using canned chickpeas, put them in a bowl with 1 tablespoon of the olive oil, toss, and set aside.

If you are using dried chickpeas, put ¾ cup dried chickpeas in a bowl with 2½ cups cold water and refrigerate overnight. Drain and rinse. Place the chickpeas in a medium saucepan and add fresh water to cover. Bring to a boil over medium heat. Reduce the heat, cover, and simmer until the chickpeas are tender but not mushy, about 1 hour. Add the salt during the last 15 minutes of cooking. Drain and transfer to a bowl. Toss with 1 tablespoon of the olive oil and set aside to cool.

Bring a pot of salted water to a boil, drop in the broccoli florets, and blanch for 3 minutes. Drain and refresh in ice water. Set aside to cool.

Bring another large pot of salted water to a boil. Add the pasta and cook al dente, about 12 minutes.

Meanwhile, heat the remaining 2 teaspoons olive oil in a large, preferably nonstick skillet, add the onion, stir, and as soon as it begins to sizzle, add the stock. Lower the heat and cook until the onion is tender. Add the chickpeas and garlic and cook for 1 minute or until the garlic just releases its fragrance and the chickpeas are warmed through. Add the tomatoes and broccoli and cook for 2 to 3 minutes more. Season with salt and pepper.

Drain the pasta and transfer to a warm serving bowl. Add the sauce and toss quickly to combine. Serve immediately, passing the cheese at the table if desired.

Serves 3 or 4

➤ *To prepare ahead, blanch the broccoli as directed and prepare the sauce, but do not cook the pasta or add the broccoli to the sauce until just before serving.*

| PER SERVING | |
| --- | --- |
| CALORIES | 560 |
| FAT | 16 GM |
| SATURATED FAT | 2 GM |
| CHOLESTEROL | 0 MG |
| SODIUM | 73 MG |
| PROTEIN | 24 GM |
| CARBOHYDRATE | 84 GM |

# Fettuccine with Shrimp and Spicy Tomato Sauce

*Shrimp makes this pasta a substantial main course that you can prepare easily and quickly. If you make the sauce ahead — say, in the morning or the night before — you can have a flavorsome and satisfying dinner on the table in the time it takes to cook the pasta.*

1 pound fettuccine
1¾–2 cups Arrabbiata Sauce without
   cheese (page 98)
1 pound small or medium shrimp,
   peeled

8–10 fresh basil leaves, torn into small
   pieces, for garnish (optional)

Bring a large pot of salted water to a boil. Add the fettucini and cook al dente, about 12 minutes. Drain.

Place the sauce over medium heat until warmed through. Add the shrimp, raise heat, and cook, stirring frequently and gently, for 5 minutes or until the shrimp turn pink and appear firm.

Divide the pasta among 4 warm dishes. Top with the sauce and shrimp and garnish with the basil if desired. Serve immediately.

**Serves 4**

➤ *I love to do this dish with* fettuccine neri — *black squid-ink pasta. The glistening black strands make an elegant presentation, and the pasta has more body and flavor than ordinary pasta.*

| PER SERVING | |
| --- | --- |
| CALORIES | 601 |
| FAT | 13 GM |
| SATURATED FAT | 1 GM |
| CHOLESTEROL | 140 MG |
| SODIUM | 460 MG |
| PROTEIN | 37 GM |
| CARBOHYDRATE | 90 GM |

# 10
# FISH and SHELLFISH

Broiled Bluefish

Bluefish with Red Pepper Relish

Cornmeal-Crusted Catfish on Mixed Greens

Pan-Grilled Sole

Oriental Sole Fillets

Teriyaki Salmon Steaks

Seared Salmon on a Bed of Fennel

Grilled Salmon Burgers

Cold Poached Salmon

Seared Tuna in a Black Pepper Crust

Crab Cakes

Hot Garlicky Shrimp

Scampi alla Busara

Allen Susser's Shrimp Shepherd's Pie

Warm Shrimp and Bean Salad

Steaming Mussels: Master Recipe

Greek-Style Cold Stuffed Mussels

Curried Mussels and Rice

Seviche of Scallops

Grilled Sea Scallops

Grilled Lobster with Vietnamese Dipping Sauce

I T'S HARD TO BELIEVE TODAY, but historically fish and shellfish were the prime source of protein for the poor. In 1622, when a new group of colonists arrived in Plymouth, the governor was deeply humiliated because his young colony was so short of food that the only dish they could present was lobster.

Today, top-quality fish and shellfish is often more expensive than meat because of the costs involved in getting fresh fish to market, not to mention shortages brought about by overfishing. Yet our belated love affair with this now very politically correct food shows no signs of abating. As a protein source, it has every virtue from both a health and a preparation standpoint: a low-fat food that is easily and quickly cooked, needs no involved treatment, and can be presented in all sorts of tasty ways.

But let's face it, fish can be less than satisfying, especially the mild flounder and soles that fish-phobic Americans look to for their lack of bones or strong taste. Whitefish boredom was handled by breading and frying, or by masking it with sauces based on flour-thickened butter and cream (or, worse, cheese). Today a wonderful variety of light, easy enhancements are available, including sauces with a vinaigrette or citrus base; a bed of fennel; a tomato coulis; a superb red pepper relish; or simply a topping of Tomatoes Concassé, very ripe tomatoes cut up and briefly cooked in a tiny bit of olive oil with shallot, savory herbs, and seasonings (see page 264). Low-Fat Tartar Sauce (page 262) is another pleasant accompaniment. All of these treatments add flavor and satisfaction with very little fat or calories. So does crusting, in which the traditional concept of breading and frying to keep moisture in and add flavor is replaced with various savory crusts of herbs, crumbs, black pepper, powdered chili peppers, or nuts (watch the fat) or with a delicate dusting of seasoned flour.

Don't overlook the oilier fishes such as bluefish, salmon, and trout, which are not only delicious but also good sources of the omega-3 fatty acids, which may help reduce the risk of heart attack and stroke. Eating only one or two servings of these fish each week is considered a protective measure.

Shellfish are another wonderful way to round out the protein picture. Shrimp, even a few, tossed into a stir-fry or pasta sauce make a satisfying dish. Their cholesterol content, though a little higher than that of other shellfish, is no longer regarded as serious, since they are so low in saturated fat, the dominant dietary factor in elevating serum cholesterol. Scallops are a healthful and sophisticated "natural fast food" (they must be cooked rapidly, or they become tough) and fabulous in a seviche. Mussels are probably one of the most underused and inexpensive sources of low-fat protein available outside the vegetable world.

# Broiled Bluefish

*So many people are convinced that they dislike this fish because it is too "fishy." The strip of dark muscle meat down the center can be strong, but only when bluefish is not impeccably fresh. In summertime, freshly caught blues (especially "snappers," or baby blues) are a delicacy and a wonderful source of healthful omega-3 fatty acids. Here is a fast, easy way to broil them, and the naysayers won't believe they're eating bluefish! This method works equally well with any "meaty" fish fillet, such as weakfish, red snapper, or grouper.*

1¾ pounds bluefish fillets, preferably "snappers," skin on
5 tablespoons reduced-fat mayonnaise
2 tablespoons white wine or vermouth
1 tablespoon reduced-sodium soy sauce
2 tablespoons minced fresh chives (optional)
1 teaspoon Dijon mustard

Preheat the broiler.

Wash the fish and pat dry with paper towels. Place on a piece of heavy-duty aluminum foil, flesh side up.

Put the mayonnaise in a small bowl, thin with the wine or vermouth, and mix in the soy sauce, chives (if using), and mustard. Spread the mixture over the fillets with the back of a spoon so that they are lightly and evenly covered.

Broil 4 to 6 inches from the heat for 7 to 9 minutes, depending on the thickness of the fish. The tops should be slightly golden and flecked with brown. Serve immediately.

**Serves 4 or 5**

*Fish and Shellfish*

► *For the quintessential easy summer dinner, accompany this recipe with fresh corn on the cob and a salad of sliced ripe tomatoes with fresh basil.*

| PER SERVING | |
| --- | --- |
| CALORIES | 268 |
| FAT | 12 GM |
| SATURATED FAT | 2 GM |
| CHOLESTEROL | 94 MG |
| SODIUM | 517 MG |
| PROTEIN | 32 GM |
| CARBOHYDRATE | 5 GM |

# Bluefish with Red Pepper Relish

*This incredibly flavorsome relish from chef Ed Brown of New York's Sea Grill makes a dramatic presentation for any broiled or grilled fish. It stands up best to a slightly oily fish such as fresh bluefish.*

2 medium sweet red peppers
1 tablespoon ground cumin
1 tablespoon crushed coriander seeds
freshly ground black pepper to taste
2 teaspoons olive oil
1 teaspoon minced fresh ginger

2 cloves garlic, minced
¼ cup dry white wine
2 heaping tablespoons chopped fresh cilantro leaves
6 five-ounce portions Broiled Bluefish (see page 113)

Roast the peppers by either of the methods described on page 207. Place in a brown paper bag and let steam for 10 minutes. Stem, seed, and finely chop.

Heat a large, heavy skillet over medium-high heat. Add the cumin, coriander, and several grindings of black pepper and pan-roast just until their fragrance is released, about 1 minute, shaking the pan several times. Do not let the spices burn.

Lower the heat. Add the oil, ginger, and garlic and cook for about 1 minute or until the garlic is soft and barely golden. Add the chopped peppers and cook over medium-low heat for about 5 minutes. Add the wine, raise the heat slightly, and continue cooking until the liquid has evaporated but the mixture is still moist. Remove from the heat, stir in the cilantro, and set aside until ready to serve.

Place a generous dollop of relish atop each portion of fish. Transfer any leftover relish to a small condiment bowl for the table.

**Makes about 1½ cups, serving 6**

➤ *The red pepper relish also can be used with grilled vegetables or as a crostini topping.*

| PER SERVING | |
|---|---|
| CALORIES | 303 |
| FAT | 2 GM |
| SATURATED FAT | 2 GM |
| CHOLESTEROL | 94 MG |
| SODIUM | 520 MG |
| PROTEIN | 33 GM |
| CARBOHYDRATE | 8 GM |

# Cornmeal-Crusted Catfish on Mixed Greens

*Farm-raised catfish has a sweet, clean flavor, unlike the muddy quality sometimes found in this denizen of river bottoms. This recipe has a nice combination of tastes and textures and supplies your salad as well.*

3 cups mixed lettuces plus arugula or mesclun
¼ cup thinly sliced Vidalia or red onion
¼ cup yellow cornmeal
salt and freshly ground black pepper to taste

2 four-ounce catfish fillets
4 teaspoons canola oil
2 tablespoons lemon juice
½ teaspoon grated lemon zest
1½ teaspoons Dijon mustard
½ teaspoon honey

Combine the greens and the onion in a bowl and set aside.

Place the cornmeal on a dinner plate. Season well with salt and pepper. Rinse the catfish and shake off water but do not dry. Lay the fish pieces on the cornmeal — first on one side, then the other — to coat evenly. Set aside.

Heat 2 teaspoons of the oil in a large nonstick skillet over medium-high heat. Add the fish and cook for 2 to 3 minutes per side, until golden brown and cooked through (turn with the aid of a plastic spatula). Remove to paper towels on a warm platter to drain.

To the skillet add the remaining 2 teaspoons oil, lemon juice, lemon zest, mustard, and honey and whisk over medium heat for 30 seconds. Remove from the heat. Add the warm dressing to the greens and onion in the bowl and toss, which will wilt the greens. Divide between 2 plates and top with the fish pieces.

**Serves 2**

➤ *Try substituting farm-raised catfish in some of your favorite fish recipes.*

| PER SERVING | |
| --- | --- |
| CALORIES | 357 |
| FAT | 19 GM |
| SATURATED FAT | 3 GM |
| CHOLESTEROL | 47 MG |
| SODIUM | 154 MG |
| PROTEIN | 24 GM |
| CARBOHYDRATES | 20 GM |

# Pan-Grilled Sole

*Since broiling invariably overcooks flatfish fillets, the only quick way to cook them (besides microwaving) is pan-grilling. The method is simple and gives the fish a delicate crust — a bit of texture that benefits it enormously.*

½ cup 1 percent milk
1 cup all-purpose flour
1 teaspoon salt (or more to taste)
freshly ground black pepper to taste
2 teaspoons unsalted butter

4 five-ounce gray or lemon sole fillets
½ cup white wine
chopped fresh parsley for garnish
lemon wedges

Place the milk in a glass pie plate and the flour on a sheet of waxed paper. Season the flour with the salt and pepper. Have a warm platter ready.

Melt the butter in a large nonstick skillet over medium-high heat. Dip each fish fillet in the milk, then lay it gently on the flour, turning once to coat both sides. Sauté the fillets on both sides until just cooked through and slightly translucent in the center. This will take about 3 minutes, and you will probably have to do them in 2 batches. Transfer to the platter.

Lower the heat, pour in the wine, and use a wooden spoon to stir and scrape up the brown bits in the pan. Reduce the liquid slightly to a syrupy glaze and spoon it over the fish. Garnish with the parsley and serve at once with the lemon wedges.

**Serves 4**

PER SERVING

| | |
|---|---|
| CALORIES | 293 |
| FAT | 4 GM |
| SATURATED FAT | 2 GM |
| CHOLESTEROL | 74 MG |
| SODIUM | 683 MG |
| PROTEIN | 31 GM |
| CARBOHYDRATE | 26 GM |

# Oriental Sole Fillets

*Sole is easy to overcook, which is why I like to do the fillets in the microwave. This recipe enhances the delicate taste and is simple and quick to prepare. Rolling the fish keeps it from overcooking.*

salt and freshly ground black pepper to taste

1-pound gray or lemon sole or flounder fillets

1 tablespoon canola oil

1 tablespoon grated or finely julienned fresh ginger

1 large scallion, white and green parts, trimmed and julienned

1 teaspoon dark sesame oil

reduced-sodium soy sauce (optional)

rice wine vinegar (optional)

Season fish lightly with salt and pepper. Fold or roll the fillets so that the thinner end is tucked under the thicker middle part. Place rolls like the spokes of a wheel in a round microwave-safe dish that can go to the table. Cover with plastic wrap and microwave on high for 2½ to 4 minutes or until the fish is completely opaque. Remove the wrap, drain off any liquid in the dish, and cover loosely with foil.

In a 2-cup glass measure, combine the canola oil, ginger, and scallion and microwave for 1 minute on high. Add the sesame oil, let cool slightly, pour over the fish, and serve. Sprinkle with soy sauce and a splash of rice wine vinegar if desired.

**Serves 2 or 3**

► *Serve with blanched snow peas or sugar snap peas and a few little red new potatoes with the skin on, which can also be cooked in the microwave. Season the vegetables with salt and pepper after cooking.*

PER SERVING

| | |
|---|---|
| CALORIES | 195 |
| FAT | 8 GM |
| SATURATED FAT | 1 GM |
| CHOLESTEROL | 73 MG |
| SODIUM | 124 MG |
| PROTEIN | 29 GM |
| CARBOHYDRATE | 1 GM |

# Teriyaki Salmon Steaks

*This is another recipe that I urge you to make in the microwave, simply because it yields salmon steaks of incomparably moist, velvety succulence. And it's so easy! Of course, the marinade has something to do with that, too. The steaks also are delicious made in the conventional oven, but the texture will be different.*

4 salmon steaks about ½ inch thick
(about 1¾ pounds)
2 tablespoons reduced-sodium soy
sauce
1 tablespoon semisweet sherry or
marsala

1 teaspoon lemon juice
1½ teaspoons sugar
1 clove garlic, crushed
2 scallions, white and green parts,
trimmed and finely sliced or
julienned

Place the salmon steaks in a shallow 2-quart microwave-safe baking dish (such as a glass pie plate) with the tails toward the center. In a cup, combine the soy sauce, sherry or marsala, lemon juice, sugar, and garlic. Pour over the fish and let marinate at room temperature for 30 minutes.

### In the Microwave

Cover tightly with plastic wrap and microwave on high for 7 minutes. Let stand, covered, for 2 to 3 minutes, then sprinkle with the scallions. Serve in the baking dish.

### In the Oven

Preheat the oven to 425°F.

Cover tightly with heavy-duty aluminum foil. Bake in the center of the oven for 15 minutes. Uncover, sprinkle with the scallions, and serve immediately.

**Serves 4**

➤ *Serve with plain white rice and blanched string beans. Enjoy some of the marinade spooned over the rice.*

| PER SERVING | |
|---|---|
| CALORIES | 269 |
| FAT | 11 GM |
| SATURATED FAT | 2 GM |
| CHOLESTEROL | 96 MG |
| SODIUM | 379 MG |
| PROTEIN | 35 GM |
| CARBOHYDRATE | 4 GM |

# Seared Salmon on a Bed of Fennel

*I've always felt that even bland fish becomes satisfying when you serve some flavorsome vegetable preparation alongside or underneath it. Here, savory baked fennel, buttery and redolent of garlic, makes a two-minute seared fillet tasty and exciting. The same magic works with any firm whitefish fillet, such as grouper or red snapper. Just remember to ask for fillets with the skin on.*

1 tablespoon olive oil
4 four- to six-ounce pieces salmon
    fillet, skin on (see Note)
salt and freshly ground black pepper
    to taste

1 recipe Braised Fennel (page 206),
    warmed

Put the oil in a glass baking dish or pie plate. Add the fish pieces and turn gently with a rubber spatula and a fork until coated on both sides. Season with salt and pepper.

Preheat a griddle or large, heavy skillet. Sear the fish, skin side down, for 1 minute. Turn carefully with a spatula and sear the other side for 1 to 1½ minutes, depending on the degree of doneness preferred.

Make a bed of fennel on each of 4 warm dinner plates. Carefully lay a fish fillet on top of each.

**Serves 4**

| PER SERVING (SALMON ONLY) | |
| --- | --- |
| CALORIES | 211 |
| FAT | 11 GM |
| SATURATED FAT | 2 GM |
| CHOLESTEROL | 70 MG |
| SODIUM | 56 MG |
| PROTEIN | 25 GM |
| CARBOHYDRATE | 0 GM |

Note: The tail section of salmon, which is often less expensive than a center cut, is ideal for this use. Serve with little steamed or boiled red new potatoes with the skin on.

# Grilled Salmon Burgers

*I never eat hamburgers anymore, although I occasionally crave one mightily. These satisfying salmon burgers are a suitable substitute, and everybody loves them.*

1-pound salmon fillet, skinned
3 large egg whites, lightly beaten
2 tablespoons finely chopped scallion
2 tablespoons chopped fresh dill
1 tablespoon Worcestershire sauce
1 tablespoon nuoc mam (Vietnamese fish sauce) (see Note)

½ cup (approximately) fresh bread crumbs (page 271)
2 teaspoons olive oil
hamburger buns or French bread

Chop the salmon by hand or in a food processor equipped with the steel blade. Place in a large mixing bowl and add the egg whites, scallion, dill, Worcestershire sauce, and nuoc mam. Mix well with a fork. Add enough bread crumbs to bind the mixture together. With a light hand, form into 4 burgers about 1 inch thick. Place on a dinner plate and chill for 30 minutes.

Heat a stove-top grill pan, charcoal grill, or broiler until very hot. Just before cooking, oil the grill or broiler and drizzle or brush the olive oil over one side of the burgers. Place the burgers, unoiled side down, on the grill and cook for about 2 minutes. Turn with a spatula and cook for 2 minutes more, being careful not to overcook. Serve immediately on a lightly toasted bun or French bread.

**Serves 4**

➤ *You can dress up these burgers with a slice of Vidalia or red onion and ketchup if you like. Serve with coleslaw on the side.*

| PER SERVING | |
| --- | --- |
| CALORIES | 331 |
| FAT | 12 GM |
| SATURATED FAT | 2 GM |
| CHOLESTEROL | 56 MG |
| SODIUM | 546 MG |
| PROTEIN | 28 GM |
| CARBOHYDRATE | 27 GM |

Note: If you don't have nuoc mam, use 1 teaspoon anchovy paste or very lightly salt the mixture.

# Cold Poached Salmon

*This is one of the most useful recipes to have in your repertoire. Not only is cold poached salmon elegant for almost any occasion, but everyone likes it, it can be made ahead, and it has no added fat. Serve with Swedish Cucumber Salad (page 85).*

**Court Bouillon**

2 quarts water

2 cups dry white wine

¼ cup wine vinegar

2 medium onions, sliced

2 carrots, scraped and cut into 1-inch chunks

6 fresh parsley stems, chopped

2 bay leaves, broken

½ teaspoon dried thyme

2 tablespoons salt

8–10 black peppercorns

**Salmon**

3 pounds center-cut salmon or 1 five-pound whole salmon, head and tail removed

Potato Vinaigrette (recipe follows)

fresh parsley or dill sprigs for garnish

To make the court bouillon, in a large nonreactive soup pot, bring all the ingredients to a boil over high heat. Partially cover, lower the heat, and simmer for 40 minutes to 1 hour. Let cool and strain. *(May be prepared up to 3 days ahead.)*

To poach the salmon, select a fish poacher, heavy pot, or oval roasting pan that will accommodate the fish nicely. Wrap the fish in a double-thick piece of damp cheesecloth that is long enough to extend several inches beyond both ends of the fish. Bring the poaching liquid to a boil and lower the salmon into it. The liquid should cover the fish by 1½ inches; add water if necessary. Cover, lower the heat, and cook for 8 minutes per pound if the fish is thick, 5 to 6 minutes per pound if it is thin. Adjust the heat so that the liquid just shivers (slightly less than a simmer).

At the end of the cooking time, remove from the heat, uncover, and let the fish stand in the liquid until both are lukewarm, about 20 minutes. Using the ends of the cheesecloth as handles, lift the fish from the liquid and unwrap carefully. (If poaching a whole fish, carefully scrape away and remove the skin and any jagged edges with a small, sharp knife.) Transfer to a serving platter, add potato vinaigrette, and garnish with parsley or dill sprigs. Serve at room temperature.

Serves 8–10

➤ *Letting the fish cool in the poaching broth is critical to soft, moist, flavorful salmon. The poaching liquid may be strained through additional cheesecloth and refrigerated or frozen for further use.*

PER SERVING (SALMON ONLY)

| | |
|---|---|
| CALORIES | 192 |
| FAT | 8 GM |
| SATURATED FAT | 1 GM |
| CHOLESTEROL | 73 MG |
| SODIUM | 243 MG |
| PROTEIN | 26 GM |
| CARBOHYDRATE | 1 GM |

# Potato Vinaigrette

*This silken sauce is a natural for poached salmon but also can be served with mussels or scallops on a bed of greens as a quick first course.*

2 cups (approximately) defatted, reduced-sodium chicken stock, preferably homemade (page 274)
1 large baking potato (about ½ pound), peeled and diced
pinch of fresh thyme leaves

1 clove garlic
2 tablespoons sherry wine vinegar
2 tablespoons light olive oil
½ teaspoon sugar (or more to taste)
salt and freshly ground black pepper to taste

In a medium saucepan, combine 2 cups of the chicken stock, the potato, thyme, and garlic. Bring to a boil, lower the heat slightly, and cook until the potato is tender, about 15 minutes. Transfer to a blender or food processor and puree until smooth. Add the vinegar, oil, sugar, and salt and pepper. Dilute with additional stock if the sauce seems too thick. (Consistency should be similar to that of mayonnaise.) Serve cold or at room temperature.

Makes about 1⅔ cups

➤ *Sprinkle with chopped fresh parsley or snipped dill for a color note if desired.*

# Seared Tuna in a Black Pepper Crust

*This is one of my favorite ways to prepare tuna. It is an adaptation of a recipe from chef Alan Harding, who used to serve it with quick-sautéed spinach and cooked navy beans dressed with a light lime vinaigrette. I love this combination of flavors and textures with the crusty tuna, but you can serve it any way you like.*

1½ pounds first-quality fresh tuna in
   one thick piece
1 tablespoon plus 1 teaspoon cracked
   black pepper

1 teaspoon olive oil
1 tablespoon canola oil

Trim off any dark parts of the tuna and cut into 4 rectangular logs. Place the pepper on a piece of waxed paper and press all four sides of each piece of fish in the pepper to make a thin, even coating.

Combine the olive oil and canola oil and heat to almost smoking in a large, heavy skillet. Add the tuna and lower the heat to medium. Sear each side of each piece for barely 1 minute, then turn and sear the remaining three sides. The fish pieces should be brown on the outside but quite rare in the middle. Remove to a warm plate.

Cut the tuna into ½-inch-thick slices, fan out on 4 dinner plates, and serve at once.

**Serves 4**

► *If you want to serve this with spinach, wipe out the pan in which you seared the tuna, add a little oil, and quick-sauté fresh spinach in it.*

| PER SERVING | |
|---|---|
| CALORIES | 291 |
| FAT | 13 GM |
| SATURATED FAT | 3 GM |
| CHOLESTEROL | 65 MG |
| SODIUM | 67 MG |
| PROTEIN | 40 GM |
| CARBOHYDRATE | 1 GM |

# Crab Cakes

*Crab cakes, which most of us think of as a restaurant item, are easy to prepare at home and make a nice change of pace from fish. The secret of these cakes is the relatively small amount of bread crumbs and the chilling before cooking.*

1 pound fresh jumbo lump crabmeat
½ cup fresh bread crumbs (page 271)
¼ cup reduced-fat mayonnaise
⅓ cup minced scallion, green part only
⅓ cup finely diced sweet green or red pepper
2 teaspoons Dijon mustard

1 tablespoon chopped fresh parsley or dill
1 large egg white, lightly beaten
salt and freshly ground black pepper to taste
½ cup fine dry bread crumbs
2 teaspoons canola oil
lemon wedges

Put the crabmeat in a large bowl and pick over to remove bits of shell and cartilage. Add the fresh bread crumbs and mix in.

In a small bowl, combine the mayonnaise, scallion, green or red pepper, mustard, and parsley or dill. Add to the crab mixture and mix in gently, taking care not to break up the crabmeat lumps. Carefully fold in the egg white with a rubber spatula just until the mixture holds together. Season with salt and pepper. Form into 8 cakes and arrange on a baking sheet lined with waxed paper. Cover with plastic wrap and refrigerate for at least 30 minutes.

Place the dry bread crumbs on a plate and coat both sides of each cake with crumbs. Place a large nonstick skillet over medium heat and warm the oil, spreading it evenly over the surface with a brush. Add the crab cakes and sauté for 5 minutes or until lightly browned and crisp. Turn carefully with a spatula and cook for 5 minutes more. Serve immediately with the lemon wedges.

Serves 4

➤ *To accompany the crab cakes, I suggest either Low-Fat Tartar Sauce (page 262) or a simple sauce made of ketchup mixed with a few drops of hot pepper sauce to taste. French Potato Salad (page 87) rounds out the meal nicely.*

| PER SERVING | |
| --- | --- |
| CALORIES | 245 |
| FAT | 8 GM |
| SATURATED FAT | 1 GM |
| CHOLESTEROL | 167 MG |
| SODIUM | 643 MG |
| PROTEIN | 27 GM |
| CARBOHYDRATE | 15 GM |

# Hot Garlicky Shrimp

*This is one of the nicest and easiest ways I know to prepare shrimp. They look and taste marvelous, and you can have them on the table in minutes!*

1 pound (about 20) large uncooked
   shrimp
salt to taste
1½ tablespoons olive oil

4 small cloves garlic, sliced
1 dried red chili pepper, cut into
   1-inch pieces

Peel the shrimp, leaving the last tail segment intact. Season the shrimp with salt.

Heat the olive oil in a large, heavy nonstick skillet. Add the garlic and chili pepper and sauté until the garlic is light brown, about 1 minute. Add the shrimp and cook over high heat, keeping the shrimp moving and turning them over with a wooden spoon, until they are pink and slightly charred in places, about 3 to 5 minutes. Lower the heat slightly and cook for about 1 minute more. Serve hot.

Serves 4

➤ *Serve with a green vegetable, rice pilaf, and a green salad.*

| PER SERVING | |
|---|---|
| CALORIES | 147 |
| FAT | 7 GM |
| SATURATED FAT | 1 GM |
| CHOLESTEROL | 140 MG |
| SODIUM | 137 MG |
| PROTEIN | 19 GM |
| CARBOHYDRATE | 2 GM |

# Scampi alla Busara

*The whole family will enjoy this extremely flavorful, quickly prepared entrée, which comes from Italy's Adriatic Coast. Serve with a green vegetable, followed by a salad. Leftover sauce can be used to dress pasta.*

2 tablespoons olive oil
1 large onion, cut into ¼-inch dice
   (about ¾ cup)
2 cloves garlic, minced
2 twenty-eight-ounce cans imported
   Italian plum tomatoes, drained,
   seeded, and chopped, or 2¼
   pounds fresh plum tomatoes,
   peeled, seeded, and chopped

½ cup beef stock or beef broth
½ teaspoon salt
freshly ground black pepper to taste
1½ pounds (about 36) large shrimp
   (see Note)
½ cup dry white wine

Heat the oil in a deep 10-inch skillet over medium heat until fragrant. Add the onion and garlic and sauté, stirring occasionally, until softened, about 5 minutes. Add the tomatoes and stock and cook, stirring occasionally, until most of the liquid is evaporated, about 30 minutes. Season to taste with salt and several grindings of black pepper.

Add the shrimp and wine and simmer, turning the shrimp occasionally, until they are firm and cooked through, about 5 minutes. (Take care not to overcook them.)

Serves 4–6

➤ *Serve the shrimp lightly covered with sauce on a bed of rice.*

| PER SERVING | |
| --- | --- |
| CALORIES | 266 |
| FAT | 8 GM |
| SATURATED FAT | 1 GM |
| CHOLESTEROL | 168 MG |
| SODIUM | 1,067 MG |
| PROTEIN | 26 GM |
| CARBOHYDRATE | 19 GM |

Note: In the original Italian recipe, the shells are left on the shrimp, which produces tastier flesh and adds flavor to the dish. To prepare, carefully cut through the shell along the back of each shrimp with a small, sharp knife or kitchen shears, leaving the shells intact. Remove the vein if you wish (I never do). As you eat the shrimp, simply flick up the shell with your knife and pull out the succulent meat with your fork. The taste is worth the extra work. Of course, you may peel the shrimp before cooking if you wish.

# Allen Susser's Shrimp Shepherd's Pie

*A contemporary low-fat take on an old favorite, adapted from a recipe by Chef Allen, one of Miami's most creative restaurateurs. A great prepare-ahead one-dish meal.*

1 pound medium shrimp, peeled and deveined
¼ teaspoon ground allspice
pinch of ground cinnamon
½ teaspoon dry mustard
2 teaspoons kosher or coarse salt
freshly ground black pepper to taste
1 tablespoon dry white wine
2 tablespoons chopped fresh parsley, preferably Italian flat-leaf parsley

1 pound (about 4 medium) potatoes, preferably Yukon Gold
½ cup 1 percent milk (approximately)
1 tablespoon prepared white horseradish
1½ teaspoons olive oil
1 teaspoon finely chopped garlic
1 pound fresh spinach, trimmed

In a glass or stainless steel bowl, combine the shrimp, allspice, cinnamon, mustard, 1 teaspoon of the salt, several grindings of pepper, wine, and parsley. Set aside.

Place the potatoes in a large pot with enough cold salted water to cover. Bring to a boil, reduce the heat to medium, cover, and cook for 20 to 25 minutes or until tender. Drain and let cool. When cool enough to handle, peel and mash roughly with the back of a large fork. (They should be somewhat lumpy.) Add the milk, horseradish, and remaining 1 teaspoon salt. Season rather highly with pepper and beat briefly to blend. Set aside.

Preheat the oven to 400°F. In a sauté pan, warm ½ teaspoon of the olive oil and add the garlic. When it releases its aroma but has not taken on any color, add the spinach, water still clinging to the leaves. Stir over medium heat until just wilted, about 2 minutes. Remove from the pan with a slotted spoon directly into an ungreased 1½-quart baking dish. Spread over the bottom and follow with a layer of the shrimp. Spread the horseradish mashed potatoes over the top and roughen with a fork. *(May be prepared ahead up to this point, refrigerated, brought to room temperature, and baked.)*

Drizzle the top with the remaining 1 teaspoon olive oil. Bake in the upper third of the oven for 15 to 20 minutes or until the shrimp turn pink. Place under the broiler (about 4 inches from the heat) for 1½ to 2 minutes or until the top becomes flecked with brown.

**Serves 2 or 3**

| PER SERVING | |
| --- | --- |
| CALORIES | 322 |
| FAT | 6 GM |
| SATURATED FAT | 1 GM |
| CHOLESTEROL | 188 MG |
| SODIUM | 1,042 MG |
| PROTEIN | 32 GM |
| CARBOHYDRATE | 35 GM |

# Warm Shrimp and Bean Salad

*One of my best recipes is not mine at all, but my version of cookbook writer Evan Kleiman's version of an Italian classic. It is almost always my first thought in summer for a satisfying luncheon dish. It is quick, easy, and gorgeous, and everyone adores it. Evan uses white cannellini beans, but I happen to love it made with* **borlotti,** *or cranberry beans.*

4 cups cooked cranberry beans or 2 fifteen-ounce cans cannellini beans, drained
½ small red onion, minced (about ½ cup)
4 inner stalks celery with leaves, thinly sliced
10–12 sprigs fresh thyme, leaves only
juice of 1 medium lemon
4 tablespoons extra-virgin olive oil
salt and freshly ground black pepper to taste

4–6 cloves garlic, minced
½ to 1 teaspoon red pepper flakes (or to taste)
24–36 large shrimp, peeled
2 bunches arugula, trimmed
2 ripe tomatoes or 4 large plum tomatoes, seeded, juiced, and finely diced
1 small handful coarsely chopped fresh Italian flat-leaf parsley
lemon wedges for garnish

In a medium bowl, mix together the beans, onion, celery, thyme, lemon juice, 3 tablespoons of the olive oil, and salt and pepper. Set aside to marinate while you cook the shrimp.

Heat the remaining 1 tablespoon olive oil in a medium nonstick skillet. Add the garlic and cook just until its fragrance is released. Do not let it brown. Add the red pepper flakes and shrimp and sauté, moving the shrimp around frequently, so they cook evenly, about 6 to 7 minutes.

Line individual salad plates with the arugula and spoon some of the seasoned beans in the center of each plate. Arrange the hot shrimp over the beans and top with the diced tomatoes and parsley. Garnish with lemon wedges and serve immediately.

Serves 4–6

➤ *Italians would drizzle additional olive oil over the tomatoes before serving. Let your conscience be your guide. Serve with crusty Italian bread and a sparkling white wine such as Italian Prosecco.*

| PER SERVING | |
|---|---|
| CALORIES | 437 |
| FAT | 14 GM |
| SATURATED FAT | 2 GM |
| CHOLESTEROL | 168 MG |
| SODIUM | 197 MG |
| PROTEIN | 37 GM |
| CARBOHYDRATE | 42 GM |

# Steaming Mussels:
# Master Recipe

1 cup white wine
1 cup water
⅓ cup finely chopped onion or 1
  shallot, chopped

a few sprigs fresh parsley
½ bay leaf
4 quarts (6 pounds) mussels

In a large kettle, combine the wine, water, onion or shallot, parsley, and bay leaf. Bring to a boil and cook for 2 to 3 minutes. Add the mussels, cover, and cook over high heat for 5 minutes or until the shells open. Give the kettle one or two shakes during the cooking time to redistribute the mussels.

Remove the mussels with a slotted spoon. After the broth has settled, strain it through a sieve lined with cheesecloth. Remove the mussels from the shells, discarding any that have not opened. They are now ready to be sauced or used as indicated in a specific recipe.

---

## CLEANING AND STEAMING MUSSELS

I am always surprised at how few cooks prepare mussels at home. I imagine this is because they can be tedious to clean, although cleaning today's farmed mussels and the lovely green mussels from New Zealand is much easier. Mussels are very versatile — wonderful in risotto, vinaigrette, or rémoulade; curried; or on the half shell with salsa. If you are lucky enough to live near some coastal outcropping pounded by a strong surf, they can be free for the gathering.

To clean mussels, place them in a plastic basin or bucket of cold water. Brush them (I use a special wire brush for this purpose, available in any hardware store) and pull out their "beards." If there is any crusted material on the shell, scrape it off with a small knife. Drain the water and fill the basin again, this time adding 2 tablespoons of salt or vinegar for each quart of mussels. Let them sit this way for 15 minutes to encourage them to give up any sand they contain. Discard any mussels with broken or open shells. Repeat the soaking process with fresh water containing salt or vinegar, drain, and rinse.

---

# Greek-Style
# Cold Stuffed Mussels

*This Lenten dish from the Greek island of Andros makes a delicious and filling hors d'oeuvre or first course. Or, by simply stirring all the mussels into the cooked rice, the same recipe can be used as a pilaf, hearty enough for a main course.*

36 large fresh mussels
coarse salt
1½ cups water
½ cup white wine
1 tablespoon olive oil
2 medium onions, finely chopped
¾ cup long-grain rice such as Carolina

½ teaspoon ground cinnamon
½ teaspoon ground allspice
⅓ cup pine nuts
⅓ cup dried currants
2 tablespoons chopped fresh parsley
freshly ground black pepper to taste
lemon wedges for garnish

Clean and debeard the mussels, scrubbing them well with a stiff brush under cold running water. Put them in a kettle with the salt, water, and wine. Cover and steam until the shells open, about 3 to 5 minutes. Discard any that remain closed. Remove from the heat and let cool. Strain and reserve the broth.

In a nonstick skillet, sauté the olive oil, onion, and 2 tablespoons of the reserved broth over low heat until the onion is soft and takes on some color. Add the rice and cook for 2 or 3 minutes more, stirring constantly.

Add 1½ cups of the reserved broth, then stir in the cinnamon, allspice, pine nuts, currants, parsley, and several grindings of pepper. Cover and bring to a boil. Lower the heat and cook for 15 minutes or until the rice is tender and all the liquid has been absorbed.

Remove the mussels from their shells, reserving the best half of each shell. Stir the mussels into the rice. Place about a tablespoon of the mixture in each shell, mounding it slightly, allowing 1 mussel per shell. Chill the stuffed mussels, then serve garnished with lemon wedges.

Serves 6 as a first course, 8 as an hors d'oeuvre

➤ *This dish is worthwhile making only with large, plump mussels in large shells. If your mussels are on the small side and you have some of the very tasty rice mixture left over, you can serve it as a side dish at another meal.*

# Curried Mussels and Rice

*Rice and mussels have a satisfying affinity, as this delicious salad illustrates.
Although it requires a little work, it is not at all hard to make, and the results
are rewarding when served as part of a buffet or to luncheon guests.*

4 quarts (6 pounds) mussels, scrubbed
and debearded

3 teaspoons good-quality curry
powder (or more to taste)

½ cup Classic Vinaigrette (page 93)

¼ teaspoon canola oil

1⅓ cups long-grain rice such as
Carolina

1 teaspoon salt (or to taste)

1 cup cooked green peas

⅓ cup reduced-fat mayonnaise

freshly ground black pepper to taste

chopped fresh cilantro or parsley
(optional)

Open the mussels by steaming them in wine as directed in the Master
Recipe on page 132. Use a slotted spoon to transfer them to a bowl. Strain the
broth into a glass measure, add enough water to make 2⅔ cups, and set
aside.

Add 1 teaspoon of the curry powder to the vinaigrette, beat in, and set
aside.

Shell the mussels, placing them in a medium bowl as you work. Toss with
half the vinaigrette. Set aside. *(May be prepared ahead up to this point.)*

Bring the mussel broth to a boil in a large saucepan. Add the oil, rice, and
salt and bring back to a boil. Cover and cook over medium heat for 18 minutes. Put a clean folded towel over the rice, replace the lid, and let sit for 10
to 15 minutes.

Put the rice in a large serving bowl and toss with two forks. Add the mussels and peas. Using two rubber spatulas, carefully toss with the remaining
vinaigrette.

In a small bowl, combine the mayonnaise with the remaining 2 teaspoons curry powder, fold into the rice mixture, season with salt and pepper, and sprinkle with the cilantro or parsley (if using). Cover with plastic wrap and chill for at least 1 hour before serving. Remove the salad from the refrigerator 15 minutes or so before serving so that it is not too cold.

**Serves 6**

| PER SERVING | |
| --- | --- |
| CALORIES | 393 |
| FAT | 14 GM |
| SATURATED FAT | 2 GM |
| CHOLESTEROL | 37 MG |
| SODIUM | 906 MG |
| PROTEIN | 20 GM |
| CARBOHYDRATE | 46 GM |

# Seviche of Scallops

*In Peru, this seviche is served with cold cooked sweet potatoes and cold corn on the cob, an exquisite play of flavors and textures. It is another of my favorite dishes to serve for lunch on a hot summer day, with crusty peasant bread to mop up the delicious juices. I also serve scallop seviche without the corn-potato accompaniment, on a large ruffled red lettuce leaf, as a first course.*

2 pounds very fresh sea scallops
¾ cup lime juice (about 4 small limes)
½ large red onion, thickly sliced
1 fresh jalapeño or green chili pepper, seeded and quartered
1 fresh red chili pepper, seeded and quartered
¼ cup fresh parsley leaves
½ cup fresh cilantro leaves

2 tablespoons fruity olive oil
salt and freshly ground black pepper to taste
2 baked sweet potatoes, cooled and each cut into 4 or 5 pieces (optional)
2 ears corn, cooked, cooled, and each cut into 4 pieces (optional)

Put the scallops in a colander and wash them by letting hot water run over them briefly. Cut each in half or, if very large, in quarters. Put in a shallow nonreactive bowl, add the lime juice, and stir to make sure all the pieces are coated. Cover with plastic wrap and refrigerate for 4 hours, stirring once or twice. Drain the scallops, discarding the juice.

Put the onion, hot peppers, parsley, and cilantro in the food processor and pulse until finely chopped. Add the oil and pulse 2 or 3 times. Pour this mixture over the scallops, toss with a rubber spatula, and season with salt and pepper. Arrange on a serving dish, surrounded by the sweet potato and corn if desired.

**Serves 6 as a first course, 4 as a main course**

➤ *Rinsing the scallops with hot water is important to help the lime juice penetrate and "cook" them.*

| PER SERVING | |
|---|---|
| CALORIES | 184 |
| FAT | 6 GM |
| SATURATED FAT | 1 GM |
| CHOLESTEROL | 50 MG |
| SODIUM | 247 MG |
| PROTEIN | 26 GM |
| CARBOHYDRATE | 6 GM |

# Grilled Sea Scallops

*Grilled scallops are great for low-fat diets. They're easy to make and require no gussying up. I love the contrast between the slightly crusty exterior and the sweet interior. If you want a sauce, Low-Fat Tartar Sauce (page 262) is perfect. Halved, this makes a quick meal for two.*

20 large sea scallops (about 1½ pounds)
4 teaspoons olive oil

salt and freshly ground black pepper to taste
lemon wedges (optional)

Preheat the broiler or a ridged stove-top cast-iron grill or pan. Put the olive oil in a small glass dish. Use a kitchen brush to paint the scallops all over with oil. Season the tops with salt and pepper. Place on the grill or broiler seasoned side down and cook for 2½ minutes. Season again with salt and pepper and turn over with a spatula. Cook 1½ to 2 minutes more or until marked by the grill. Serve immediately with lemon wedges if desired.

Serves 4

> ➤ *Be careful not to overcook scallops. Like all foods consisting of muscle tissue, they can toughen easily from too much heat. They should be a bit translucent in the center (check one with the tip of a small, sharp knife). Buy the biggest, most well shaped scallops you can find so that the tender flesh stays moist when exposed to the intense heat of the grill.*

| PER SERVING | |
|---|---|
| CALORIES | 190 |
| FAT | 6 GM |
| SATURATED FAT | 1 GM |
| CHOLESTEROL | 56 MG |
| SODIUM | 274 MG |
| PROTEIN | 29 GM |
| CARBOHYDRATE | 4 GM |

# Grilled Lobster with Vietnamese Dipping Sauce

*Lobsters have always been a summertime treat, but the melted butter for dipping that was de rigueur has gone the way of the dodo for health-conscious diners. The savory, fat-free Vietnamese dipping sauce known as nuoc cham is the perfect alternative.*

1 small fresh red chili pepper or "bird" pepper, seeded and minced
6 tablespoons lime juice (2 or 3 limes)
¼ cup nuoc mam (Vietnamese fish sauce)

3 tablespoons sugar (or to taste)
1 tablespoon minced garlic
2 tablespoons water (approximately)
4 1½-pound lobsters
1 teaspoon canola oil

In a small bowl, combine the chili pepper and lime juice and let sit for 2 minutes. Add the nuoc mam, sugar, garlic, and water and stir to dissolve the sugar. You should have about 1 cup sauce. Divide among 4 small bowls and set aside.

Put a lobster steamer with water on to boil. Prepare a medium-hot fire in a charcoal grill. Steam the lobsters for 5 minutes. When cool enough to handle, twist off the claws and tails. Remove the little swimmerets on the undersides of the tails, split the tails in half lengthwise, spread slightly, and use a small basting brush to paint the exposed meat with the oil. Discard the main parts of the bodies after removing and reserving any coral (red roe).

Place the tails and claws on the grill — claws in the center, tails facing outward. Place tails shell side down and cook for 2 to 3 minutes, then turn the tails over and cook for 5 to 6 minutes more or until the flesh is lightly browned and cooked through. Remove to a plate. Continue cooking the claws for about 15 minutes total, turning once. Serve warm with the dipping sauce and pass the roe if desired.

Serves 4

➤ *Corn on the cob and a sliced tomato salad with shredded fresh basil or mint is a nice accompaniment.*

| PER SERVING | |
| --- | --- |
| CALORIES | 243 |
| FAT | 4 GM |
| SATURATED FAT | 1 GM |
| CHOLESTEROL | 108 MG |
| SODIUM | 1,166 MG |
| PROTEIN | 34 GM |
| CARBOHYDRATE | 17 GM |

Note: Nuoc mam can be bought in oriental markets.

# 11
# POULTRY AND MEAT

Balsamic Glazed Chicken Breasts

Chicken Cutlets Milanese

Moroccan Broiled Chicken

Soy-Roasted Chicken

Oven-"Fried" Chicken

Tandoori Chicken

Curry of Lamb or Chicken

Curried Chicken Salad

Chicken Chili

Thai Beef Salad

Grilled Butterflied Leg of Lamb

Leftover Meat with Peruvian Red Onion Sauce

Oven-Braised Lamb Shanks

Veal Stew with Tomatoes and Peas

Veal Picatta

Marinated Pork Tenderloin

FOREHEAD FURROWS RELAX and I can sense an almost audible sigh of relief when I tell people that yes, you *can* eat meat and maintain a healthfully low-fat diet. The keys are frequency and quantity.

Meat has its virtues: it contributes complete protein, iron, and many other essential nutrients. But once you get used to eating a great variety of tasty and satisfying foods, you probably won't crave it that much or plan it for dinner as often just because you can't think of anything else. Try to get out of the habit of thinking only of meat for your main course. Plan meals so that when you do eat meat, it more often plays a supporting role rather than being the star.

When choosing meat, select from the leanest cuts, such as chuck, round, loin, or leg. Avoid the prime cuts, such as sirloin, which are usually highest in fat. Grilled marinated flank steak, however, can be sliced paper thin so that a small portion is every bit as satisfying as a steak.

Think about "the other white meat," pork — not the fatty cuts, but pork tenderloin or center loin, which have 4.1 and 6.1 grams of fat, respectively, in a three-ounce cooked serving. This compares favorably with a similar-sized portion of skinless chicken breast. (By contrast, lean ground beef has nearly 16 grams of fat in the same size serving.)

Try lean veal (yes, it's expensive, but that means you won't be tempted too often!) in thin scaloppine, in stews, or ground for a meat loaf.

Very little needs to be said about chicken, apart from the obvious caveats such as avoiding the skin (as tempting as it may be) and exercising portion control. Chicken is probably the most versatile flesh food, and there are many delicious low-fat ways to prepare it. Judging from the number of menus on which it appears, roast chicken is the new American favorite. I'd serve Soy-Roasted Chicken (page 144) to anyone, although I acknowledge that it's not typical company fare, especially if you're not keen on carving. I have found, though, that individual servings of half a small bird, redolent of a lemon-garlic marinade and grilled or broiled, usually delight guests. And almost everyone is happy with a moist, tasty chicken breast, as in elegant Balsamic Glazed Chicken Breasts (page 141). Chicken Chili (page 152) or a good chicken curry (page 149) is fine for informal occasions.

# Balsamic Glazed Chicken Breasts

*Chicken breasts top everyone's list of low-fat main courses. The trick is to find ways to make them that are still moist and flavorful. This unusually tasty and elegant preparation more than meets the requirements, with a beautifully silky amber sauce that looks for all the world as if it contains butter (though it hasn't a drop).*

3 teaspoons olive oil

2 whole boneless, skinless chicken breasts, halved (about 4 ounces each), slightly flattened by pounding

½ cup finely diced carrot

½ cup finely diced onion

1 teaspoon minced garlic

1 tablespoon balsamic vinegar

1 tablespoon tomato paste

1 teaspoon sugar

1 cup defatted, reduced-sodium chicken stock, preferably homemade (page 274)

⅛ teaspoon salt (or to taste)

freshly ground black pepper to taste

1 tablespoon finely chopped parsley

Warm a platter plus a dinner serving plate. Cut a round piece of heavy aluminum foil the size of your skillet. Set aside.

In a large nonstick skillet, heat 1 teaspoon of the olive oil and spread over the bottom with a brush. Add the chicken and cook over medium-high heat, turning once, for about 5 minutes total. Remove to the warm plate and set aside.

In the same pan, heat the remaining 2 teaspoons oil and add the carrot, onion, and garlic. Press the sheet of foil down on the vegetables and cook over medium heat, stirring once or twice, until the carrot is tender and the onion is lightly colored, about 5 minutes.

Add the vinegar, turn the heat to high, and cook until reduced, about 30 seconds. Add the tomato paste, sugar, and chicken stock and stir to blend. Add the reserved chicken breasts and any juices that have collected in the dish. Simmer gently, uncovered, over medium-low heat, turning the chicken once, for 12 minutes or until tender. Season with salt and pepper and transfer to the warmed serving platter with the sauce spooned over and around. Garnish with the parsley and serve immediately.

Serves 4

➤ *Serve with rice, with some of the sauce spooned over, and a delicate green vegetable such as zucchini that will not compete with the delectable sauce.*

| PER SERVING | |
|---|---|
| CALORIES | 202 |
| FAT | 5 GM |
| SATURATED FAT | 1 GM |
| CHOLESTEROL | 64 MG |
| SODIUM | 345 MG |
| PROTEIN | 28 GM |
| CARBOHYDRATE | 6 GM |

# Chicken Cutlets Milanese

*This recipe came about when we were lamenting how much we missed that Italian restaurant staple, veal cutlet Milanese (breaded and fried), piled high with diced tomatoes and basil. I tried a chicken version, marinating the breasts for added flavor since it was to be grilled rather than fried, and my family and guests loved it. The flavors mingle well, and the combination is especially appealing when you can't look at another pale chicken breast.*

2 whole boneless, skinless chicken breasts, halved (about 4 ounces each), flattened
½ cup lemon juice (about 1½ medium lemons)
2 tablespoons olive oil
1 large clove or 2 medium cloves garlic, crushed

pinch of dried thyme
2 medium-ripe tomatoes
6 fresh basil leaves, washed, dried, and shredded
salt and freshly ground black pepper to taste

Put the breasts in a glass baking dish that will hold them in one layer. In a small bowl, beat the lemon juice, olive oil, garlic, and thyme with a fork and pour over the chicken. Cover with plastic wrap and refrigerate for 2 hours, turning the chicken pieces once during that time.

Just before you cook the chicken, core, seed, and dice or roughly cut up the tomatoes and mix with the basil in a small bowl. Season with salt and pepper and set aside.

Preheat the broiler or a stove-top ridged grill. Broil or grill the chicken for 4 minutes on each side (3 minutes per side or just until nicely marked if you are using a really hot stove-top grill). Place one cutlet on each of 4 dinner plates. Divide the tomato mixture among them, spooning it right on top of the chicken, and serve at once.

**Serves 4**

➤ *Fans will recognize the Lemon-Thyme Chicken Breasts from* Low Fat & Loving It.

➤ *You must use fresh ripe tomatoes and fresh basil, so consider this a dish to be savored in summer or whenever both are available.*

| PER SERVING | |
| --- | --- |
| CALORIES | 210 |
| FAT | 8 GM |
| SATURATED FAT | 1 GM |
| CHOLESTEROL | 66 MG |
| SODIUM | 81 MG |
| PROTEIN | 27 GM |
| CARBOHYDRATE | 7 GM |

# Moroccan Broiled Chicken

*I suddenly realized one day that I almost never grill or roast chicken without first marinating it. This is nothing I deliberately set out to do, but it evolved because marinating imparts such flavor and tenderness. And with such satisfying flavor, you don't need the skin for taste or moisture.*

2 small frying chickens (2½–3 pounds each), quartered
salt and freshly ground black pepper to taste

4 large cloves garlic, crushed
½ cup lemon juice
3 tablespoons fruity olive oil
1 tablespoon chopped fresh parsley

Wash the chicken thoroughly, dry, and season lightly with salt and pepper. In a shallow glass dish, mix together the garlic, lemon juice, olive oil, and parsley. Roll the chicken pieces in this mixture and marinate, refrigerated, for 1 to 4 hours.

Preheat the broiler. Drain the chicken, reserving the marinade. Place the chicken, skin side down, on the broiler rack and broil about 7 inches from the heat for 10 minutes, basting once with the marinade. Turn over and broil for 10 minutes more, basting again with the marinade. During the final 5 minutes of cooking, turn twice more, basting each time. Discard the marinade.

Transfer the chicken to a serving platter, pour the pan juices over, and serve at once. Remove the skin before eating.

**Serves 6**

➤ *This chicken is delicious cooked on a charcoal grill, in which case each bird should be cut in half, backbone removed, then cut into parts after cooking. Adjust the cooking time according to the manufacturer's directions for your type of grill. Butterflied squab chickens or Cornish hens also are delicious this way.*

| PER SERVING | |
| --- | --- |
| CALORIES | 306 |
| FAT | 13 GM |
| SATURATED FAT | 3 GM |
| CHOLESTEROL | 133 MG |
| SODIUM | 128 MG |
| PROTEIN | 43 GM |
| CARBOHYDRATE | 1 GM |

# Soy-Roasted Chicken

*This recipe produces the most exquisite, burnished-mahogany bird that will ever grace your table. And even more important, the marinade, with its oriental overtones combined with the high-heat roasting method, exerts some subtle magic on the flesh so that it is incredibly tender and moist and remains that way even the next day, making leftovers pure pleasure. Though tempting, try to resist eating the skin.*

1 four-pound roasting chicken

⅓ cup reduced-sodium soy sauce

¼ cup light olive oil

1 tablespoon dark sesame oil

1 clove garlic, crushed

1 teaspoon salt

½ teaspoon finely grated fresh ginger

Remove and discard any excess fat from the cavity of the chicken and wash and dry the bird. In a small bowl, combine the soy sauce, olive oil, sesame oil, garlic, salt, and ginger. Rub the chicken inside and out with the mixture. Place the chicken in a sturdy plastic bag, pour the marinade over, squeeze out any excess air, and seal securely. Refrigerate for at least 2 hours (up to 24 hours). When you think of it, turn the chicken over to redistribute the marinade.

Preheat the oven to 450°F. Remove the chicken from the refrigerator and let it come to room temperature. Remove the chicken from the bag, wipe well, and place on a rack in a roasting pan. Truss the legs if desired.

Strain the marinade through a sieve, discard the solids, and spoon or brush the liquid over the chicken to coat the skin lightly. Roast, basting frequently with marinade, for 45 to 50 minutes or until a meat thermometer inserted in the thigh registers 158°F to 160°F. (Alternatively, test by piercing the thickest part of the thigh with a skewer or fork. If the juices are only faintly pink, the chicken is done.) Remove from the oven and allow to rest for 10 minutes before carving.

Serves 4–6

➤ *If pan drippings begin to burn or smoke, pour about ¼ cup water in the pan from time to time.*

| PER SERVING | |
| --- | --- |
| CALORIES | 179 |
| FAT | 9 GM |
| SATURATED FAT | 2 GM |
| CHOLESTEROL | 63 MG |
| SODIUM | 366 MG |
| PROTEIN | 21 GM |
| CARBOHYDRATE | 1 GM |

# Oven-"Fried" Chicken

*In its original version, this was our family's hands-down favorite dish, made for all important occasions. Originally, the chicken was dipped in egg, then crumbs anointed with a quarter pound of melted butter. And, of course, we ate the skin; that was the best part. This low-fat version, made with neither the skin nor the butter, is surprisingly moist and delicious.*

juice of 1 medium lemon (about ¼ cup)

1 tablespoon canola oil

1 3½-pound frying chicken, cut into 8 pieces, skin removed

salt and freshly ground black pepper to taste

vegetable cooking spray

Dijon mustard

2 large egg whites, lightly beaten

1½ cups fresh bread crumbs from homestyle or French bread

paprika

Preheat the oven to 400°F.

In a small bowl, combine the lemon juice and canola oil and set aside.

Season the chicken parts on both sides with salt and pepper. Select a baking dish large enough to hold all the chicken parts in one layer; spray it well with vegetable cooking spray and set aside.

Place several good dollops of mustard in a small bowl and use a basting brush to paint the chicken pieces with it. Dip each piece in the egg whites.

On a dinner plate, season the bread crumbs with salt and pepper. Roll each chicken piece in the mixture and arrange in the baking dish. Sprinkle the lemon juice mixture over the chicken, sprinkle lightly with paprika, and bake for 50 minutes. Baste once or twice with the pan juices after 30 minutes.

**Serves 4**

| PER SERVING | |
| --- | --- |
| CALORIES | 332 |
| FAT | 10 GM |
| SATURATED FAT | 2 GM |
| CHOLESTEROL | 134 MG |
| SODIUM | 618 MG |
| PROTEIN | 44 GM |
| CARBOHYDRATE | 10 GM |

# Tandoori Chicken

*Tandoori chicken, tender and moist from its flavorful marinade, is always cooked without the skin, making it a natural candidate for a great low-fat dinner. Although no home oven can approximate the intense heat of the Indian tandoor, which cooks with amazing rapidity, high-heat roasting is a good substitute. My version omits the traditional red-orange dye.*

2 small broiler/fryer chickens (about 2½ pounds each), halved, skin removed, or 4 small breasts and 4 small legs and thighs, preferably unseparated, skin removed
1 cup nonfat yoghurt
¼ cup white vinegar
2½ teaspoons ground cumin
2 teaspoons pure chili powder (see Appendix)
1½ teaspoons garam masala (see Note)

1½ teaspoons salt
1 tablespoon freshly ground black pepper
¼ cup evaporated skim milk or light cream
2 cloves garlic, crushed
1 small (walnut-size) piece fresh ginger, minced
12 soft lettuce leaves
thin lemon slices
yellow or red onion rings
fresh cilantro sprigs for garnish

Cut off and discard all visible fat from the chicken pieces. Wash them and dry on paper towels. Place bone side down on a board, and with a large, very sharp knife make three deep diagonal gashes in each breast and one long gash down the length of each leg and thigh. (This allows the marinade to penetrate.)

Combine all but the final four remaining ingredients in a large glass baking dish that will hold all the chicken in one layer. Add the chicken and marinate for at least 6 hours, preferably overnight, turning occasionally.

Preheat the oven to 500°F for at least 30 minutes. Remove the chicken pieces from the marinade and put them in a shallow roasting pan breast side up. Roast in the upper third of the oven until almost crusty, about 20 minutes. Turn and roast for 5 to 7 minutes more. The chicken should be crusty but not scorched.

To serve, arrange a bed of lettuce leaves on a large, warm platter and place the chicken pieces on top. Decorate with alternating lemon slices and onion rings. Garnish with the cilantro and serve immediately.

**Serves 4**

*Charcoal-Grilled Tandoori Chicken:* This preparation is excellent on the charcoal grill. Wait until the coals have a gray ash, then blow away the ash to reveal the red coals. Wipe the grill with oil so that the chicken won't stick, brush the chicken with marinade, sprinkle with lemon juice, and grill for about 15 minutes. Turn over and grill for 10 minutes more, basting again with the lemon juice. The yoghurt marinade tenderizes the meat considerably, so allow less cooking time than you would for ordinary chicken halves.

➤ *Serve this dish with basmati rice. Eat the lettuce, onion, and cilantro sprigs with the chicken. My Indian friends wouldn't think of eating this dish without green chili peppers as well.*

| PER SERVING | |
| --- | --- |
| CALORIES | 355 |
| FAT | 9 GM |
| SATURATED FAT | 2 GM |
| CHOLESTEROL | 192 MG |
| SODIUM | 661 MG |
| PROTEIN | 61 GM |
| CARBOHYDRATE | 5 GM |

Note: Garam masala is a ground spice mixture available in Indian and gourmet food shops.

# Curry of Lamb or Chicken

*This Westernized curry is ideal for maximizing a small amount of leftover meat or poultry. It can be made an hour or so ahead and kept warm until mealtime. Serve over rice and pass your favorite chutney.*

2 tablespoons canola oil
2 cups cooked lamb or chicken cut
    into bite-size pieces (about ¾
    pound)
1 cup chopped onion
1 cup coarsely chopped apple
¾ cup chopped celery
2 or 3 cloves garlic, minced
2 tablespoons all-purpose flour
¼ cup good-quality curry powder
1 cup peeled and diced fresh tomatoes
    or 5 canned tomatoes, diced

¼ cup raisins
1 cup defatted, reduced-sodium
    chicken stock, preferably
    homemade (page 274)
salt and freshly ground black pepper
    to taste
½ cup evaporated skim milk
2 tablespoons chopped fresh cilantro
    (optional)

Heat the oil in a large, preferably nonstick skillet. Warm the lamb or chicken, but do not let it get hard or brown. Add the onion, apple, celery, and garlic and cook, stirring, until most of the moisture evaporates.

Combine the flour and curry powder and sprinkle over the meat mixture, mixing well until the meat is coated. Add the tomatoes, raisins, chicken stock, and salt and pepper. Bring almost to a boil, then add the milk and correct the seasoning. Sprinkle with the cilantro (if using) and serve.

**Serves 4**

| PER SERVING (LAMB) | | PER SERVING (CHICKEN) | |
|---|---|---|---|
| CALORIES | 418 | CALORIES | 408 |
| FAT | 17 GM | FAT | 15 GM |
| SATURATED FAT | 4 GM | SATURATED FAT | 2 GM |
| CHOLESTEROL | 75 MG | CHOLESTEROL | 77 MG |
| SODIUM | 353 MG | SODIUM | 370 MG |
| PROTEIN | 29 GM | PROTEIN | 31 GM |
| CARBOHYDRATE | 40 GM | CARBOHYDRATE | 40 GM |

# Curried Chicken Salad

*This low-fat chicken salad is a staple in our house for lunches, help-yourself dinners when family members are eating at different times, or anytime a prepare-ahead meal is needed. It's a good buffet dish, too. The curry and cilantro add bright flavor notes, and the moistness generated by the chutney means less mayonnaise is needed.*

6 chicken breast halves, bone in, skin on

4 cups (approximately) water or defatted, reduced-sodium chicken broth, preferably homemade (page 274)

salt and freshly ground black pepper to taste

3 or 4 scallions, white and green parts, finely chopped

3 slender stalks celery, strings removed and thinly sliced

¼ cup golden raisins

2 tablespoons good-quality curry powder

3 heaping tablespoons reduced-fat mayonnaise

3 heaping tablespoons nonfat yoghurt

3 tablespoons white wine (approximately)

½–¾ cup chutney, such as Major Grey's

2 tablespoons chopped fresh cilantro or parsley (optional)

Preheat the oven to 350°F.

Place the chicken breasts in a baking pan that will hold them comfortably in one layer. Pour in enough chicken stock, water, or a combination of the two so that the chicken is almost submerged. Cook for about 45 minutes in the center of the oven, adjusting the heat so that the liquid just shivers but does not boil. Remove the chicken from the oven and let cool in the broth.

Skin the breasts and tear, rather than cut, the meat into bite-size pieces. Layer them in a large mixing bowl, spooning some of the broth over each layer. Refrigerate for at least 1 hour. Strain the remaining broth and refrigerate or freeze for another use.

Toss the chilled chicken pieces with two wooden spoons. Season lightly with salt and pepper. Add the scallion, celery, and raisins and toss.

Place the curry powder in a small skillet over medium heat and toast for about 1½ minutes. Do not let it burn. Set aside.

In a small bowl, mix together the mayonnaise and yoghurt. In a cup, mix together the toasted curry powder and wine to make a slurry, adding more wine if needed. Blend into the mayonnaise mixture. Stir in the chutney. Pour over the chicken mixture and toss well. Adjust the seasoning. Turn out into a serving dish and sprinkle with the cilantro or parsley (if using).

**Serves 6–8**

➤ *The secret to incredibly moist meat for this or any chicken salad is allowing the breasts to cool in the broth and spooning more broth over the torn pieces before mixing. Try to allow enough preparation time for this if you can.*

| PER SERVING | |
|---|---|
| CALORIES | 267 |
| FAT | 6 GM |
| SATURATED FAT | 1 GM |
| CHOLESTEROL | 63 MG |
| SODIUM | 510 MG |
| PROTEIN | 24 GM |
| CARBOHYDRATE | 27 GM |

# Chicken Chili

*Chili fans will love this new "white" chili, which combines low-fat chicken with dazzling colors and spices. It offers the perfect blueprint for people who like to get a little personal with their chili. You can play with the heat; add or subtract spices, beans, or garnishes; or have it alone or over rice.*

3 whole boneless, skinless chicken
  breasts (about 2 pounds), halved
2 tablespoons plus 2 teaspoons olive
  oil
1½ large onions, chopped
7 or 8 cloves garlic, finely chopped
⅓ cup pure ground chili (see Appendix)
4 teaspoons ground cumin
1 teaspoon cayenne pepper or ½
  teaspoon red pepper flakes
1 cup dark beer
1 sweet green pepper, seeded and cut
  into ½-inch chunks
1 sweet red pepper, seeded and cut
  into ½-inch chunks

2 cups canned whole tomatoes in
  puree
2 tablespoons tomato paste
1 tablespoon sugar (or to taste)
3 cups (approximately) reduced-
  sodium defatted chicken broth,
  preferably homemade (page 274)
1 nineteen-ounce can cannellini
  beans, rinsed and drained
1 cup canned chickpeas, rinsed and
  drained
salt and freshly ground black pepper
  to taste
lime wedges (optional)

Using a sharp knife, trim away any fat or gristle from the chicken. Cut di-agonally into ½-inch strips, then cut diagonally the other way to make ½-inch cubes.

Heat the 2 tablespoons of olive oil in a Dutch oven or other large, heavy pot. When very hot, add the chicken and toss lightly over high heat until opaque and cooked through, about 4 minutes. Use a slotted spoon to trans-fer to paper towels to drain.

Reheat the pot, add the remaining 2 teaspoons olive oil, and sauté the onion and garlic over medium heat until the onion is tender, about 3 min-utes. Be careful that they do not burn. Stir in the ground chili, cumin, and cayenne or red pepper flakes and cook for 4 to 5 minutes. Add the beer and cook until reduced by one-half.

Add the green and red peppers, tomatoes, tomato paste, and sugar, break-ing up the tomatoes against the side of the pot with a wooden spoon. Add the broth, stir well, and bring to a boil. Cover, reduce the heat to medium, and simmer for 30 minutes. Add the reserved chicken, cannellini beans, and chickpeas. Stir to combine, then simmer for 15 minutes. Add more stock if mixture seems too dry. Season with salt and pepper. If you would like more heat, make cautious additions of cayenne or red pepper flakes. Serve with lime wedges if you wish.

**Serves 8–10**

➤ *You may serve this dish alone or over rice. Garnish with a good sprinkling of chopped scallions or nonfat sour cream, or serve with warm flour tortillas.*

| PER SERVING | |
| --- | --- |
| CALORIES | 258 |
| FAT | 6 GM |
| SATURATED FAT | 1 GM |
| CHOLESTEROL | 53 MG |
| SODIUM | 623 MG |
| PROTEIN | 28 GM |
| CARBOHYDRATE | 22 GM |

# Thai Beef Salad

*We eat very little meat at our house, but every once in a while, when the desire surfaces, I turn to this supremely delicious dish, which gives each person a big two and a quarter ounces of lean flank steak. In fact, I think I now make it for the unique flavors alone; the meat is somehow secondary! A great make-ahead dish.*

vegetable cooking spray
1 one-pound flank steak
6 medium cloves garlic, roughly chopped
2 tablespoons reduced-sodium soy sauce
¼ cup plus 2 tablespoons lime juice
1 tablespoon sugar
¼ cup chopped fresh cilantro
¼ cup chopped fresh mint

1 teaspoon freshly ground black pepper
2 fresh jalapeño peppers
3 scallions
1 large tomato
1 medium cucumber, halved lengthwise, seeded, and thinly sliced
1 small head red leaf lettuce
½ small head radicchio
2 cups cooked rice

Preheat the broiler with the pan close to the heat.

Spray the broiler rack with vegetable cooking spray and broil the steak until medium-rare, about 4 minutes per side. Remove from the oven, let cool slightly, and refrigerate until chilled, about 1 hour.

While the steak is chilling, make the dressing. In a blender or food processor, combine the garlic, soy sauce, lime juice, and sugar. Transfer to a bowl and add the cilantro, mint, and black pepper. Set aside.

Stem and seed the jalapeños and cut into 1-inch julienne strips. Trim the scallions and thinly slice. Seed and juice the tomato and cut into ½-inch dice. Add these ingredients to the dressing along with the cucumber.

Slice the steak thinly across the grain. Tear up the lettuce and radicchio, combine in a bowl, and divide among 4 plates. Divide the beef slices among the plates. Top with the dressing and serve immediately with room-temperature rice on the side.

**Serves 4**

| PER SERVING | |
|---|---|
| CALORIES | 326 |
| FAT | 7 GM |
| SATURATED FAT | 3 GM |
| CHOLESTEROL | 43 MG |
| SODIUM | 367 MG |
| PROTEIN | 22 GM |
| CARBOHYDRATE | 43 GM |

# Grilled Butterflied Leg of Lamb

*There's a certain moment in the summer when the idea of a grilled leg of lamb is irresistible. And if we don't make pigs of ourselves, we can enjoy this occasional treat without guilt, especially if we fill up on the accompaniments.*

1 seven-pound leg of lamb, boned, butterflied, and trimmed of fat inside and out

salt and freshly ground black pepper to taste

¼ cup olive oil

1 tablespoon minced garlic

1 teaspoon cracked black pepper

1 bunch fresh parsley, chopped

2 tablespoons mixed dried thyme, rosemary, and oregano

1 tablespoon orange juice

1 tablespoon lemon juice

¼ teaspoon ground cumin

¼ teaspoon ground cardamom

Lay the lamb flat on a work surface and season with salt and pepper on both sides. In a small bowl, mix all the remaining ingredients into a paste. Rub on both sides of the lamb so that it is evenly coated and refrigerate for about 6 hours. Let come to room temperature before cooking.

Preheat a charcoal or gas grill or the broiler. Place the lamb flat on the grill over a medium fire. If using the broiler, place 4 to 5 inches from the heat. Grill or broil until medium-rare, about 10 to 12 minutes on one side, then 6 minutes on the other. For medium or well-done meat, cook longer, turning as needed to prevent scorching. Transfer to a cutting board and let rest for 10 minutes before slicing thinly.

Serves 8–10

➤ *Serve with Grilled Zucchini (page 228) and oven-roasted potatoes.*

| PER SERVING | |
| --- | --- |
| CALORIES | 170 |
| FAT | 7 GM |
| SATURATED FAT | 2 GM |
| CHOLESTEROL | 76 MG |
| SODIUM | 58 MG |
| PROTEIN | 24 GM |
| CARBOHYDRATE | 0 GM |

# Leftover Meat with Peruvian Red Onion Sauce

*Peruvians use this incredibly delicious yet simple sauce with all kinds of foods, including slices of leftover chicken or meat, small fried fish similar to our smelts, or hard-boiled egg slices and potatoes. It makes a meal out of anything, and after eating it once, you'll be addicted.*

½ cup chopped red onion
1 tablespoon white or cider vinegar
1 tablespoon lemon juice
2–3 tablespoons olive oil
⅓–½ cup chopped fresh cilantro
    leaves
½ teaspoon salt (or to taste)
freshly ground black pepper to taste

½ pound (approximately) cooked lean
    leg of lamb, lean beef such as
    London broil, or pork loin, thinly
    sliced
lettuce leaves
5 or 6 unpeeled new potatoes boiled
    and cut into ½-inch-thick slices

Combine the onion, vinegar, and lemon juice in a medium bowl. Let stand for 10 minutes to soften the onion slightly. Stir in the olive oil, cilantro, salt, and liberal grindings of pepper. You should have about 1¼ cups of sauce.

Arrange the meat slices down the center of a serving platter. Place the lettuce leaves around the perimeter of the platter. Arrange the potato slices in an overlapping pattern around the meat, on top of the lettuce leaves. Spoon the sauce over the meat and serve.

Serves 3 or 4

*Poached Chicken with Red Onion Sauce:* Poach 4 chicken breast halves. Let cool, then remove and discard the skin, slice the meat thinly, and serve as above. Alternatively, you may use leftover sliced chicken breast.

*Poached Fish and Red Onion Sauce:* Slice ¾ pound of any poached or left-over lean whitefish and serve as above.

| PER SERVING | |
| --- | --- |
| CALORIES | 285 |
| FAT | 13 GM |
| SATURATED FAT | 3 GM |
| CHOLESTEROL | 51 MG |
| SODIUM | 324 MG |
| PROTEIN | 19 GM |
| CARBOHYDRATE | 23 GM |

# Oven-Braised Lamb Shanks

*If I had to choose one favorite recipe that keeps me from a total commitment to vegetarianism, it would be sweet, tender, meat-almost-falling-off-the-bone lamb shanks. This is a hearty, easy-to-make cold-weather dish that is not excessively high in fat. Accompany it with Tuscan-Style Beans (page 187), bean puree, or boiled potatoes.*

4 lamb shanks (about 1 pound each), trimmed of fat and membrane
2 or 3 cloves garlic, finely minced
1 teaspoon dried thyme
salt and freshly ground black pepper to taste
2 small carrots, cut into thin 2-inch strips
2 medium onions, thinly sliced

2 stalks celery, cut into thin 2-inch strips
2 bay leaves
1 cup reduced-sodium tomato sauce
½ cup dry red wine
½ cup water or reduced-sodium defatted beef broth
1 tablespoon olive oil

Preheat the oven to 300°F.

Wipe the shanks with a damp paper towel. In a small bowl, combine the garlic, thyme, and salt and pepper. Rub on the lamb shanks.

Sprinkle the bottom of a Dutch oven with the carrots, onions, celery, and bay leaves. Arrange the shanks on top. In a small bowl, mix together the tomato sauce, wine, water or broth, and olive oil. Pour over the meat. Cover tightly and bake in the center of the oven for 1½ to 2 hours, depending on the size of the shanks. Check the pot from time to time; it is important that the meat gently simmers.

During the last 20 minutes of cooking, uncover the pan and raise the oven temperature to 400°F. Baste the shanks frequently. The meat should be fork-tender.

When the shanks are done, use tongs to transfer them to a large warm platter. Cover loosely with aluminum foil and keep warm. Remove the bay leaves from the sauce and skim off the fat. Put the sauce through a food mill or push it through a sieve. Heat, correct the seasoning, and serve in a warm sauceboat with the shanks.

**Serves 4**

➤ *Make this ahead — the flavor only improves. And if you refrigerate it overnight, you can easily remove almost all of the fat.*

| PER SERVING | |
|---|---|
| CALORIES | 499 |
| FAT | 17 GM |
| SATURATED FAT | 5 GM |
| CHOLESTEROL | 200 MG |
| SODIUM | 314 MG |
| PROTEIN | 67 GM |
| CARBOHYDRATE | 17 GM |

# Veal Stew with Tomatoes and Peas

*This fabulous dish, which is my current favorite for company and special occasions, started out with a dreadful mistake. A kitchen helper mistakenly cut the meat off the bone of some veal shanks meant for my husband's favorite osso buco. This "rescue" effort received such raves that it is now my first choice for winter entertaining. It merits a fine wine.*

1½ pounds lean boneless veal from the shank or shoulder

2 tablespoons canola oil

1 tablespoon butter

3 tablespoons chopped onion

2 teaspoons salt

freshly ground black pepper to taste

1 cup Italian plum tomatoes, coarsely chopped (liquid reserved)

1 ten-ounce package frozen petit peas, thawed, or 2 pounds fresh peas, shelled

1 recipe Gremolata (recipe follows)

Cut the veal into 1½-inch cubes and dry the pieces thoroughly.

Put the oil, butter, and onion in a heavy casserole and sauté over medium heat until pale gold. Add the veal, browning the pieces well on all sides. (Do not crowd the pot, or the veal will not brown. Cook in 2 batches if necessary.) (Remove the first batch to a warm plate.)

Return all the meat to the pot. Add the salt, pepper, tomatoes, and reserved tomato liquid. When the mixture begins to boil, cover the pot and adjust the heat so that the stew is barely simmering. Cook until the veal is very tender when pricked with a fork, about 1 to 1½ hours. *(May be prepared ahead up to this point and refrigerated for up to 2 days. Reheat over medium heat.)*

When you judge the stew to be about 15 minutes short of being done, add the peas, allowing 15 minutes for fresh peas or 5 minutes for thawed frozen peas. Taste and add salt if necessary. Sprinkle on the Gremolata.

Serves 4–6

➤ *Serve with rice or soft white polenta.*

PER SERVING (STEW ONLY)

| | |
|---|---|
| CALORIES | 265 |
| FAT | 10 GM |
| SATURATED FAT | 3 GM |
| CHOLESTEROL | 112 MG |
| SODIUM | 266 MG |
| PROTEIN | 32 GM |
| CARBOHYDRATE | 9 GM |

# GREMOLATA

2 teaspoons grated lemon zest
½ teaspoon very finely chopped garlic

2 tablespoons finely chopped fresh
parsley

Combine all the ingredients in a small bowl and set aside.

**Makes 3 tablespoons**

PER TABLESPOON

| | |
|---|---|
| CALORIES | 8 |
| FAT | 0 GM |
| SATURATED FAT | 0 GM |
| CHOLESTEROL | 0 MG |
| SODIUM | 3 MG |
| PROTEIN | 0 GM |
| CARBOHYDRATE | 2 GM |

# Veal Picatta

*Veal scaloppine offer a lovely and satisfying way to enjoy meat occasionally without overdoing it. While expensive, a pound feeds four and can be stretched with pleasing accompaniments such as haricots verts, squash puree, and oven-roasted potatoes. Aside from having less butter, this is the traditional recipe.*

1 pound veal scaloppine, thinly sliced
    and pounded flat
¾ cup all-purpose flour
1 tablespoon canola oil
1 tablespoon plus 1 teaspoon butter
salt and freshly ground black pepper
    to taste

3 tablespoons lemon juice
2 tablespoons finely chopped fresh
    parsley
⅓ cup white wine
4 thin lemon slices for garnish

Select a large, heavy 10-inch skillet. If the scaloppine are large, cut them in half or just a bit larger than playing cards. You should have about 10 pieces.

Spread the flour on waxed paper and set aside. Heat the oil and the 1 tablespoon butter over medium-high heat. (The pan should be hot enough so that the meat sizzles as soon as it touches the pan.) Quickly dip both sides of 3 or 4 scaloppine (or as many as will fit in the pan easily without overlapping) in flour, shaking off any excess. Cook until lightly browned on one side, about 1 minute. Turn and brown the other side. (The scaloppine will shrink slightly.) When done, transfer to a warm platter and season with salt and pepper. Cook the remaining scaloppine the same way.

Remove the pan from the heat and add the lemon juice, scraping up any loose brown bits with a wooden spoon. Swirl in the remaining 1 teaspoon butter and add the parsley. If it seems as if there will not be enough sauce to coat the meat, add some wine (up to ⅓ cup). Return the scaloppine to the pan, turn gently to coat with sauce, and heat just long enough to warm the sauce and veal together. Transfer the scaloppine to the platter, pour the sauce over, and garnish with the lemon slices. Serve immediately.

Serves 4

➤ *I suggest making scaloppine in a regular heavy sauté pan rather than a non-stick one; they require quick cooking over really high heat, or they will become rubbery. Also, dip the scaloppine with flour just prior to cooking them; if the flour gets soggy, the meat will not brown properly.*

| PER SERVING | |
| --- | --- |
| CALORIES | 276 |
| FAT | 10 GM |
| SATURATED FAT | 3 GM |
| CHOLESTEROL | 99 MG |
| SODIUM | 116 MG |
| PROTEIN | 27 GM |
| CARBOHYDRATE | 20 GM |

# Marinated Pork Tenderloin

*Not all of "the other white meat" is high in fat; in fact the pork tenderloin, a small, lean cut from the top of the loin that is relative high in price (hence the phrase "high on the hog"), has a fat content that compares favorably with that of chicken breast. It cooks rapidly, is delicious at any temperature, and takes well to all sorts of marinades. The following, my favorite, is another winner from my friend Dale Loy. I serve it with low-fat mashed Yukon Gold potatoes and roasted carrots.*

3 cloves garlic
4 or 5 bay leaves, crumbled
1 tablespoon olive oil
⅓ cup reduced-sodium soy sauce

2 tablespoons balsamic vinegar
1 small pork tenderloin (about ¾–
   1 pound)

In a small bowl, combine the garlic, bay leaves, olive oil, soy sauce, and vinegar. Place in a sealable plastic bag with the pork. Marinate for 2 hours.

Preheat the oven to 425°F. Remove the pork from the bag, reserving the marinade. Roast for about 30 minutes, basting once or twice with the marinade. Let sit for 10 minutes at room temperature before slicing thinly, slightly on the diagonal. Strain the remaining marinade, heat to boiling, and use as a dipping sauce.

**Serves 2 or 3**

| PER SERVING | |
| --- | --- |
| CALORIES | 239 |
| FAT | 11 GM |
| SATURATED FAT | 3 GM |
| CHOLESTEROL | 78 MG |
| SODIUM | 1,244 MG |
| PROTEIN | 30 GM |
| CARBOHYDRATE | 5 GM |

# 12
# GRAINS

Foolproof White Rice

Basic White Rice Cooking Method

Mexican Red Rice

Melanie Barnard's Yellow Rice and
Black Bean Pilaf

Middle Eastern Rice Salad

Basmati Rice with Turmeric

Fragrant Rice

Risotto Technique

Risotto of Wild Mushrooms

Risotto with Asparagus

Bulgur Wheat Pilaf with Lentils

Barley, Mushroom, Scallion, and Parsley Pilaf

Quinoa Salad

Vegetable Couscous Salad

G RAINS ARE AMONG the most virtuous of foods: low in fat, free of saturated fat and cholesterol, and high in dietary fiber. This food has sustained a major portion of the world's populations since biblical times, but most people in Westernized industrial countries are not used to thinking of grains as main-course fare, even though they lend themselves to casseroles, main-dish salads, and bases for stews. The one exception I can think of is Italy, in which grains (in the form of pasta, made from wheat; polenta, made from cornmeal; and rice, used in risottos) form a major part of the diet.

Probably the grain Americans are most comfortable with is rice. It is easy to prepare and unmatched in versatility. It can be main-course fare, as the base of many stews; turned into a delicious salad, as in Middle Eastern Rice Salad (page 169); or used as a fabulous dessert, as in Low-Fat Rice Pudding (page 233). And it can accompany just about any other food. In addition to our splendid long-grain rice (such as Carolina), there is the distinctively flavored basmati rice for pilafs and to accompany Indian food, and the peerless Arborio rice, from Italy's Po Valley, for risottos.

Brown rice, which still retains the bran, is more nutritious than white rice but takes longer to cook. It may be used in place of the rice called for in many of the recipes in this section (except the risottos), following package instructions for cooking times. Nutty, chewy wild rice is not really rice at all, but an aquatic grass. It is expensive and best used mixed with regular rice as a side dish. Check the package for cooking directions.

In addition to rice, there is a wide range of other nourishing grains, many of which can be served like rice, such as barley, bulgur wheat, wheat berries, kasha, and polenta. Amaranth and quinoa, while not botanically classified as grains, can be used in the same ways and are becoming increasingly popular for their interesting flavors and high protein content.

Store rice in a tightly covered container, preferably in a dark cool place. (One Middle Eastern cook I know swears that a bay leaf or two buried in the rice keeps weevils away.) Other whole grains, such as cornmeal and bulgur, do best in the refrigerator because of their oil content.

# FOOLPROOF WHITE RICE

So many readers have told me that they could never cook rice properly until they followed these foolproof instructions, which appeared in *Low Fat & Loving It,* that I include them again here, since rice is such an important component of healthy meals. If you are confident that you won't have a disaster, you won't hesitate to plan a meal around it. Do note, however, that making risotto, which calls for Arborio rice, requires a different method, which is explained on page 172.

For perfect rice every time, here are the simple principles to apply to the cooking method that follows.

**Learn the basic procedure.** It applies to making any amount of rice, whether with water, or stock, and with any herbs or seasonings.

**Always keep the same proportions** — two measures of liquid (water, broth, or stock) to one measure of rice.

**Use the right pan.** Cook in a heavy-bottomed pot with a tight-fitting lid.

**Time accurately and don't stir.** Cook rice for 18 minutes from the *boil.* Never stir rice while it is cooking, and keep the heat at medium-low to prevent scorching.

**Use the Middle Eastern towel trick at the end.** When the rice has finished cooking, turn off the heat, remove the lid, and put a clean, folded kitchen towel on top of the pot. Set the lid back on top and let the pot sit this way for about 10 minutes. The rice will not get cold, and the steam it contains will be absorbed by the cloth instead of condensing and falling back onto the rice (which is what makes it gummy). Then fluff with a fork and serve. The rice will be beautifully fluffy, with each grain separate.

These instructions are for long-grain rice. They do not apply to Arborio rice or short-grain rice. Basmati rice has slightly different rules as well, explained in the recipe on page 170).

# Basic White Rice Cooking Method

1 teaspoon butter
2 teaspoons canola oil
1½ cups long-grain rice, such as
    Carolina

3 cups boiling water or defatted,
    reduced-sodium broth or chicken
    stock, preferably homemade (page
    274)
salt to taste

In a heavy saucepan with a tight-fitting lid, combine the butter and oil over medium heat. Add the rice and stir for no more than 1 minute to coat it with butter and oil. Pour in the water or stock, add the salt, and bring to a boil, stirring. Cover, reduce the heat to low, and cook for 18 minutes or until all the liquid is absorbed and the rice is tender but firm. Remove from the heat, remove the lid, lay a clean, folded kitchen towel over the pot, and replace the lid. Let sit for 10 minutes. Fluff the rice with two forks and serve.

**Makes 3 cups, serving 4–6**

| PER SERVING | |
| --- | --- |
| CALORIES | 188 |
| FAT | 2 GM |
| SATURATED FAT | 0 GM |
| CHOLESTEROL | 2 MG |
| SODIUM | 32 MG |
| PROTEIN | 3 GM |
| CARBOHYDRATE | 37 GM |

# Mexican Red Rice

*A beautiful and delicious way to prepare rice, especially when you want to feed a lot of people. Leftovers are even better the next day!*

3 cups reduced-sodium defatted
   chicken stock, preferably
   homemade (page 274)
¼–½ teaspoon saffron threads
2 tablespoons canola oil
1 medium onion, finely chopped
2 large cloves garlic, finely chopped
1½ cups long-grain rice, such as
   Carolina

3 medium ripe tomatoes (¾–1
   pound), seeded and chopped
1 small sweet red pepper, seeded and
   cut into thin strips
salt and freshly ground black pepper
   to taste
2 tablespoons chopped fresh cilantro

In a saucepan, bring the stock to a boil, then reduce the heat to a simmer. In a small bowl, soak the saffron in 2 tablespoons of hot stock for 10 minutes.

Heat the oil in a heavy saucepan or large skillet with a tight-fitting lid. Add the onion and garlic and sauté, stirring, until the onion is translucent but has not taken on color. Add the rice and cook, stirring to coat, for about 45 seconds. Add the tomatoes and red pepper and stir together for 1 to 2 minutes.

Add a ladleful of stock and stir in. Add the saffron and stir again. Add the balance of the stock and the salt and pepper, bring to a boil, cover, reduce the heat to low, and cook for 18 minutes. Fluff with two forks and taste for seasoning. Turn out into a serving dish and garnish with the cilantro.

Makes about 5 cups, serving 6–8

➤ *You can omit the saffron if you wish and still have a lovely, tasty dish. One Mexican friend serves it this way for buffets, omitting the sweet red pepper and garnishing it instead with pomegranate seeds.*

| PER SERVING | |
|---|---|
| CALORIES | 211 |
| FAT | 4 GM |
| SATURATED FAT | 0 GM |
| CHOLESTEROL | 0 MG |
| SODIUM | 284 MG |
| PROTEIN | 5 GM |
| CARBOHYDRATE | 38 GM |

# Melanie Barnard's Yellow
# Rice and Black Bean Pilaf

*This just might be the most valuable addition to your healthy cooking repertroie. It's easy, colorful, and tasty, and all the ingredients can be kept on hand. It's also useful to flesh out a meal of leftovers or for a really quick but filling meal on its own, accompanied by a salad.*

1 tablespoon olive oil
⅓ cup finely chopped onion
½ teaspoon ground turmeric or ¼
   teaspoon crushed saffron threads
½ teaspoon ground cumin
¼ teaspoon cayenne pepper
½ teaspoon salt

1 cup long-grain rice, such as Carolina
2 cups defatted, reduced-sodium
   chicken stock, preferably
   homemade (page 274)
1½ cups canned black beans, rinsed
   and drained

In a medium saucepan with a tight-fitting lid, heat the oil. Add the onion and sauté over medium heat, stirring frequently until softened, about 4 minutes. Stir in the turmeric, cumin, cayenne, salt, and rice. Toss for 1 minute to coat the rice with oil. Add the stock, bring to a boil, cover the pan, and reduce the heat to low. Cook for 10 minutes. Add the beans but do not stir them into the rice. Cover and cook until the rice is tender and the stock is absorbed, about 10 minutes more. Gently stir the beans into the rice before serving.

Serves 4–6

| PER SERVING | |
| --- | --- |
| CALORIES | 310 |
| FAT | 5 GM |
| SATURATED FAT | 0 GM |
| CHOLESTEROL | 8 MG |
| SODIUM | 821 MG |
| PROTEIN | 10 GM |
| CARBOHYDRATE | 49 GM |

# Middle Eastern Rice Salad

*This is one of those dishes that goes with everything. It's particularly nice in summer, at outdoor lunches and on picnics. The only company it needs is cold roast chicken, some crusty bread, and cold white wine. Also keep it in mind for buffets.*

1 recipe Basic White Rice (page 166)

1 large cucumber, peeled, seeded, and cubed (see Note)

2 medium ripe tomatoes, diced, or 8 cherry tomatoes, halved

5 or 6 scallions, white and green parts, thinly sliced

½ teaspoon red pepper flakes (or to taste)

3 tablespoons finely chopped fresh parsley

3 tablespoons finely chopped fresh mint (see Note)

3 tablespoons olive oil

2 tablespoons lemon juice

salt and freshly ground black pepper to taste

dash of cayenne pepper (optional)

8 pitted black olives for garnish (optional)

Let the rice sit for 20 minutes after cooking. Transfer to a large bowl and fluff with two forks. Add the cucumber, tomatoes, scallions, pepper flakes, parsley, mint, olive oil, and lemon juice. Toss well. Season with salt and pepper and cayenne (if using). Garnish with the black olives if desired.

**Serves 6**

Notes: Use 2 Kirby cucumbers, unpeeled, if available. They are sweeter, and you don't need to seed them.

Do not use commercial dried mint, which has a harsh flavor.

| PER SERVING | |
|---|---|
| CALORIES | 376 |
| FAT | 11 GM |
| SATURATED FAT | 2 GM |
| CHOLESTEROL | 0 MG |
| SODIUM | 18 MG |
| PROTEIN | 6 GM |
| CARBOHYDRATE | 63 GM |

# Basmati Rice with Turmeric

*For flavor and texture, delicately fragrant basmatic rice is unsurpassed. It must be cooked with more care than ordinary rice and is best soaked in cold water before cooking. Serve it with Indian vegetables or any sauced dish.*

1¼ cups basmati rice

1 tablespoon plus 1 teaspoon canola
  oil

1 medium onion, finely chopped

1 bay leaf

½ teaspoon ground turmeric

2 whole cloves

2½ cups water

½ teaspoon salt (or to taste)

freshly ground black pepper to taste

Put the rice in a bowl and cover with cold water. Let soak for 15 to 30 minutes. Drain in a colander, rinse under cold water, and drain again.

In a large, heavy saucepan or skillet with a tight-fitting lid, heat the oil almost to smoking. Add the onion and bay leaf and sauté until the onion is glossy but does not brown. Stir in the turmeric, cloves, and water. When the mixture comes to a boil, stir in the rice and salt. When tiny "wells" begin to appear on the surface, stir gently and cover. Turn the heat down to its lowest setting and cook for 15 minutes.

Remove from the heat and let sit, covered for several minutes. *Do not remove the cover at any time during this steaming period.* When you remove the lid, use 2 forks to lift the rice gently from the bottom and fluff it. Remove the cloves and bay leaf and discard. Season with pepper and additional salt if desired.

**Serves 4**

VARIATION:

*Plain Basmati Rice:* Omit the bay leaf, turmeric, and cloves.

| PER SERVING | |
| --- | --- |
| CALORIES | 252 |
| FAT | 6 GM |
| SATURATED FAT | 0 GM |
| CHOLESTEROL | 0 MG |
| SODIUM | 27 MG |
| PROTEIN | 7 GM |
| CARBOHYDRATE | 49 GM |

# Fragrant Rice

*This is a particularly lovely way to present rice to guests, especially on a nonmeat buffet. People are often surprised that rice can be so delicate and flavorsome.*

2 cups basmati rice

1 tablespoon plus 2 teaspoons canola oil

9 cardamom seeds

2 cinnamon sticks

10 whole cloves

3 bay leaves

1 cup chopped onion

1¼ tablespoons finely chopped garlic

1½ tablespoons finely chopped fresh ginger

2 teaspoons sea salt or kosher salt

⅓ cup chopped fresh cilantro (optional)

Put the rice in a bowl and cover with cold water. Let soak for 15 to 30 minutes. Drain in a colander, rinse under cold water, and drain again. Or, for a faster method, place the rice in a bowl, then place the bowl under cold running water, letting the water fill the bowl and flow gently over the rim until the water is clear, about 5 minutes. Drain in a colander, return to the bowl, cover with 4 cups cold water, and let soak for 30 minutes. Drain again, reserving the water.

Heat the oil in a heavy 3-quart saucepan having a tight-fitting lid. Add the cardamom, cinnamon sticks, cloves, and bay leaves and cook until the seeds jump. Add the onion, garlic, ginger, and salt. Stir and cook for 1 minute. Cover and cook over medium heat for 2 minutes or until the onion is soft and translucent.

Add the drained rice and stir until the rice begins to color, 2 to 3 minutes. Add the reserved rice water and bring to a boil, stirring. Turn the heat down to the lowest setting and cook, covered, for 10 minutes. *Do not stir.* Use a trivet to raise the pot above the heat and let steam for 10 minutes more.

Turn off the heat and leave the covered rice undisturbed for at least 15 minutes. Place a clean, folded kitchen towel on top of the pot, replace the lid, and cool for 5 minutes more. Sprinkle with the cilantro (if using) and serve.

**Serves 10**

| PER SERVING | |
| --- | --- |
| CALORIES | 258 |
| FAT | 5 GM |
| SATURATED FAT | 0 GM |
| CHOLESTEROL | 0 MG |
| SODIUM | 521 MG |
| PROTEIN | 7 GM |
| CARBOHYDRATE | 52 GM |

## RISOTTO TECHNIQUE

Wholesome, nutritious, versatile, and addictively delicious, risotto, the classic rice dish of northern Italy is not really hard to make, although the ingredients list may seem forbiddingly long and you cannot stray too far from the stove while making it. But the hands-on experience of making a risotto and the joy on the faces of those who taste it are more than just compensation. Have all the ingredients ready before you begin, as risotto cooks quickly.

Making risotto is not an exact science (for me this is one of its pleasures). You watch, sense, smell — and once you are familiar with the basic technique, you will develop a feel for the right moment to make the next addition of liquid or when the rice is just al dente.

Risotto is considered a first-course dish in Italy (except risotto Milanese, served with osso buco), but with the increased emphasis on filling main courses that do not involve meat, I find it a satisfying main course at lunch or dinner with the addition of a first course or an accompanying vegetable and a salad.

Here's what you have to know.

The creamy quality of a real risotto does not come from cream, but from the very high starch content of Arborio rice. Use only Italian Arborio.

The stock or other liquid is added slowly and stirred in one-half cup at a time as the risotto cooks, rather than all at once as in conventional rice cookery.

The risotto should be stirred frequently but not constantly. You kind of hang around the stove keeping an eye on it so that it doesn't stick and you catch the moment when the next addition is required.

The finished product should always be a little soupy, though each grain is separate and firm to the bite. If the rice gets mushy, you've overcooked it.

The basic technique never changes; once you learn it, you can make a risotto out of anything that strikes your fancy.

All risottos have (1) a *liquid* which can be wine or stock, in which the rice is cooked; (2) *condimenti,* the seafood, vegetable, meat, or other ingredients that give the risotto its flavor; (3) a *soffrito,* usually finely minced onion sautéed in butter, oil, or a combination of both. Sometimes carrots, parsley, garlic, and other ingredients may be added to the *soffrito,* depending on the recipe. A little liquid, set aside and stirred in at the last minute before serving, enhances the creamy quality and means that you can omit the usual last-minute addition of butter.

# Risotto of Wild Mushrooms

*In my view, a good risotto must contain some butter, but the overall fat and saturated fat content is still within acceptable limits for a main course, especially for such an extraordinary treat!*

½ ounce dried porcini mushrooms
1 cup very hot water
2 tablespoons unsalted butter
6 ounces fresh shiitake or other wild mushrooms, stemmed and sliced (about 2 cups)
½ cup evaporated skim milk
salt and freshly ground black pepper to taste
dash of cayenne pepper
4 cups vegetable or reduced-sodium defatted chicken stock, preferably homemade (pages 272, 274)

**Soffrito**

1 tablespoon unsalted butter
1 tablespoon olive oil
½ cup finely chopped onion
1 clove garlic, minced
1½ cups Arborio or Vialone rice
½ cup white wine
⅓ cup freshly grated aged Parmesan cheese
1 tablespoon chopped fresh parsley
freshly grated aged Parmesan cheese (optional)

Place the porcini and water in a small bowl and let stand for 30 minutes. Strain the porcini liquid into a medium saucepan that will hold all the cooking liquid. Coarsely chop the porcini and set aside.

Heat the butter in a small skillet. When it begins to foam, add the fresh mushrooms and cook, stirring, for 3 to 5 minutes or until the mushrooms are soft and the liquid they give off is almost completely evaporated. Add the porcini and continue cooking for about 2 minutes more. Add the milk and simmer until slightly reduced and thickened. Season with salt and pepper and cayenne. Set aside.

Add the stock to the porcini liquid and bring to a gentle simmer.

To make the soffrito, heat the butter and oil in a heavy 4-quart saucepan or casserole. Add the onion and cook gently for 2 minutes or until it is translucent. Stir in the garlic. Add the rice and cook for 2 minutes, stirring with a wooden spoon to coat all the grains. Add the wine and cook until it is almost completely evaporated. Begin to add the hot broth, ½ cup at a time, stirring frequently. Wait until each addition is almost completely absorbed before adding the next ½ cup, reserving about ¼ cup to add at the end. Stir frequently as the risotto cooks to prevent sticking.

After about 18 to 20 minutes, when the rice is tender but still has some "tooth," add the reserved broth and mushrooms, then vigorously stir in the ⅓ cup Parmesan and the parsley. Serve immediately. Pass additional grated Parmesan if you wish.

Serves 4

VARIATION:

*Risotto with Wild Mushrooms and Peas:* Add 1 cup cooked frozen or fresh peas with the cooked mushrooms at the end.

| PER SERVING | |
| --- | --- |
| CALORIES | 503 |
| FAT | 15 GM |
| SATURATED FAT | 7 GM |
| CHOLESTEROL | 30 MG |
| SODIUM | 760 MG |
| PROTEIN | 15 GM |
| CARBOHYDRATE | 72 GM |

# Risotto with Asparagus

*Few dishes say "spring" as eloquently as a risotto with fresh asparagus. This one incorporates a trick I learned from Francesco Antonucci, the brilliant chef of Remi, who uses part of the asparagus to make a puree in which he cooks the risotto, guaranteeing that the flavor permeates every grain.*

1 pound very fresh slender
   asparagus
½ baking potato, peeled and
   coarsely chopped
2 cups water
½ teaspoon salt
3 cups (approximately) vegetable or
   reduced-sodium defatted
   chicken stock, preferably
   homemade (pages 272, 274)

2 tablespoons olive oil
½ cup finely chopped onion
1 clove garlic, minced
1½ cups Arborio or Vialone rice
½ dry white wine
1 tablespoon butter (optional)
freshly ground black pepper
¼ cup freshly grated aged
   Parmesan cheese

Wash the asparagus and snap off the bottom stems where they break naturally. Peel the stems if necessary. Cut off about 1¼ inches of the tips and reserve. Cut the stems into 1-inch pieces and place in a medium saucepan. Add the potato, water, and salt and bring to a boil. Adjust the heat and cook until the asparagus and potato are tender, about 10 to 15 minutes. Puree, along with any remaining liquid, in a food processor or food mill. Add enough water to make 2 cups. Taste and add more salt if needed. Set aside 12 of the reserved asparagus tips and add the rest to the puree. Set aside. (May be prepared ahead up to this point.)

Put the stock in a saucepan and place over low heat, heating it so that it barely simmers. Heat the oil in a heavy 4-quart saucepan over medium heat. Add the onion and sauté gently for 1 to 2 minutes or until translucent. Do not let it brown. Stir in the garlic. Add the rice and cook for about 2 minutes, stirring with a wooden spoon to coat all the grains. Add the wine and cook, stirring, until it is completely absorbed. Add ¼ cup of the asparagus puree and continue cooking over moderate heat, adding more puree as the liquid in the pan is absorbed. When all the puree is added, continue cooking, adding the warm stock a ladleful at a time until only ¼ cup remains. After about 18 to 20 minutes, when the rice is tender but still chewy, stir in the butter (if using) and remaining stock, garnish with the reserved asparagus tips, and serve at once. Pass a pepper mill and the Parmesan cheese on the side.

**Serves 4–6**

| PER SERVING | |
| --- | --- |
| CALORIES | 337 |
| FAT | 7 GM |
| SATURATED FAT | 2 GM |
| CHOLESTEROL | 3 MG |
| SODIUM | 336 MG |
| PROTEIN | 12 GM |
| CARBOHYDRATE | 55 GM |

# Bulgur Wheat Pilaf with Lentils

*For committed or occasional vegetarians, a grain-legume combination is an important source of complete protein. Here is a tasty and filling candidate, which also makes a nice light meal with a tomato and cucumber salad.*

4 cups (approximately) vegetable or defatted, reduced-sodium chicken or beef stock, preferably homemade (pages 272, 274)
1 cup brown or green lentils, washed and drained

1 cup coarse bulgur
salt and freshly ground black pepper to taste
2 teaspoons butter
1 tablespoon canola oil
2 medium onions, thinly sliced

In a heavy 3-quart saucepan, combine the stock and lentils and bring to a boil over high heat. Reduce the heat to medium and cook for 15 to 20 minutes or until the lentils are tender. Add the bulgur and salt and pepper. Bring to a boil, stirring. Reduce the heat to low, cover, and simmer for 15 minutes or until the liquid is absorbed and the bulgur is tender. Should the liquid be absorbed before the bulgur is done, add a little more hot stock or water.

Meanwhile, heat the butter and oil in a nonstick skillet over medium heat. Add the onion and sauté gently, stirring frequently, for 5 minutes or until golden. When the bulgur is done, add the onion and mix in well. Cover and let stand in a warm place for 5 to 10 minutes.

**Serves 6 as a side dish, 4 as a main course**

> ➤ *I have used a tiny amount of butter because it is part of the characteristic taste of this pilaf. It's only a small splurge, however, as the original recipe calls for 6 tablespoons butter.*

| PER SERVING | |
| --- | --- |
| CALORIES | 379 |
| FAT | 6 GM |
| SATURATED FAT | 2 GM |
| CHOLESTEROL | 5 MG |
| SODIUM | 677 MG |
| PROTEIN | 22 GM |
| CARBOHYDRATE | 62 GM |

# Barley, Mushroom, Scallion, and Parsley Pilaf

*"Just yummy!" says my number one taster about this delicious dish, which should also please the barley fans who want a pilaf that can be made on top of the stove. The balsamic vinegar does something magical.*

1 cup medium pearl barley
2 teaspoons olive oil
¼ pound shiitake or white mushrooms, stemmed and sliced
1 medium onion, thinly sliced
3½ cups vegetable stock, preferably homemade (page 272)

2 scallions, white and green parts, minced
2 tablespoons chopped fresh parsley
freshly ground black pepper to taste
1 tablespoon balsamic vinegar

Place the barley in a fine sieve and wash under cold running water until the water runs clear, about 3 minutes. Drain and set aside.

Put the olive oil in a heavy 3-quart saucepan and place over medium-high heat. Add the mushrooms and onion and sauté until softened, about 5 minutes. Add the stock and bring to a boil. Stir in the barley, partially cover, reduce the heat, and let simmer for 35 minutes. Remove from the heat and let stand, uncovered, for 5 minutes. Stir in the scallion, parsley, several good grindings of black pepper, and vinegar.

Serves 4–6

▶ Pearl barley is barley from which the double outer husk and bran layer have been removed. Though not quite as nutritious as Scotch barley, which retains some of the bran, the cooking time is considerably reduced.

| PER SERVING | |
| --- | --- |
| CALORIES | 189 |
| FAT | 2 GM |
| SATURATED FAT | 0 GM |
| CHOLESTEROL | 0 MG |
| SODIUM | 107 MG |
| PROTEIN | 5 GM |
| CARBOHYDRATE | 38 GM |

# Quinoa Salad

*Once considered a sacred grain by the Incas, who called it the "mother grain," quinoa (KEEN-wah) isn't really a grain at all, but a seed belonging to the spinach family. It becomes light and crunchy, much like bulgur wheat, when cooked. Highly nutritious, quinoa contains all the essential amino acids that make up protein, plus iron and other nutrients.*

1 cup quinoa
1¼ cups water or vegetable or
    defatted, reduced-sodium chicken
    stock, preferably homemade
    (pages 272, 274)
½ teaspoon salt (or to taste)
1½ tablespoons lime juice
¼ cup olive oil

1 tablespoon finely minced fresh
    ginger
freshly ground black pepper to taste
½ cup finely diced sweet red pepper
2–3 tablespoons finely chopped
    scallions
¼ cup minced fresh cilantro

Rinse the quinoa briefly in a colander and set aside.

Bring the water or stock to a boil in a 2½- to 3-quart saucepan. Add the quinoa and return to a boil. Reduce the heat and simmer, covered, for 15 minutes or until all the liquid is absorbed. Remove from the heat and let sit, covered, for 5 minutes. Fluff with a fork and turn out into a large bowl.

While the quinoa cooks, make the dressing. In a small bowl, dissolve the salt in the lime juice, whisk in the oil, and add the ginger and black pepper. Add the dressing to the quinoa and toss to coat. Add the red pepper, scallion, and cilantro. Adjust the seasoning and toss again. Let stand for about 30 minutes before serving or refrigerating. Adjust the seasoning again before serving. Serve at room temperature.

**Makes about 5 cups, serving 8–10**

➤ *Quinoa, which can be found in health food stores and many supermarkets, is delicious mixed with corn or any other grain as a side dish. Note that it expands to four times its volume when cooked.*

| PER SERVING | |
|---|---|
| CALORIES | 129 |
| FAT | 7 GM |
| SATURATED FAT | 1 GM |
| CHOLESTEROL | 0 MG |
| SODIUM | 223 MG |
| PROTEIN | 3 GM |
| CARBOHYDRATE | 14 GM |

# Vegetable Couscous Salad

*Inspired by New York chef Matthew Kenney, this tasty prepare-ahead dish is attractive, nourishing, and filling, and it can accompany just about any food. It's very easy to eat, and it keeps for at least two days in the refrigerator, which is why I make a lot at one time.*

2 cups defatted, reduced-sodium
  chicken stock, preferably
  homemade (page 274)
1 tablespoon plus 2 teaspoons olive oil
1 cup finely chopped red onion (1
  medium onion)
1 tablespoon minced garlic
2 carrots, scraped and finely diced
1 sweet red pepper, seeded and finely
  diced
1 medium zucchini, finely diced

pinch of saffron threads
1 tablespoon ground turmeric
2 cups medium-grain couscous (about
  1 pound)
1 cup canned chickpeas
grated zest of 1 medium orange
juice of 1 medium lemon
salt and freshly ground black pepper
  to taste
¼ cup chopped fresh parsley or
  cilantro (optional)

Bring the stock to a simmer in a saucepan. Heat the oil in a large nonstick saucepan, add the onion and garlic, and cook over medium-high heat just until the garlic releases its fragrance. Add the carrot, red pepper, zucchini, and 2 tablespoons of the hot stock. Lower heat to medium and cook the vegetables slowly, stirring continuously with a wooden spoon, until they soften without coloring, about 7–8 minutes. Add the saffron and turmeric to the stock, then add the stock to the vegetables.

Place the couscous in a large bowl and stir in the hot vegetable mixture. Add the chickpeas, orange zest, and lemon juice. Cover with plastic wrap and let sit for about 15 minutes. Fluff the couscous with a fork and season with salt and pepper. Sprinkle with parsley or cilantro if desired. Serve at room temperature.

**Makes 8 cups, serving 6–8**

➤ *Serve this dish on its own, on lettuce leaves, for a light, filling lunch, or in combination with other room-temperature dishes, such as grilled fish.*

| PER SERVING | |
| --- | --- |
| CALORIES | 292 |
| FAT | 3 GM |
| SATURATED FAT | 0 GM |
| CHOLESTEROL | 0 MG |
| SODIUM | 218 MG |
| PROTEIN | 10 GM |
| CARBOHYDRATE | 54 GM |

# 13

# BEANS and LEGUMES

Basic Bean Cooking

Basic Beans

Black Bean Salsa

Tuscan-Style Beans

Turkish Beans

Bean Curd with Watercress

Ma Po's Tofu

Korean Scallion Pancakes with Bean Sprout Salad

Other bean and legume recipes in other sections in this book include: Hummus (pp. 50–51), No-Fat Black Bean Dip (pp. 51–52), Bruschetta of White Beans and Rosemary (pp. 44–45), Chickpea Soup with Swiss Chard (p. 64), Pasta e Fagioli with Chicken (pp. 66–67), Orecchiette with Broccoli, Chickpeas, Onions, and Tomatoes (pp. 108–109), Bulgur Wheat Pilaf with Lentils (p. 176), Warm Shrimp and Bean Salad (pp. 130–131), and Melanie Barnard's Yellow Rice and Black Bean Pilaf (p. 168).

A S A CHILD and well into my adulthood, my favorite food was the Boston baked beans at a now-extinct chain of restaurants called Horn and Hardart's. The beans were rich and crusty, sweet with molasses and smoky pork overtones. I ate them with boiled carrots and steamed cabbage, and that may have been the start of my realization that you could be supremely satisfied just eating vegetables if beans accompanied them. My bean passion continues today. I can be perfectly happy with a meal of Turkish Beans (pages 188–189) with some good bread and a salad. Hummus (pages 50–51) on *anything* is my favorite snack food. And now that beans are politically correct, they appear on many restaurant menus, as more and more people discover what vegetarians and the very poor have always known: beans are a filling accompaniment and a hearty and healthful substitute for meat, extremely satisfying and enormously versatile. Nutritionists will point out further virtues: they are low in fat, high in protein and soluble fiber, and thought to have certain cholesterol-lowering and anticarcinogenic properties as well.

When buying dried beans, search out a store with a high turnover; it's hard to calculate the correct cooking time of old beans. For the same reason, don't buy more than you will use in a short time. Although canned beans can be a great convenience when you're in a hurry or need them for a last-minute dish, they will never replace, in taste or consistency, dried beans cooked from scratch. Dried beans have a "tooth" that makes canned beans seem mushy by comparison. Cooking dried beans is not difficult; it just requires planning. You can always use the quick-soak method, and if you have a pressure cooker, even the presoaking and long cooking ceases to be a consideration. If you do use canned beans, rinse and drain them to get rid of the gooey juice and excess salt.

# BASIC BEAN COOKING

*A few points to note when cooking dried beans:* Dried beans need to be picked over and rinsed before using, to remove dust, bits of dirt, and small pebbles. The easiest way to do this is to spread them out in a large pan such as a baking sheet. Then put the beans in a bowl, cover with water, and swish around with your hand. Drain and discard the water.

The next step is soaking. (Only lentils, split peas, and black-eyed peas need not be soaked. Simply rinse and cook them as directed.) Soaking speeds the cooking time. Many recipes say to soak overnight, but tests have shown that beans absorb all the water they can hold in four hours. You also may use the quick-soak method described below. In either case, discard the soaking water before cooking.

Soak beans in cold water to cover and use fresh water for the actual cooking. This helps to remove some of the complex sugars (oligosaccharides) that can cause flatulence. Changing the water two or three times is an additional help.

Soak beans in at least three to four times their volume of water.

Don't add salt to the soaking water or the cooking water; this causes the skin to toughen and become impermeable so that liquids will not be absorbed. For the same reason, do not add any acidic flavoring, such as wine, vinegar, or tomatoes. Salt should be added once beans become tender — during the last five minutes of cooking.

For use as a side dish, allow 1 cup of dried beans to serve four. Dried beans double in volume and weight after soaking and cooking. Therefore, 1 cup (8 ounces) dried equals 2 to 2½ cups (1 to 1¼ pounds) soaked and cooked.

Don't allow beans to boil. Rather, simmer them over low heat. Cook beans partially covered to prevent foaming.

Cooking times for beans are only a guide. About fifteen minutes before you expect them to be done, taste one. If the center is still dense, taste again five minutes later, continuing to taste every five minutes until they are done.

### Quick Soak
Place washed and picked-over beans in a large pot. Cover with two inches of unsalted water, or three times their volume. Bring to a boil and boil for 2 minutes. Remove from the heat and let sit, covered, for 1 hour. Drain and rinse the beans. They are now ready for use.

# COOKING TIMES FOR BEANS

*The times are for beans that have been soaked for at least four hours. All of the following should be soaked before cooking. The times are approximate, as older beans may require more cooking, freshly dried ones less.*

| Bean | Regular Cooking | Pressure Cooker |
|---|---|---|
| Black beans | 1 to 1½ hours | 8 to 10 minutes |
| Chickpeas | 1½ to 2 hours | 10 to 12 minutes |
| Cranberry beans (*borlotti*) | 40 to 50 minutes | 6 to 8 minutes |
| Fava beans | 2 hours | 16 to 18 minutes |
| Great Northern beans | 1 hour | 10 to 12 minutes |
| Kidney beans (red) | 1½ hours | 10 to 12 minutes |
| Cannellini beans (white kidney beans) | 1½ hours | 10 to 12 minutes |
| Lima beans or flageolets | 50 minutes | 6 to 8 minutes |
| Navy or pea beans | 1½ hours | 6 to 8 minutes |
| Pigeon peas | 20 minutes | 4 to 6 minutes |
| Pinto beans | 1½ to 2 hours | 6 to 8 minutes |

The following do not require soaking.

| Bean | Regular Cooking | Pressure Cooker |
|---|---|---|
| Black-eyed peas | 30 minutes | 4 to 6 minutes |
| Lentils | 20 minutes | 8 minutes |
| Split peas | 30 minutes | 15 minutes |

NOTE: Do not use the microwave to cook dried beans. However, the microwave may be used as an alternative to the quick-soak method. Put the washed, picked-over beans in a wide, microwave-safe bowl, cover with plastic wrap, punch two holes in the plastic, and microwave on high for 15 to 20 minutes. Remove and let sit, covered, for 10 minutes. Drain and cook according to the recipe. These instructions are for one pound of beans. Cook a smaller amount for proportionately less time.

# Basic Beans

*You may flavor beans with almost any herb you like. For Italians, sage and cannellini beans are almost inseparable. A bay leaf, an onion studded with two whole cloves, or parsley is never amiss.*

1 cup dried beans
1 bay leaf
1 small onion, peeled and studded
  with 2 whole cloves

salt to taste

Spread the beans out on a baking sheet and pick through them to remove any debris or pebbles. Rinse in a colander, place in a large bowl, and cover with 8 cups water. Let sit for at least 4 hours or overnight.

Drain the beans and discard the water. Transfer the beans to a large, heavy pot. Add the bay leaf, onion, and 12 cups water. Cover and simmer for the amount of time listed in the chart on page 184. Add water as necessary to keep the beans covered with liquid. Test the beans for doneness, squeezing one between your thumb and forefinger. It should be tender — rather soft but not mushy. Add salt during the last 5 minutes of cooking.

**Makes about 2½ cups**

# Black Bean Salsa

*Salsas are one of the foods that characterize the nineties and with good reason. We have become hooked on strong flavors, which a salsa easily adds to simple grilled fish or chicken. Bean salsa also enhances the protein picture in any vegetarian meal that includes a pasta or grain dish.*

2 cups canned or cooked black beans (page 185)
1 large ripe tomato, lightly seeded and diced (about 1 cup)
½ cup finely chopped red onion
1 fresh jalapeño or serrano pepper, stemmed, seeded, and finely chopped

2 tablespoons fresh lime juice
2 tablespoons olive oil
salt and freshly ground black pepper to taste
½ cup coarsely chopped fresh cilantro

Combine the beans, tomato, onion, hot pepper, lime juice, and oil in a medium bowl. Season with salt and pepper. Cover and refrigerate. *(May be prepared up to this point up to 3 hours ahead.)*

An hour or so before serving, add the cilantro and let come to room temperature.

**Makes about 3 cups, serving 8**

VARIATIONS:

*Black Bean–Mango Salsa:* Substitute 1 cup peeled and coarsely chopped fresh, ripe mango for 1 cup of the beans and prepare as above.

*Black Bean–Papaya Salsa:* Substitute 1 cup peeled and coarsely chopped fresh, ripe papaya for 1 cup of the beans and prepare as above.

PER SERVING BLACK BEAN SALSA

| | |
|---|---|
| CALORIES | 97 |
| FAT | 4 GM |
| SATURATED FAT | 1 GM |
| CHOLESTEROL | 0 MG |
| SODIUM | 4 MG |
| PROTEIN | 4 GM |
| CARBOHYDRATE | 13 GM |

*Recipes*

# Tuscan-Style Beans

*The Tuscans love beans, so much so that other Italians refer to them as "bean eaters." Certainly no one makes better beans than those found in Tuscany. The secret? Slow, careful cooking in the oven, which makes them tender without becoming mushy. Beans made this way can be served as is, drizzled with olive oil, or used in other recipes calling for cooked beans. They also can be mashed, flavored, and used for bruschetta (page 44).*

| | |
|---|---|
| 1 pound dried cannellini or Great Northern beans, rinsed and picked over | 1 sprig fresh sage |
| | 1 tablespoon extra-virgin olive oil |
| 1 large clove garlic | ½ teaspoon salt or more to taste |
| | freshly ground black pepper |

Place the beans in a bowl. Add cold water to cover by 3 inches. Refrigerate for 4 hours or overnight.

Preheat the oven to 300°F. Drain the beans, transfer to an ovenproof casserole, and add cold water to cover by 1 inch. Add the garlic, sage, and olive oil and bring to a simmer over low heat. Place in the center of the oven and cook for 45 minutes to 1 hour or until the beans are very tender. (Depending on the age of the beans, the cooking time may vary by as much as

30 minutes.) Add salt and cook for 5 minutes more. Drain and serve warm or at room temperature, drizzled with a little additional olive oil if you like and with liberal grindings of pepper.

**Makes about 6 cups, serving 10–12**

| PER SERVING | |
|---|---|
| CALORIES | 151 |
| FAT | 2 GM |
| SATURATED FAT | 0 GM |
| CHOLESTEROL | 0 MG |
| SODIUM | 105 MG |
| PROTEIN | 9 GM |
| CARBOHYDRATES | 26 GM |

# Turkish Beans

*This is one of my best recipes. It was love at first bite when the mother of my friend Dale Loy served it with a garlicky leg of lamb thirty years ago. I've no idea whether it is authentically Turkish or only someone's fancy, but it is good! I've made it for picnics and to take to the country on weekends, as it travels well. It's good at any temperature, easily doubled or tripled, and great as a main vegetarian dish or as a side dish with meat loaf or barbecued or roast chicken.*

1 cup dried large white beans such as Great Northern, or 1 twenty-ounce can cannellini beans
1 tablespoon plus 1 teaspoon olive oil
3 carrots sliced ¼ inch thick
½ cup diced sweet green or red pepper
1 cup celery cut in medium dice
2 large cloves garlic, finely chopped

3 tablespoons finely chopped fresh parsley
2 medium ripe tomatoes, peeled, seeded, and chopped, or 4 canned Italian plum tomatoes, chopped (liquid reserved)
salt and freshly ground black pepper to taste
dash of cayenne pepper (optional)

If using dried beans, soak, drain, and cook as directed on pages 183–184. If using canned beans, drain well and rinse.

Heat the olive oil in a heavy nonstick skillet. Sauté the carrots, sweet pepper, celery, garlic, and parsley until the garlic releases its fragrance, about 3 minutes. Add the tomatoes and 2 tablespoons tomato liquid or water and continue cooking until the vegetables are softened but still firm and not browned. Add the beans, salt and pepper, and cayenne (if using). Stir together gently, cover, and simmer for 15–20 minutes or until the vegetables are tender, adding a little more tomato liquid or water if necessary to prevent sticking.

**Serves 4**

➤ *This dish tastes better made early in the day so that the flavors have a chance to develop. Leftovers are great stuffed into a warm pita bread pocket.*

| PER SERVING | |
| --- | --- |
| CALORIES | 232 |
| FAT | 5 GM |
| SATURATED FAT | 1 GM |
| CHOLESTEROL | 0 MG |
| SODIUM | 49 MG |
| PROTEIN | 11 GM |
| CARBOHYDRATE | 37 GM |

# Bean Curd with Watercress

*Esteemed in the Orient but ignored here because of its blandness, healthful, low-calorie, iron- and calcium-rich tofu (or bean curd) is redeemed by its chameleon-like quality of taking on the flavor of whatever it is cooked or dressed with. Serve this dish with rice.*

1 large bunch watercress (about 5 ounces)
1 fresh red chili pepper or jalepeño pepper, seeded and minced
½ sweet red pepper, seeded and diced
½ teaspoon salt
8 ounces firm tofu
1¼ cups vegetable or defatted, reduced-sodium chicken stock, preferably homemade (pages 272, 274)

½ teaspoon cornstarch
2 teaspoons reduced-sodium soy sauce
1 teaspoon dark sesame oil
¼ teaspoon sugar
2 tablespoons vegetable oil
2 cloves garlic, slightly crushed
1-inch piece fresh ginger, finely chopped
1 teaspoon toasted sesame seeds (page 268)

Wash, dry, and mince the watercress (stalks and all) and put in a small bowl. Add the hot pepper and sweet pepper, sprinkle with the salt, and mix well. Let stand for 30 minutes.

Meanwhile, put the tofu in a small pot, add 1 cup of the stock, and bring to a very gentle simmer over low heat. Simmer for 10 minutes. Turn off the heat and let sit on the stove.

Put the cornstarch in a small cup, slowly add the remaining ¼ cup stock, and blend. Add the soy sauce, sesame oil, and sugar and mix well.

Heat the vegetable oil in a heavy skillet over high heat. When the oil is hot, add the garlic and stir-fry, pressing down on it with the back of a wooden spoon. As soon as it begins to turn dark, remove and discard. Add the ginger and stir-fry for 20 seconds or just until the flavor is released.

Add the watercress mixture and stir-fry for 1 minute or just until the watercress has wilted. Lower the heat, give the cornstarch mixture a quick stir, and pour over the watercress mixture. Stir and cook for 30 seconds more or until slightly thickened. Remove from the heat.

Carefully lift the tofu out of the stock and transfer to a serving dish. Cut into ¾- to 1-inch cubes. Discard the stock. Pour the watercress over the tofu, sprinkle with the sesame seeds, and serve.

**Serves 4 as part of an oriental meal**

➤ *Fresh tofu usually comes in 5-ounce cakes, so you need to buy two for this recipe. Packaged tofu usually comes in 1-pound packages. Refrigerate leftover tofu, keeping it in a covered container filled with water. Change the water every other day.*

| PER SERVING | |
| --- | --- |
| CALORIES | 139 |
| FAT | 11 GM |
| SATURATED FAT | 1 GM |
| CHOLESTEROL | 0 MG |
| SODIUM | 705 MG |
| PROTEIN | 6 GM |
| CARBOHYDRATE | 5 GM |

# Ma Po's Tofu

*This spicy, aromatic preparation is popular throughout China, a classic dish that dates back to the Manchu dynasty. Ma Po (the name means "pockmarked") was the wife of a famous Szechuan chef, who apparently made up in cooking skills what she lacked in physical beauty. It is, hands down, the most delicious tofu dish I've ever encountered.*

1 tablespoon reduced-sodium soy sauce
2 tablespoons sherry
1 tablespoon dark miso paste
  (optional) (see Note)
½ teaspoon sugar
1–1½ teaspoons hot chili paste with
  garlic (see Note)
2 teaspoons cornstarch
2 pieces firm tofu (1 pound)
1 tablespoon peanut or canola oil

¼ pound lean ground pork
2 teaspoons minced fresh ginger
1 teaspoon minced garlic
⅓ cup coarsely chopped scallion
  (white and part of the green) (2 or
  3 scallions)
½ cup defatted, reduced-sodium
  chicken stock, preferably
  homemade (page 274)
1 teaspoon dark sesame oil

In a small bowl, combine the soy sauce, 1 tablespoon of the sherry, miso, sugar, and chili paste. Set aside.

In another small bowl, mix together the cornstarch and remaining 1 tablespoon sherry and set aside.

Drain the tofu and dry on paper towels. Cut into ½-inch cubes and set aside.

Place a wok or heavy skillet over high heat for about 1 minute. Add the peanut or canola oil and heat until hot but not smoking. Add the pork and stir-fry, breaking it up into small pieces, for 2 to 3 minutes or until it turns white. Use a slotted spatula to transfer to paper towels to drain.

To the oil remaining in the pan, add the ginger, garlic, and scallions. Stir-fry for 30 seconds. Stir the seasoning sauce and add it to the pan all at once. Stir-fry for about 30 seconds more. Pour in the stock and bring to a boil. Add the tofu and cooked pork and toss briefly until heated through. Add the cornstarch mixture and heat, stirring, just until the sauce thickens. Remove from the heat and add the sesame oil. Transfer to a heated serving dish and serve immediately.

**Serves 4 as a main course, 6 as part of a Chinese meal**

➤ *Leftovers make an unusually delicious, hearty sandwich. Spread lightly mashed bean curd on toasted seven-grain bread and add lettuce and a few thin slices of cucumber.*

| PER SERVING | |
| --- | --- |
| CALORIES | 181 |
| FAT | 11 GM |
| SATURATED FAT | 2 GM |
| CHOLESTEROL | 13 MG |
| SODIUM | 209 MG |
| PROTEIN | 16 GM |
| CARBOHYDRATE | 6 GM |

Note: Miso paste is found in oriental markets and keeps in the refrigerator for at least 6 months. Chili paste with garlic also is found in oriental markets and the Chinese food section of some supermarkets. It has a long shelf life.

# Korean Scallion Pancakes

*Elizabeth Alston, whose delightful book* **Pancakes and Waffles** *is the source for this adaptation, advises making the salad first so that the flavors have time to blend. You can spoon some salad on top of a pancake, roll it, and eat it out of hand, or plate and serve the pancakes with the salad on top or on the side.*

½ cup all-purpose flour

1 large egg plus 1 large egg white

2 tablespoons water

1 tablespoon plus 2 teaspoons canola oil

½ teaspoon salt

5 scallions

1 small fresh hot chili pepper or 1 pickled jalapeño pepper, seeded and minced as finely as possible

1 recipe Bean Sprout Salad (recipe follows)

Put the flour, egg and egg white, water, 1 tablespoon oil, and salt in a medium bowl. Beat with a wire whisk or hand-held electric mixer to make a smooth, quite thick batter.

Trim the scallions, leaving the white and about 3 inches of the green tops. Cut in half lengthwise, then slice thinly crosswise. Add to the batter along with the hot pepper.

Brush 1 teaspoon of the remaining oil over a round iron griddle or non-stick skillet that measures 8 to 9 inches *across the bottom*. Place over medium-high heat. When the pan is very hot, pour in half the batter, about ½ cup. With a metal spatula, spread the batter quickly to form an 8-inch pancake about one-eighth inch thick. Cook for about 1 minute or until the bottom is lightly browned. Flip the pancake and cook for 1 to 2 minutes more. Slide the pancake out of the pan and onto a warm plate. Make a second one with the remaining 1 teaspoon oil and ½ cup batter. Serve immediately with Bean Sprout Salad.

**Serves 2**

| PER SERVING (PANCAKE ONLY) | |
| --- | --- |
| CALORIES | 274 |
| FAT | 14 GM |
| SATURATED FAT | 2 GM |
| CHOLESTEROL | 106 MG |
| SODIUM | 289 MG |
| PROTEIN | 9 GM |
| CARBOHYDRATE | 28 GM |

# BEAN SPROUT SALAD

| | |
|---|---|
| 1 tablespoon sesame seeds | 2 tablespoons reduced-sodium soy |
| 1½ cups (4 ounces) mung-bean | sauce |
| sprouts (see Note) | 1 teaspoon sugar |
| 2 tablespoons rice wine vinegar or | 1 teaspoon dark sesame oil |
| cider vinegar | ½ teaspoon minced garlic |

Toast the sesame seeds in a small, heavy dry skillet over medium heat for 4 to 5 minutes, tossing frequently until golden brown. Transfer to a medium bowl, add all the remaining ingredients, and toss to mix. Let stand at room temperature for about 30 minutes, but not more than 1 hour, to allow the flavor to develop.

**Makes 1½ cups, serving 2**

| PER SERVING | |
|---|---|
| CALORIES | 84 |
| FAT | 5 GM |
| SATURATED FAT | 1 GM |
| CHOLESTEROL | 0 MG |
| SODIUM | 605 MG |
| PROTEIN | 3 GM |
| CARBOHYDRATE | 9 GM |

Note: Mung-bean sprouts, the kind used in Chinese cooking, are available in most supermarkets.

# 14
# VEGETABLES

Basic Broccoli

Sautéed Broccoli Rabe

Roasted Brussels Sprouts

Oven-Roasted Carrots

Carrots and Celery with Caraway Seeds

Crumbed Cauliflower with Anchovies,
Capers, and Olives

Indian-Style Spiced Cauliflower with Potatoes

Braised Fennel

Roasted Sweet Red Peppers

Roasted Sweet Peppers Marinated with
Capers and Anchovies

Sweet Pepper, Ham, and Onion Omelet

Roasted New Potatoes with Thyme and Garlic

Anchovied Potatoes, Tomatoes, and Zucchini

Spiced Potatoes and Eggplant

Potato-Vegetable Gratin

Buttermilk Mashed Potatoes

Stir-Fried Mushrooms, Peppers,
Broccoli, and Shrimp

Thai Spinach and Watercress

Pan-Grilled Radicchio

Butternut Squash and Ancho Chili Puree

Baked Acorn Squash

Yellow Squash Casserole

Roasted Sweet Potatoes

Baked Stuffed Tomatoes

Mixed Roasted Vegetables

Roasted Fall Vegetables

Zucchini Râpé

Grilled Zucchini with Mint

ADDING A GREATER variety of vegetables to your diet and preparing them in interesting ways that go beyond the usual steaming or boiling is one positive step toward increasing your consumption of healthy plant foods and enjoying doing it. Each day aim to include at least one serving of a cruciferous vegetable (broccoli, cabbage, cauliflower, kohlrabi, mustard greens, turnips) and one of the beta-carotene vegetables or fruits (again broccoli, carrots, kale, spinach, sweet potatoes). The prescribed minimum of five helpings a day may seem like a lot, but it really isn't when you bear in mind that a helping is only half a cup. (To see how easily this can be accomplished, read the five-a-day suggestions in chapter 4.)

Beginning or ending a meal with a salad is another easy way to incorporate vegetables into your diet. Just make sure you don't drench it with high-fat dressing, probably the largest single hidden or unconsidered source of fat in people's diets today.

This section contains some marvelous ways to prepare a variety of vegetables and none is particularly difficult. If you're like me, you'll find that the more you eat these tasty dishes, the more you'll crave them. At least two nights a week, we have all-vegetable dinners (which include a filling grain or starch). Although I must admit that preparing vegetables is more labor-intensive than just throwing a chop on the grill and a potato in the oven, the bonuses — in both taste satisfaction and the knowledge that we are eating healthfully — are more than worth the extra effort.

If you're in a hurry or not inclined to cook, get your blanching technique down pat and just serve broccoli or string beans with a dash of olive oil or a squeeze of lemon juice. But I'm hoping that after you read these recipes, you won't want to stop there!

# Basic Broccoli

*This is simply blanched broccoli — the best way, in my opinion, to cook this healthful and useful vegetable. The broccoli can be finished in various ways or seasoned and used as is, as a side dish, a component of a salad, or a snack food.*

1 head very fresh broccoli (about 1½ pounds)
salt and freshly ground black pepper to taste

lemon wedges (see Note)

Rinse the broccoli in cool water. Cut off the head at the point where the stems of the florets meet the central stalk. Discard the stalk or prepare it separately according to the instructions below. Separate the florets into manageable clusters at the point where the small stems end — about 2½ inches below the base of the head. Depending on how you will use the broccoli, you can leave the stems attached to the clusters or remove them and cook separately.

Bring a large pot of salted water to a boil. (Add a good handful of salt, as it will help keep the broccoli green and will be washed off at the end.) If you are cooking the stems separately, add them 1 to 2 minutes before the florets. Add the florets and boil uncovered until tender but crisp, about 4 to 5 minutes after the water returns to a boil. Drain in a colander, then plunge briefly into a basin of cold water or spray with cold water to stop the cooking and set the color.

To cook the stalks, cut off and discard the woody bottom end, then remove the tough outer skin by peeling up from the base, using the thumb as a guide so the cut is not too deep. Cut into half-inch disks or 1½-inch-long sticks and add to the boiling water 2 minutes before you add the florets. Serve immediately, seasoned with salt and pepper and a good squeeze of lemon juice.

Serves 4

➤ *Broccoli cooked this way may be prepared ahead of time, spread on a towel to cool, and then refrigerated, covered by a damp paper towel. Finish off by warming* in a nonstick pan in a small amount of oil flavored with a crushed clove or two of garlic.

➤ *The use determines how you should cut the broccoli. For stir-frying and with pasta, you may wish to use just the florets or the florets and stems separated. If you are serving broccoli as a side dish, you may wish to keep the stems attached. They will be a little more resilient than the florets, but the contrast is pleasant. Some people peel the stems; I don't.*

| PER SERVING | |
|---|---|
| CALORIES | 32 |
| FAT | 0 GM |
| SATURATED FAT | 0 GM |
| CHOLESTEROL | 0 MG |
| SODIUM | 25 MG |
| PROTEIN | 4 GM |
| CARBOHYDRATE | 6 GM |

Note: Omit the lemon juice if you are planning to use the broccoli as part of another preparation (a stir-fry, pasta dish, or salad).

# Sautéed Broccoli Rabe

*Also known as broccoli raab, rapini, and stem broccoli, this pungent green is really more closely related to the turnip family. Highly esteemed by the Chinese and the Italians, its slightly bitter flavor is an acquired taste, which can quickly become an addiction. Many cooks steam-sauté it with the water clinging to the leaves before finishing it in garlic-flavored olive oil, but I find that a brief blanching first removes some of the bitterness.*

2 bunches broccoli rabe (about 1½–2 pounds)
2 tablespoons extra-virgin olive oil

2 large cloves garlic (or more to taste), slightly crushed
freshly ground black pepper to taste

Bring 4 quarts of salted water to a boil.

Remove the thick stems of the broccoli rabe and trim, leaving about 2 inches of stalks. Cut the leaves, sprouts, and stems into 2- to 3-inch pieces. Fill the sink with cold water and dunk well several times to get rid of any sand. Drain in a colander and drop by handfuls into the boiling water. Boil for 4 minutes (it will shrink considerably), drain, run cold water over briefly, and drain on a towel.

Put the olive oil in a large skillet and add the garlic. Cook over medium heat for about 30 seconds or until it softens and releases the flavor, but do not let it brown. Holding the skillet cover as a shield (water on the leaves may spatter the oil), stand back and quickly add the broccoli rabe to the pan. Toss with tongs or a pot fork until wilted and tender but still bright green. Season with pepper, toss, and cook for 1 minute more.

**Serves 4**

➤ *Leftovers make a fabulous sandwich with roasted sweet red or yellow peppers and a slice of mozzarella.*

| PER SERVING | |
|---|---|
| CALORIES | 89 |
| FAT | 7 GM |
| SATURATED FAT | 1 GM |
| CHOLESTEROL | 0 MG |
| SODIUM | 26 MG |
| PROTEIN | 4 GM |
| CARBOHYDRATE | 6 GM |

# Roasted Brussels Sprouts

*I adore brussels sprouts cooked this way. The high heat makes them miraculously sweet, with a crispy, slightly charred exterior and a meltingly tender interior. I have to make lots of extras because no one in my family (myself included) can resist nibbling on them as soon as they're made!*

2 ten-ounce containers brussels
    sprouts
2 tablespoons olive oil

salt and freshly ground black pepper
    to taste

Preheat the oven to 425°F.

Rinse the brussels sprouts, remove any loose or discolored leaves, and cut a thin slice off the bottom of the stem, leaving the leaves attached. With the tip of a small, sharp knife, make a shallow cross in the bottom of each.

Place the olive oil in a heavy baking dish, add the sprouts, roll and toss to coat with oil, and season well with salt and pepper. Place the pan on the lowest rack of the oven and roast for 35 minutes, turning the sprouts once or twice during cooking. They are done when they are slightly charred outside and can be easily pierced in the center with a knife tip. If they are larger or older than usual, they may need a little more time.

**Serves 4**

➤ *Look for brussels sprouts that are firm and compact. Those with yellow- or brown-tipped leaves are older and can be slightly bitter.*

| PER SERVING | |
| --- | --- |
| CALORIES | 104 |
| FAT | 7 GM |
| SATURATED FAT | 1 GM |
| CHOLESTEROL | 0 MG |
| SODIUM | 26 MG |
| PROTEIN | 3 GM |
| CARBOHYDRATE | 9 GM |

# Oven-Roasted Carrots

*An accompaniment that goes with everything and could not be easier, these carrots can be made in any quantity. Though absolutely lovely plain, they also can be dressed up with snipped fresh dill or mint.*

vegetable cooking spray
1 bunch firm unblemished carrots
  (6–8 carrots)

1 tablespoon olive oil
salt and freshly ground black pepper
  to taste

Preheat the oven to 400°F. Spray a 2- or 3-quart oval gratin dish with vegetable cooking spray.

Scrape the carrots and cut them on the diagonal into ¾-inch slices. Pile them in the dish, add the oil, and toss well to coat. Season with salt and pepper and toss again. Place the dish on the bottom rack of the oven and bake for about 35 minutes or until the carrots are soft and some are lightly browned or charred on the edges.

**Serves 4**

➤ Since carrots shrink as their flavor intensifies, you may want to double the recipe to make sure there are enough for seconds.

| PER SERVING | |
|---|---|
| CALORIES | 75 |
| FAT | 4 GM |
| SATURATED FAT | 0 GM |
| CHOLESTEROL | 0 MG |
| SODIUM | 35 MG |
| PROTEIN | 1 GM |
| CARBOHYDRATE | 10 GM |

# Carrots and Celery with Caraway Seeds

*The origins of this useful recipe are lost in time (I think it was originally made with cream), but I do know that when I haven't had time to shop for fresh vegetables for dinner, this is a good bet, as carrots and celery are almost always on hand. It's quick, easy, and incredibly tasty.*

1 tablespoon olive or canola oil
¼ cup chopped onion
3 cups celery thinly sliced on the diagonal
3 cups carrots thinly sliced on the diagonal

¼ cup defatted, reduced-sodium chicken stock, preferably homemade (page 274)
½ teaspoon salt (or to taste)
freshly ground black pepper to taste
1 teaspoon caraway seeds

Heat the oil in a heavy nonstick skillet having a lid. Add the onion and sauté until soft but not brown. Add the celery, carrots, stock, salt, and pepper. Bring to a boil, cover, and lower the heat so that the vegetables simmer for 10 to 15 minutes or until tender but still slightly crisp. Uncover, raise the heat slightly, and cook for 2 to 3 minutes to evaporate any excess liquid. Toss with the caraway seeds just before serving.

Serves 6–8

➤ The caraway seeds add a subtle dimension — if you like caraway. If not, leave them out. It's good either way.

| PER SERVING | |
|---|---|
| CALORIES | 50 |
| FAT | 2 GM |
| SATURATED FAT | 0 GM |
| CHOLESTEROL | 0 MG |
| SODIUM | 222 MG |
| PROTEIN | 1 GM |
| CARBOHYDRATE | 7 GM |

# Crumbed Cauliflower with Anchovies, Capers, and Olives

*Soggy, flavorless, and to be avoided at all cost was the view I had of cauliflower growing up. Then I tasted a dish like this in Italy that changed my mind forever. It is so richly flavored and satisfying that we often have it as a main course.*

1 large head cauliflower (about 2 pounds)

6 flat anchovy fillets

1 or 2 dried red chili peppers, seeded

2 cloves garlic

1½ teaspoons capers, rinsed

1 tablespoon plus 2 teaspoons extra-virgin olive oil

1 cup fresh bread crumbs (page 271) (see Note)

6–8 imported black olives, pitted and cut into strips

freshly ground black pepper to taste

salt to taste (optional)

Divide the cauliflower into small florets and cut the tender stalks into small pieces. Wash carefully. Bring a large pot of salted water to a boil and add the cauliflower. Bring back to a boil and cook for 5 minutes, uncovered, timed from the second boil. Drain, run cold water over, and dry on paper towels.

While the cauliflower cooks, chop the anchovies, chili pepper(s), garlic, and capers and set aside.

Heat the oil in a large nonstick skillet, add the bread crumbs, and cook, stirring, for 3 minutes or until pale gold and coated with oil. Add the cauliflower and cook, stirring frequently with a fork, until tender but still crunchy, about 3 minutes.

Add the anchovies, chili pepper(s), garlic, capers, and olives and cook for about 1 minute more. Stir gently but well. Add the black pepper and salt if desired.

**Makes 6–7 cups, serving 6 as a side dish, 4 as a main course**

| PER SERVING | |
| --- | --- |
| CALORIES | 87 |
| FAT | 5 GM |
| SATURATED FAT | 1 GM |
| CHOLESTEROL | 2 MG |
| SODIUM | 261 MG |
| PROTEIN | 3 GM |
| CARBOHYDRATE | 8 GM |

Note: Fresh bread crumbs are a must for this dish. Use Italian or whole wheat bread if possible.

# Indian-Style Spiced Cauliflower with Potatoes

*Another filling vegetable main course for meatless meals.*

1 large head cauliflower (1½–2 pounds)
1-inch piece fresh ginger
3 small cloves garlic
¾ teaspoon ground turmeric
½ teaspoon red pepper flakes (or to taste)
½ teaspoon salt

freshly ground black pepper to taste
4 medium potatoes, such as Yukon Gold, peeled
2 tablespoons canola oil
1 teaspoon cumin seeds
4 canned Italian plum tomatoes (liquid reserved)
2 tablespoons chopped fresh cilantro

Cut the cauliflower into florets and set aside.

Grate the ginger; you should have about 1 teaspoon. Place in a small dish. Put the garlic through a press. Add to the ginger and mix together to make a smooth paste. Set aside.

In another small dish, combine the turmeric, red pepper flakes, salt, and liberal grindings of pepper. Set aside.

Cut the potatoes in half lengthwise and then slice each half into six pieces.

In a heavy nonstick skillet, heat the oil. Add the cumin and sauté for 45 seconds to 1 minute or until the seeds begin to dance. Stir in the garlic-ginger paste. Add the potatoes and stir-fry over medium heat for 3 minutes. Add the turmeric mixture and stir-fry for 3 minutes more.

Add the tomatoes, breaking them up with your fingers. Add about ½ cup of the reserved tomato liquid, cover, and simmer for 5 minutes. Add the cauliflower and stir-fry over high heat for 1 minute. If the pan appears dry, add a little more tomato liquid. Turn the heat to low, cover, and cook gently for 15 minutes. Uncover, and if there is any excess moisture in the pan, turn up the heat to evaporate. Taste; you may wish to add a little more salt. Sprinkle with the cilantro and serve.

**Serves 8 as a side dish, 6 as a main course**

➤ *Drying the spices first (tumeric, red pepper flakes, etc.) by brief, constant stirring over high heat (watch for scorching!) makes them "bloom" and penetrate the vegetable they are being cooked with, thus lending their full flavor.*

| PER SERVING | |
|---|---|
| CALORIES | 145 |
| FAT | 5 GM |
| SATURATED FAT | 0 GM |
| CHOLESTEROL | 0 MG |
| SODIUM | 242 MG |
| PROTEIN | 3 GM |
| CARBOHYDRATE | 23 GM |

# Braised Fennel

*Either you like fennel or you don't. I'm very fond of it braised with garlic, which gives it a sweet, buttery quality. This easy, low-calorie recipe is an excellent accompaniment to simply cooked fish.*

1 large head firm, unblemished fennel (about 1 pound)
1 tablespoon plus 1 teaspoon canola oil

4 cloves garlic, sliced
salt and freshly ground black pepper to taste

Preheat the oven to 350°F.

Remove the feathery tops and stalks of the fennel, trim the bottom, and cut into quarters.

Heat the oil in a heavy ovenproof casserole. Gently sauté the garlic until golden, then remove and discard. Add the fennel and cook uncovered over medium heat, turning occasionally, until lightly browned, about 7 to 8 minutes. Season with salt and pepper.

Cover the casserole and bake for 20 minutes or until the fennel is soft through and through. Remove one quarter at a time and slice. Place in a serving dish, pour the savory juices from the casserole over the fennel, and serve.

Serves 4

➤ *Fennel is packed with nutrients. One cup provides one and a half times the recommended daily allowance (RDA) of vitamin C, one-third the RDA of iron and potassium, plus some folic acid, calcium, and phosphorus.*

| PER SERVING | |
| --- | --- |
| CALORIES | 62 |
| FAT | 5 GM |
| SATURATED FAT | 0 GM |
| CHOLESTEROL | 0 MG |
| SODIUM | 103 MG |
| PROTEIN | 1 GM |
| CARBOHYDRATE | 4 GM |

# Roasted Sweet Red Peppers

*What did we do before sweet red peppers were available all year round? Hardly a week goes by when I don't eat roasted peppers in some form — marinated, as a first course, in a vegetable sandwich, as a garnish, chopped and spiced as a relish, and on and on. Here's how to make roasted red peppers — of course, you can include yellow peppers, too.*

4 medium well-shaped sweet red peppers

Lay the peppers on a heated broiler rack about 2 to 3 inches from the heat source and turn frequently with tongs or two wooden spoons as they blister and blacken, until almost completely charred. This will take 7 to 10 minutes. (See Note.)

Immediately put the peppers in a brown paper bag and twist tightly to seal. Set aside to steam for 10 to 15 minutes. When the peppers can be handled, rub off the charred skin with a paper towel or scrape it off with the edge of a paring knife. *Do not rinse the peppers, or they will become soggy.* Then cut off the tops, cut the peppers in half, and scrape out the seeds and ribs. If not using immediately, wrap the peppers in plastic wrap and store in the refrigerator for up to 4 days.

**Serves 4**

| PER SERVING | |
|---|---|
| CALORIES | 20 |
| FAT | 0 GM |
| SATURATED FAT | 0 GM |
| CHOLESTEROL | 0 MG |
| SODIUM | 1 MG |
| PROTEIN | 1 GM |
| CARBOHYDRATE | 5 GM |

Note: If you only need 1 or 2 peppers or don't wish to heat the broiler, they can also be "roasted" on top of a gas stove by placing them directly on the gas ring. You have to watch these closely and turn them quickly as the skin chars. Then proceed as above.

# Roasted Sweet Peppers Marinated with Capers and Anchovies

*I always used to order this as a first course in Italian restaurants until I realized that I could make it at home. It's a great opener in summer and delicious with several thin slices of fresh mozzarella as a light lunch on a day when no other saturated fat is planned. Serve with plenty of crusty bread.*

3 or 4 sweet red peppers
3 or 4 sweet yellow peppers
wine vinegar
salt and freshly ground black pepper
   to taste

2 tablespoons capers
2 tablespoons fruity olive oil
1 two-ounce can flat anchovy fillets

Roast the peppers as described in Roasted Sweet Red Peppers (page 207). Peel the peppers over a bowl to catch any of the caramelized pepper juice. Cut the pepper halves into quarters if they are large. Arrange a layer of pepper in a shallow glass or porcelain serving dish. Sprinkle with a teaspoon or so of wine vinegar, a dash of salt, and several good grindings of black pepper. Repeat the layers until all the peppers are used. Sprinkle the top with the capers and olive oil, season with salt and pepper, and add any reserved pepper juice. Cover with plastic wrap and refrigerate for 4 hours. Let come to room temperature. Drain the anchovies, crisscross them in pairs over the peppers, and serve.

Serves 4–6

➤ *Yellow peppers do not need as much roasting as red, so watch those carefully.*

| PER SERVING | |
|---|---|
| CALORIES | 95 |
| FAT | 6 GM |
| SATURATED FAT | 1 GM |
| CHOLESTEROL | 5 MG |
| SODIUM | 436 MG |
| PROTEIN | 4 GM |
| CARBOHYDRATE | 7 GM |

# Sweet Pepper, Ham, and Onion Omelet

*You could call this the kitchen sink omelet because I have made it with just about every odd bit of leftover food I find in the kitchen. I might add half a jalapeño pepper one day, some asparagus tips another, diced tomatoes and basil, chopped herbs — you get the idea. Sweet red pepper is a constant, though, because it adds such flavor and substance. Be careful not to overcook — egg whites can get rubbery very quickly.*

3 large egg whites
1 teaspoon water (approximately)
salt and freshly ground black pepper
  to taste
1 teaspoon olive or canola oil
⅓ cup chopped onion

¼ sweet red pepper, seeded and diced
2 thin slices Black Forest or other lean
  ham (about 1 ounce cut up)
1 small handful chopped fresh cilantro
  or parsley
vegetable cooking spray

Combine the egg whites, water, and salt and pepper in a small bowl. Stir briskly with a fork.

Heat a 10-inch nonstick skillet over low heat, add the oil, and brush it around. Add and slowly sauté the onion, red pepper, and ham. When the vegetables are soft and a little brown, add the cilantro or parsley and cook for 30 seconds more. Turn the mixture out into a small bowl and wipe out the pan with a paper towel.

Heat the pan again over low heat. When hot, remove from the heat, spray with vegetable cooking spray, and pour the egg whites into the pan. Tilt to coat the bottom evenly, then cook until the bottom is set, about 10 seconds. Tilt the pan and use a plastic spatula to lift the edge of the omelet and let the uncooked portion run underneath. Cook for a few seconds more until the omelet is almost set and a little golden on the bottom. (Don't overcook; too high a heat or too long a cooking time will toughen the egg whites.)

Spoon the cooked mixture down the center of the omelet. Use a spatula to loosen and fold in the sides to the center, then tip out onto a plate, bottom side up.

**Serves 1**

▶ *You can make this omelet with 1 egg and 1 egg white. It will look more like a "real" omelet, but you'll add 5 fat grams to the fat count.*

| PER SERVING | |
| --- | --- |
| CALORIES | 164 |
| FAT | 7 GM |
| SATURATED FAT | 1 GM |
| CHOLESTEROL | 15 MG |
| SODIUM | 508 MG |
| PROTEIN | 17 GM |
| CARBOHYDRATE | 7 GM |

# Roasted New Potatoes with Thyme and Garlic

2–2½ pounds small (about 2½ inches in diameter) red-skinned new potatoes
vegetable cooking spray
1 tablespoon olive oil

1 tablespoon minced fresh thyme or 1 teaspoon dried
10–12 cloves garlic, unpeeled
sea salt and freshly ground black pepper to taste

Preheat the oven to 425°F. Place the oven rack in the lowest position.

Wash the potatoes, cut in half, wash again, and dry thoroughly with a kitchen towel or paper towels.

Spray a 12-by-8-inch shallow baking dish lightly with vegetable spray. Place in the oven to heat for about 5 minutes. Add the potatoes and olive oil and toss well to coat each potato piece lightly with oil. Return to the oven and roast for 15 minutes.

Add the thyme and garlic, turn the potatoes with a spatula or metal spoon to redistribute them, season with salt and pepper, and return to the oven for 15 minutes more. The potatoes should be golden on the cut side and easily pierced with the tip of a sharp knife. Make sure each serving includes a few garlic cloves.

**Serves 6 as a side dish**

PER SERVING

| | |
|---|---|
| CALORIES | 160 |
| FAT | 2 GM |
| SATURATED FAT | 0 GM |
| CHOLESTEROL | 0 MG |
| SODIUM | 13 MG |
| PROTEIN | 3 GM |
| CARBOHYDRATE | 31 GM |

# Anchovied Potatoes, Tomatoes, and Zucchini

*The ancient Romans used to cure small anchovy-like fish in the sun to make a condiment called garum, which they loved for the way it accented other flavors. You will enjoy the way canned anchovies work the same way to enhance quite ordinary foods, as in this tasty vegetable accompaniment.*

¾ pound small new potatoes
½ pound small zucchini
¾ pound ripe tomatoes
2 or 3 flat anchovy fillets

1 teaspoon olive oil
1 large clove garlic, minced
freshly ground black pepper to taste

Scrub but do not peel the potatoes. Put in a pot with water to cover. Cover the pot and cook until done, about 20 minutes.

While potatoes cook, scrub, trim, and slice the zucchini about ¼ inch thick. Cut the tomatoes in half vertically and slice ½ inch thick. Wash and dry the anchovies and mince. Set aside.

Heat the oil in a medium nonstick skillet and sauté the garlic until it releases its fragrance. Add the zucchini, and tomatoes and cook for 5 minutes. Add the anchovies and cook for about 10 minutes. Drain the potatoes and cut into large pieces. Add to the vegetables, stirring to coat well. Season with pepper.

**Serves 2 or 3**

PER SERVING

| | |
|---|---|
| CALORIES | 148 |
| FAT | 3 GM |
| SATURATED FAT | 0 GM |
| CHOLESTEROL | 2 MG |
| SODIUM | 144 MG |
| PROTEIN | 5 GM |
| CARBOHYDRATE | 28 GM |

# Spiced Potatoes and Eggplant

*Indian cooking often combines vegetables in unusual and delightful ways that are infinitely more satisfying than the same two vegetables served independently on a plate. Indian-Style Spiced Cauliflower with Potatoes (page 204) is one example. Here is another, especially good with simply cooked whitefish of any kind, though I often serve it as the main component of a vegetarian meal.*

3 medium Yukon Gold or Maine
    potatoes
1 medium firm, glossy eggplant
    (about 1 pound)
1 tablespoon canola oil
¾ cup chopped onion (1 medium
    onion)
1 quarter-size slice fresh ginger,
    minced

1½ teaspoons dry mustard
½ teaspoon ground turmeric
1 teaspoon salt
1 dried red chili pepper, seeded and
    crumbled
1 cup water or vegetable stock,
    preferably homemade (page 272)
2 tablespoons chopped fresh cilantro
    (optional)

Peel the potatoes and cut into 1-inch cubes. Do not peel the eggplant but cut into the same size pieces.

In a heavy skillet, preferably nonstick, having a lid, heat the oil. Add the onion and sauté until lightly browned, about 2 to 3 minutes. Add the potatoes, eggplant, ginger, mustard, turmeric, salt, and chili pepper. Cook over medium-high heat, stirring constantly, until the vegetables are uniformly coated with the spices, about 5 minutes.

Add the water or stock, cover, and simmer over medium heat until the vegetables are tender but not mushy and all the liquid is absorbed, about 15 to 20 minutes. Turn the vegetables once or twice in the sauce during this time so that all are evenly colored. If much liquid is left in the pan at the end, cook uncovered over fairly high heat for 2 minutes to evaporate it. Transfer to a serving dish, sprinkle with the cilantro (if using), and serve at once.

Serves 4–6

| PER SERVING | |
| --- | --- |
| CALORIES | 143 |
| FAT | 3 GM |
| SATURATED FAT | 0 GM |
| CHOLESTEROL | 0 MG |
| SODIUM | 502 MG |
| PROTEIN | 4 GM |
| CARBOHYDRATE | 26 GM |

# Potato-Vegetable Gratin

*My hard-to-please vegetarian daughter pronounces this dish a winner. Accompanied by a side dish of fresh green beans and followed with a hearty salad, it makes a superdelicious vegetarian meal.*

vegetable cooking spray
2 tablespoons olive oil
1 medium onion, sliced
¼ cup plus 2–3 tablespoons vegetable or defatted, reduced-sodium chicken stock, preferably homemade (pages 272, 274)
1 sweet red pepper, seeded and sliced ⅛ inch thick
1 sweet yellow pepper, seeded and sliced ⅛ inch thick

1 pound ripe tomatoes, peeled, seeded, and chopped
3 cloves garlic, minced
¼ teaspoon red pepper flakes (optional)
salt and freshly ground black pepper to taste
¼ cup chopped fresh basil
2 pounds Yukon Gold or russet potatoes
½ cup shredded Monterey Jack cheese

Preheat the oven to 400°F. Lightly spray a 14-by-8-by-2-inch (3-quart) oval gratin dish with vegetable cooking spray and set aside.

In a large frying pan, heat 1 tablespoon of the oil, add the onion, and start sautéing. Add ¼ cup of the stock and continue sautéing, stirring constantly, until the onion is soft, about 3 to 5 minutes. Add the red and yellow peppers and sauté for 3 minutes more, adding 2 to 3 tablespoons stock as needed.

Add the tomatoes and cook, stirring, until all the excess moisture evaporates. Add the garlic and cook for 1 minute. Add the red pepper flakes (if using), salt and pepper, and half the basil. Remove from heat.

Peel the potatoes and cut into ¼-inch-thick slices. Spread half the potatoes on the bottom of the baking dish, season lightly with salt and pepper, and follow with half the vegetable mixture and half the cheese. Repeat these three layers, drizzling the remaining 1 tablespoon olive oil on top.

Cover the dish lightly with aluminum foil, place on a baking sheet, and bake in the upper third of the oven for 35 minutes. Remove the foil and continue baking until the potatoes are tender and the top is browned, about 15 to 20 minutes. Sprinkle with the remaining basil and serve.

**Serves 4–6**

➤ *Buttery yellow Yukon Gold potatoes, with their firm texture, make this dish particularly delicious. They are worth going out of your way to find.*

| PER SERVING | |
| --- | --- |
| CALORIES | 266 |
| FAT | 10 GM |
| SATURATED FAT | 3 GM |
| CHOLESTEROL | 12 MG |
| SODIUM | 115 MG |
| PROTEIN | 8 GM |
| CARBOHYDRATE | 39 GM |

# Buttermilk Mashed Potatoes

*Garlic and a tiny amount of butter mixed with low-fat buttermilk (a trick I learned from* **Eating Well Magazine***) make the most luxurious low-fat mashed potatoes I know. They are heavenly with* **Soy-Roasted Chicken** *(page 144).*

2 pounds all-purpose potatoes, preferably Yukon Gold, peeled and cut into chunks

6 cloves garlic

salt to taste

2 teaspoons butter

1 cup low-fat buttermilk

freshly ground black pepper to taste

Place the potatoes and garlic in a large, heavy saucepan. Add water to cover and season with salt. Bring to a boil, reduce the heat, and cook for 10 to 15 minutes or until the potatoes are tender but not mushy.

Meanwhile, in a small saucepan, melt the butter over low heat. Cook just until it begins to turn light brown, about 1 minute. Stir in the buttermilk and heat until just warm. (Do not overheat, or the buttermilk will curdle.)

When the potatoes are done, drain in a colander (along with the garlic) and return to the pot. Place the pot over low heat and shake for 1 minute to dry the potatoes. Mash the potatoes and garlic with a potato masher. For a finer puree, use a handheld electric mixer. Add enough of the buttermilk mixture to make a smooth puree. Season with salt and pepper and serve hot.

**Serves 6**

➤ *Contrary to popular belief, buttermilk is not "buttery" but is so called because it was the liquid that remained after the butter was churned. Today it is made by adding special bacteria to nonfat or low-fat milk to give it the characteristic tang.*

| PER SERVING | |
| --- | --- |
| CALORIES | 147 |
| FAT | 2 GM |
| SATURATED FAT | 1 GM |
| CHOLESTEROL | 4 MG |
| SODIUM | 42 MG |
| PROTEIN | 4 GM |
| CARBOHYDRATE | 30 GM |

# Stir-Fried Mushrooms, Peppers, Broccoli, and Shrimp

*Stir-fried dishes are a great low-fat way to eat healthful foods in tasty, attractive combinations. Although the list of ingredients is long, the cooking takes only a few minutes after the initial, quite easy preparations. This particular dish is exceptionally beautiful and appealing in color and texture, and unlike many Chinese dishes, it is quite satisfying served as a main course with rice.*

½ cup water or reduced-sodium defatted chicken stock, preferably homemade (page 274)

2 tablespoons reduced-sodium soy sauce

2 tablespoons rice wine vinegar

2 teaspoons honey

1 tablespoon cornstarch

2 teaspoons minced garlic

2 teaspoons minced fresh ginger

1 tablespoon peanut or canola oil

½ pound medium raw shrimp, peeled and deveined

3 cups small broccoli florets

1 tablespoon water

½ sweet red pepper, seeded and cut into 1-inch squares

3 cups sliced shiitake mushrooms (about 12–15 mushrooms)

2 cups thinly shredded bok choy leaves

1 teaspoon dark sesame oil

2 tablespoons chopped fresh cilantro leaves

In a small saucepan, combine the water or stock, soy sauce, vinegar, honey, and cornstarch, stirring until the cornstarch has dissolved. Add the garlic and ginger. Bring to a boil over medium heat and cook, stirring constantly, for 2 minutes or until the sauce thickens. Set aside.

Place a large nonstick skillet or wok over high heat for 1 minute. Add the oil and heat over medium-high heat until hot. Swirl to coat the bottom. Add the shrimp and stir-fry for 2 to 3 minutes or until they turn pink. Remove the shrimp with a slotted spoon and set aside.

Add the broccoli and water to the pan and stir-fry for 1 minute or until the broccoli is bright green. Add the red pepper and mushrooms and stir-fry for another 3 minutes or until the broccoli is crisp-tender. Add the bok choy and stir-fry only to soften, about 30 seconds. Add the reserved shrimp and mix well.

Stir in the sauce and mix well to coat the ingredients. Add the sesame oil, toss, and turn out onto a warm platter. Sprinkle with the cilantro and serve immediately with hot rice.

**Serves 3 or 4**

➤ *This dish is undersalted. You may wish to pass soy sauce at the table for those who wish a little more seasoning.*

| PER SERVING | |
| --- | --- |
| CALORIES | 170 |
| FAT | 6 GM |
| SATURATED FAT | 1 GM |
| CHOLESTEROL | 71 MG |
| SODIUM | 498 MG |
| PROTEIN | 16 GM |
| CARBOHYDRATE | 16 GM |

**VARIATION:**

*With Sesame Seeds:* Omit the cilantro and sprinkle on 2 tablespoons toasted sesame seeds (page 268) at the end.

# Thai Spinach and Watercress

*This recipe is for two, to encourage you to make it, because it is quite simple and delicious. Double it for four, but don't be put off by the amount of greenery; the volume shrinks considerably when cooked.*

6 cups fresh spinach (about 1 pound)
2 cups watercress (about 1 bunch)
1 tablespoon olive oil
2 cloves garlic, minced
1 small fresh red chili pepper, seeded and minced

1 tablespoon nuoc mam (Vietnamese fish sauce) (see Note)
½ teaspoon sugar

Wash the spinach well, dry, and break off any coarse lower stems. Wash the watercress and cut into 2-inch lengths. Set aside.

Heat the oil in a large nonreactive pan with a lid. Add the garlic and sauté for 45 seconds or until the garlic softens. Add the greens and cook, covered, for 1 minute or until they just wilt. Add the chili pepper, nuoc mam, and sugar, stirring to distribute. Cover and cook for 4 minutes over medium heat, stirring once. Serve hot.

**Serves 2**

➤ *You may make this with all spinach or all watercress — just make sure you have 8 cups of greens in all.*

| PER SERVING | |
| --- | --- |
| CALORIES | 130 |
| FAT | 8 GM |
| SATURATED FAT | 1 GM |
| CHOLESTEROL | 0 MG |
| SODIUM | 442 MG |
| PROTEIN | 7 GM |
| CARBOHYDRATE | 10 GM |

Note: Nuoc mam is available in oriental groceries and Middle Eastern markets.

# Pan-Grilled Radicchio

*Remember when no one on this side of the Atlantic had ever even heard of radicchio? This Italian specialty is now virtually a household and restaurant staple in salads.*

2 heads radicchio, tough outer leaves
   removed
1 tablespoon olive oil

Salt and freshly ground black pepper
   to taste
balsamic vinegar

Cut each head of radicchio into 1-inch-wide wedges, as you would cabbage. Heat the oil in a large, heavy (preferably cast-iron) skillet over medium-high heat. Add the radicchio and sauté, turning the pieces with a metal spatula, until browned on the edges and heated through. Season with salt and pepper, splash with a little balsamic vinegar, and serve.

**Serves 4**

➤ *Use this dish to add texture and flavor to a plate of roasted or grilled vegetables or as a garnish for any main course.*

PER SERVING

| | |
|---|---|
| CALORIES | 64 |
| FAT | 3 GM |
| SATURATED FAT | 0 GM |
| CHOLESTEROL | 0 MG |
| SODIUM | 103 MG |
| PROTEIN | 0 GM |
| CARBOHYDRATE | 23 GM |

# Butternut Squash and Ancho Chili Puree

*Ancho chilies have a delightful raisiny/nutty flavor and gentle heat that combines well with many vegetables, especially butternut squash. Serve with great fanfare alongside roasted chicken.*

1 medium butternut squash (about 2 pounds)
¼ cup water
1 dried ancho chili

¼ teaspoon ground cumin
1 teaspoon salt (or more to taste)
cayenne pepper (optional)

Preheat the oven to 350°F.

Cut the squash in half lengthwise, scoop out the seeds and strings, and place cut side down on a rimmed baking sheet. Add the water to pan so squash does not stick and bake for 30 to 45 minutes or until a toothpick pierces the skin easily.

While the squash bakes, place the chili in a small saucepan and cover with water. Bring to a boil, reduce the heat, and simmer until soft, about 10 minutes. Remove the chili and save the liquid for soup or discard. When the chili is cool enough to handle, stem and seed it.

When the squash is done, remove it from the oven and let cool slightly. Scoop the flesh out of the shell and place in the bowl of a food processor. Add the chili and cumin and process until smooth, stopping to scrape down the sides of the bowl. Add the salt and a dash of cayenne (if using).

Serves 4

➤ *The chili will make the puree darker than usual.*

| PER SERVING | |
| --- | --- |
| CALORIES | 98 |
| FAT | 1 GM |
| SATURATED FAT | 0 GM |
| CHOLESTEROL | 0 MG |
| SODIUM | 559 MG |
| PROTEIN | 2 GM |
| CARBOHYDRATE | 24 GM |

# Baked Acorn Squash

*One of the nicest ways to get your beta-carotene is acorn squash, which can be kept on hand throughout the fall and winter months. This dish is easy to make in both the conventional oven and even easier in the microwave.*

2 glossy, dark green acorn squash
    (about 1¼ pounds each)
salt and freshly ground black pepper
    to taste

4 tablespoons brown sugar, firmly
    packed, or maple syrup
freshly grated nutmeg
4 teaspoons whipped butter

### In the Oven

Preheat the oven to 325°F.

Cut the squash in half through the middle, discard any seeds and strings, and slice a very thin piece off the bottom skin side of each half so they will stand upright. Place cut side down on a baking sheet and bake in the center of the oven for 25 minutes. Turn cut side up and sprinkle with salt and pepper. Into each cavity put 1 tablespoon brown sugar or maple syrup, a grating of nutmeg, and 1 teaspoon butter. Bake for 15 minutes more or until the flesh is tender and the skin is easily pierced from the outside with a toothpick.

### In the Microwave

Prepare the squash halves as above, place ingredients in each cavity as directed, and cover each half with plastic wrap. Microwave on high for 6 to 10 minutes or until tender. Let sit for 5 minutes before serving.

Serves 4

| PER SERVING | |
| --- | --- |
| CALORIES | 161 |
| FAT | 3 GM |
| SATURATED FAT | 2 GM |
| CHOLESTEROL | 7 MG |
| SODIUM | 38 MG |
| PROTEIN | 2 GM |
| CARBOHYDRATE | 36 GM |

# Yellow Squash Casserole

*I am always running into people who say, "I still make your yellow squash casserole!" — as if I never wrote another recipe! This recipe, which appeared in my first cookbook twenty-odd years ago, has apparently become a standby for lots of families besides mine. The simple, sweet, cornlike goodness appeals to just about everyone, and it's easy to make, light, and surprisingly substantial. The original recipe had double the butter and another egg yolk.*

vegetable cooking spray
3 pounds yellow summer squash
¾ cup fresh bread crumbs (page 271)
2 tablespoons butter
1 tablespoon canola oil
½ cup minced onion

1 large egg plus 1 large egg white,
  lightly beaten
1 teaspoon salt (or to taste)
freshly ground black pepper to taste
1 tablespoon sugar

Preheat the oven to 375°F. Spray a 1½-quart baking dish, such as a soufflé dish, with vegetable cooking spray and set aside. Melt the butter in the oil and set aside.

Wash and dry the squash, trim the ends, and cut roughly into 1-inch pieces. Cook in boiling salted water, covered, for 10 minutes or until tender. Drain and puree coarsely in a food processor.

In a medium bowl, combine the bread crumbs with the butter-oil mixture. Set aside ¼ cup of the crumbs. To the remaining crumbs add the squash puree, onion, egg and egg white, salt, pepper, and sugar. Pour into the prepared dish, scatter the reserved crumbs on top, and bake for 1 hour or until the squash is puffed and the crumbs are golden brown.

**Serves 6**

➤ *This accompanies any food admirably and also makes a delightful meatless meal along with herb-flavored rice and fresh spinach.*

| PER SERVING | |
| --- | --- |
| CALORIES | 147 |
| FAT | 8 GM |
| SATURATED FAT | 3 GM |
| CHOLESTEROL | 46 MG |
| SODIUM | 458 MG |
| PROTEIN | 4 GM |
| CARBOHYDRATE | 15 GM |

# Roasted Sweet Potatoes

*One sweet potato will provide you with more than five times the recommended daily allowance (RDA) of vitamin A and half that of vitamin C, not to mention a healthy dose of beta-carotene. When you tire of eating sweet potatoes baked, try roasting them instead. It turns them into a genuine side dish that is much easier to serve.*

vegetable cooking spray
3 large sweet potatoes (about 1½ pounds), peeled

1 tablespoon plus 1 teaspoon olive oil
salt and freshly ground black pepper to taste

Arrange one oven rack in the highest position. Preheat the oven to 425°F. Spray a 9-by-13-inch baking dish with vegetable cooking spray.

Cut each potato crosswise into approximately 1-inch-thick rounds. Cut each round into quarters. It is not important that all the pieces be exactly the same size and shape.

In a large bowl, toss the potato pieces with the olive oil, then spread them out in the baking dish. Sprinkle with salt and pepper. Roast in the upper third of the oven for about 30 minutes or until the potatoes are tender and some edges have begun to char slightly. Serve hot or warm.

**Serves 4–6**

| PER SERVING | |
| --- | --- |
| CALORIES | 205 |
| FAT | 4 GM |
| SATURATED FAT | 0 GM |
| CHOLESTEROL | 0 MG |
| SODIUM | 21 MG |
| PROTEIN | 3 GM |
| CARBOHYDRATE | 40 GM |

# Baked Stuffed Tomatoes

*Though stuffed tomatoes are not new, this reading offers a complex layering of flavors from the herbs and the wonderful absorptive powers of Arborio rice. Don't even attempt to make this dish with anything less than fresh, ripe summer tomatoes.*

vegetable cooking spray
6 large fresh, ripe tomatoes
¾ cup Arborio rice
1 large clove garlic, minced
½ cup snipped fresh basil leaves
½ teaspoon sugar

1 teaspoon fresh marjoram or ½
    teaspoon dried oregano
salt and freshly ground black pepper
    to taste
2 tablespoons extra-virgin olive oil
1 tablespoon fresh rosemary leaves

Preheat the oven to 350°F. Lightly spray a baking dish that will hold the tomatoes comfortably with vegetable cooking spray.

Cut a "lid" from the top of each tomato and reserve. With a spoon, remove the pulp and puree in a food processor.

In a medium bowl, combine the pureed pulp with the rice, garlic, basil, sugar, marjoram or oregano, and salt and pepper. Stuff the mixture into the tomatoes and replace the lids. Place in the prepared baking dish, sprinkle with the olive oil and rosemary, and bake for 30 to 35 minutes.

**Serves 6**

➤ *These tomatoes can be served hot, warm, or at room temperature to accompany grilled fish or as part of a light lunch or picnic. They are even better the second day.*

| PER SERVING | |
| --- | --- |
| CALORIES | 184 |
| FAT | 6 GM |
| SATURATED FAT | 1 GM |
| CHOLESTEROL | 0 MG |
| SODIUM | 21 MG |
| PROTEIN | 4 GM |
| CARBOHYDRATE | 32 GM |

# Mixed Roasted Vegetables

*This ravishingly beautiful mixture looks like more work than it is, and once you prepare the vegetables, the rest is a snap. I serve it as an accompaniment to broiled chicken and eat the leftover vegetables stuffed into a pita bread pocket for lunch the next day. It's easy to make in quantity, and people go crazy when it appears as part of a buffet.*

vegetable cooking spray
5 baby Italian eggplant or 1 medium eggplant (about 1 pound)
2 small zucchini
2 small yellow squash
1 sweet red pepper
1 sweet yellow pepper
1 medium red onion

1 medium yellow onion
2 or 3 large cloves garlic, minced
2 tablespoons fruity extra-virgin olive oil (approximately)
salt to taste
⅓ cup chopped fresh basil
generous pinch of crushed red pepper

Preheat the oven to 400°F. Spray 2 large rectangular Pyrex baking dishes or one lasagna pan with vegetable cooking spray and set aside.

Prepare the vegetables, placing them in a large bowl as you work. Cut the eggplant lengthwise into 1-inch-wide slices, then stack the slices and cut into 1-inch cubes. Cut the zucchini and yellow squash in half lengthwise and cut into 1-inch cubes. Cut the red and yellow peppers in half, seed, and cut into 1-inch strips; stack the strips and cut into 1-inch cubes. Peel the red and yellow onions. Cut in half, into thick wedges, and then into 1-inch pieces. Scatter the garlic over the vegetables. Drizzle with 2 tablespoons olive oil and sprinkle with salt.

Divide the vegetables between the 2 baking dishes so that they are pretty much in one layer. (Set the bowl aside for later.) Bake for about 1 hour or until the eggplant is very soft and the vegetables are lightly browned.

Let cool for 5 minutes, then return vegetables to the bowl. Add the basil, crushed pepper, and more salt if necessary and toss. You also may add more olive oil at this time. Let sit at room temperature for 1 hour before serving. Serve warm by gently reheating or at room temperature.

**Serves 6**

➤ *This will look like an enormous amount of raw vegetables, but they will lose a good third of their volume in cooking. To make a double or triple batch, use several lasagna pans or rimmed baking sheets.*

| PER SERVING | |
| --- | --- |
| CALORIES | 108 |
| FAT | 5 GM |
| SATURATED FAT | 1 GM |
| CHOLESTEROL | 0 MG |
| SODIUM | 10 MG |
| PROTEIN | 3 GM |
| CARBOHYDRATE | 15 GM |

# Roasted Fall Vegetables

*This is a very forgiving recipe; you can use more or less of any vegetable or leave it out altogether. Or add some brussels sprouts or peeled white or cipolline onions. Doubled, it's a reliable and delicious way to feed a holiday crowd.*

vegetable cooking spray

10 cloves garlic, unpeeled

6–8 carrots, scraped and cut into 1½-inch pieces

1 pound new potatoes, scrubbed and halved

4 parsnips (about 1 pound), scraped and cut into chunks (see Note)

2 tablespoons extra-virgin olive oil

sea salt and freshly ground black pepper to taste

2 tablespoons chopped fresh rosemary leaves or 1 tablespoon dried rosemary

Preheat the oven to 400°F. Spray a large baking pan with vegetable cooking spray.

Place the garlic, carrots, potatoes, and parsnips in the pan, add the olive oil, and mix lightly to coat. Season with salt and pepper and sprinkle with the rosemary. Bake for 30 minutes. Stir to redistribute, then bake for 15 to 20 minutes more or until one of the largest potatoes is tender when pierced with the tip of a small, sharp knife. Season again before serving.

**Serves 6–8**

| PER SERVING | |
| --- | --- |
| CALORIES | 167 |
| FAT | 5 GM |
| SATURATED FAT | 1 GM |
| CHOLESTEROL | 0 MG |
| SODIUM | 36 MG |
| PROTEIN | 3 GM |
| CARBOHYDRATE | 30 GM |

Note: As parsnips tend to be very narrow at the tip and quite fat at the other end, halve them and cut the fat end into quarters to that all the pieces cook evenly.

# Zucchini Râpé

*A quick, easily made accompaniment that can garnish almost any food. You can make it with zucchini that may not be as small, uniform, or attractive as you'd like.*

2½ pounds medium zucchini
1 teaspoon salt
1 tablespoon butter
1 tablespoon canola oil

freshly ground black pepper to taste
2 tablespoons chopped fresh parsley
(optional)

Wash the zucchini well and dry. Grate the zucchini on the largest hole of a box grater or with the shredding disk of a food processor. Transfer to a colander or sieve set over a bowl, mix in the salt, and let sit for 30 minutes, stirring once or twice. Drain and squeeze out the juice.

Heat the butter and oil in a large nonstick skillet (the larger the better to allow any excess moisture to evaporate). Add the zucchini and sauté quickly, tossing it about with a wooden spoon or spatula until it is hot and very lightly browned, about 6 to 7 minutes. Season with pepper, adding more salt only if needed. Sprinkle with the parsley and serve immediately.

**Serves 6**

➤ *For low-salt diets, rinse the zucchini quickly before squeezing it dry.*

| PER SERVING | |
| --- | --- |
| CALORIES | 63 |
| FAT | 4 GM |
| SATURATED FAT | 1 GM |
| CHOLESTEROL | 5 MG |
| SODIUM | 207 MG |
| PROTEIN | 2 GM |
| CARBOHYDRATE | 5 GM |

# Grilled Zucchini with Mint

*Grilled zucchini strips make a wonderful sandwich, on a good sourdough roll combined with roasted red or yellow peppers and a thin slice of smoked mozzarella cheese. Fresh mint enhances the delicate flavor. These strips also make a nice side dish to any meal.*

4 medium firm, straight zucchini
    (about 1¾ pounds)
1 tablespoon plus 1 teaspoon olive oil
1 clove garlic

salt and freshly ground black pepper
    to taste
⅓ cup fresh mint leaves (optional)

Wash the zucchini, dry, and trim off the stem and blossom ends. With a sharp knife, cut each lengthwise into 5 or 6 thin slices.

Put the olive oil in a small bowl and add the garlic, running it through a press. Stir and set aside.

Heat a heavy ridged stove-top grill or pan. Have a basting brush handy. Set the grill or pan over high heat and when hot enough to make a drop of water dance and evaporate almost instantly, brush the oil mixture over enough zucchini slices to cover the grill. Place them on the grill and cook until nicely seared, about 3 minutes. Brush the tops with oil and turn each piece with tongs to cook the other side. Repeat until all the zucchini is cooked, seasoning with salt and pepper and removing the slices to a platter as cooked. Sprinkle with mint leaves if desired and serve at room temperature.

**Makes about 20 slices, serving 4**

| PER SERVING | |
| --- | --- |
| CALORIES | 69 |
| FAT | 5 GM |
| SATURATED FAT | 1 GM |
| CHOLESTEROL | 0 MG |
| SODIUM | 6 MG |
| PROTEIN | 2 GM |
| CARBOHYDRATE | 6 GM |

# 15

# DESSERTS

Strawberries in Red Wine Syrup

Compote Andalouse

Low-Fat Rice Pudding

Pumpkin Flan

Crustless Apple Pie à la Mode

Apple Crisp

Pear and Ricotta Pie

Blueberry-Peach Cobbler

Cranberry Crisp

Fruit Sorbet with Orange-Mango-Peach "Salsa"

Blood Orange Sorbet

Rosemary Lime Sorbet

Grapefruit Sorbet

Espresso Granita

Thin Spice Cookies

Chocolate Mousse Cake with Raspberry Coulis

Cinnamon Streusel Coffee Cake

Shaker Lemon Nut Tea Bread

Fontina with Ripe Pears and Walnuts

Chocolate-Dipped Strawberries

DESSERTS ARE A food category of almost universal appeal. Sadly, however, simple fruits aside, most desserts are disproportionately fat- and calorie-dense, two good reasons to monitor how much of them you eat. Here is one place where you can really say no, and you should unless faced with something devastatingly appealing. When it's your house, you can always stick to plain fruit or at least a fruit dessert; these desserts are, for the most part, low in fat, and the trick is to find those that have a fabulous flavor. One I make all the time and absolutely love is Strawberries in Red Wine Syrup (page 231). It's bright and appealing, the taste is fabulous, and it's not too high in calories.

Of course, chocoholics can always make dessert out of one piece of divine chocolate, as I often do. Another delightful way to get that hit of chocolate is Chocolate-Dipped Strawberries (page 253), easy to make and impressive as well. For the family that feels dessert isn't dessert if it's not chocolate, I offer the splendidly satisfying Chocolate Mousse Cake (page 248), which is delightfully low in fat.

Regular old-fashioned cakes — those that depend on eggs and butter or oil for lightness, texture, and moistness — are another matter. I've almost never met a low-fat cake I liked, and I've tried many. There are reasons why most low-fat cakes are angel food, chiffon, or cheesecake made with ersatz sour cream and cream cheese. I find that using more than one egg white as a substitute for whole eggs makes cakes rubbery and cutting way back on butter or oil produces a cake that turns rock hard in a day. The ploy of substituting fruit puree for moistness may work technically, but I do not find it pleasing. Since pleasure is the name of the game, my solution is this: have a couple of good "real" cakes in your repertoire in which the fat content is *slightly* lower (try Cinnamon Streusel Coffee Cake [page 250] and Shaker Lemon Nut Tea Bread [page 251]) and don't overdo it. Avoid big, gooey cakes with gobs of icing, butter cream filling, and nuts. And, of course, avoid second helpings, and alternate with really light desserts that don't depend on fat at all.

I never tire of a delicious sorbet, especially if it's accompanied by a good cookie. Fruit sorbets, such as Blood Orange Sorbet (page 243) and Grapefruit Sorbet (page 245), are always refreshing and satisfying, and Rosemary Lime Sorbet (page 244) is an unusual and stunning end to any meal with intense flavors.

Other fruit desserts include Apple Crisp (page 237) or, in season, Cranberry Crisp (page 241). In summer, try fruit cobblers such as Blueberry-Peach Cobbler (page 240) or swap the peaches for nectarines. You can, in fact, make a cobbler out of many pretty combinations of fruits that provide both sweet and tart sensations. My number one favorite in the fruit department is Crustless Apple Pie à la Mode (page 236), which gives you all the goodness of that American classic without the fatty crust and makes people giggle with delight. And if you want a really impressive dessert, try Pear and Ricotta Pie (page 238). It's heavenly!

# Strawberries in Red Wine Syrup

*During that all-too-brief time when local strawberries are available — ruby red throughout, without the sour, white pithy center we've become used to — I can't resist buying quarts and quarts at roadside stands. Here's a simple recipe for those times of abundance, which also improves the off-season berries mightily. A good, easy make-ahead dessert.*

| | |
|---|---|
| 1 cup red wine | 6 whole allspice |
| 1 cup water | 6 whole cloves |
| ½ cup sugar | 3 pints ripe strawberries, hulled |
| 2 cinnamon sticks | fresh mint sprigs for garnish |
| 12 black peppercorns | (optional) |

Place the wine, water, sugar, cinnamon sticks, peppercorns, allspice, and cloves in a medium nonreactive saucepan. Cover, set over low heat, and cook until the sugar has dissolved completely, about 3 to 5 minutes. Uncover, bring to a boil, adjust the heat, and cook at a gentle boil for 5 to 7 minutes or until slightly reduced to about 1 cup.

Remove from the heat and cool completely. Remove and discard the peppercorns, allspice, cloves, and one of the cinnamon sticks. (*May be prepared up to this point 5 days in advance and refrigerated in a tightly covered container.*)

Place the strawberries in a serving bowl, pour the syrup over them, and toss gently. Let the berries marinate in the syrup for at least 30 minutes before serving. (Leave in the remaining cinnamon stick for extra flavor.) Garnish with mint sprigs if desired.

Serves 6

➤ *Accompany the berries with a bowl of Yoghurt Cheese (page 260) or crème fraîche and Thin Spice Cookies (page 247).*

| PER SERVING | |
|---|---|
| CALORIES | 142 |
| FAT | 1 GM |
| SATURATED FAT | 0 GM |
| CHOLESTEROL | 0 MG |
| SODIUM | 4 MG |
| PROTEIN | 1 GM |
| CARBOHYDRATE | 29 GM |

# Compote Andalouse

*On a trip through the south of Spain, I found fruit desserts astonishingly absent from menus, except for one, found in every parador: some version of a prune compote with citrus. This recipe is far and away the most delicious; even non–prune fanciers like it.*

grated zest of 1 medium lemon
juice of 1 lemon (about ¼ cup)
grated zest of 1 medium orange
juice of 1 orange (⅓–½ cup)
2 whole cloves

1 cinnamon stick
⅓ cup Simple Syrup (page 277)
½ cup red wine, preferably burgundy
1 bay leaf
1 pound pitted prunes

In a small saucepan, combine the lemon zest and juice, orange zest and juice, cloves, cinnamon stick, syrup, wine, and bay leaf, and bring just to a boil. Lower the heat and simmer, partially covered, for 20 minutes. Discard the cinnamon stick and bay leaf and strain the mixture, pressing down on the solids to extract all the flavor. Discard the solids. Place the prunes in a medium bowl, pour the wine mixture over them, and stir. Chill for several hours. Bring to room temperature before serving.

Serves 6

*Recipes*

➤ *Combine with other fruits and serve for breakfast or as a dessert over vanilla frozen yoghurt.*

# Low-Fat Rice Pudding

*This low-fat version of my favorite comfort food evolved over a year, and now I like it better than the original, which was made with heavy cream, half-and-half, and two additional egg yolks.*

1 quart 1 percent milk
½ cup long-grain rice, such as Carolina
½ cup raisins
2 large eggs
½ cup sugar

1 twelve-ounce can evaporated skim milk
1½ teaspoons pure vanilla extract
2 tablespoons rum (optional)
freshly grated nutmeg

In a medium saucepan, combine the 1 percent milk, rice, and raisins. Cook over medium heat, stirring occasionally, until the mixture comes to a gentle boil. Reduce the heat and simmer gently, uncovered, until the rice is tender, about 25 minutes. Stir often so that the rice does not stick to the bottom of the pan. A skin will form from time to time, but it will dissolve when you stir.

In a large bowl, beat the eggs lightly, then whisk in the sugar until blended. Stir in the evaporated milk. Stir about 1 cup of the hot rice mixture into the egg mixture. Pour the egg mixture back into the saucepan containing the remaining rice. Cook, stirring constantly, over low heat until the pudding is slightly thickened and coats a spoon, about 4 minutes. Remove from the heat and stir in the vanilla and rum (if using). Transfer to a large serving bowl and grate nutmeg lightly over the top. Let come to room temperature, then chill before serving.

**Makes about 2 quarts, serving 8**

*Lemon Rice Pudding:* Add 2 teaspoons grated lemon zest with the evaporated milk and omit the vanilla extract.

| PER SERVING | |
|---|---|
| CALORIES | 166 |
| FAT | 2 GM |
| SATURATED FAT | 1 GM |
| CHOLESTEROL | 44 MG |
| SODIUM | 97 MG |
| PROTEIN | 7 GM |
| CARBOHYDRATE | 30 GM |

# Pumpkin Flan

*Here's a holiday dessert that will not break the fat bank, despite its luxurious taste. And it's rich in beta-carotene besides. If pumpkins are not available, substitute a pureed cooked winter squash such as butternut or Hubbard.*

1¼ cups granulated sugar
3 tablespoons water
1 cup canned or fresh pumpkin puree
2 large eggs plus large egg white
2 cups evaporated skim milk
1 teaspoon pure vanilla extract
½ cup firmly packed dark brown
    sugar

2 teaspoons cornstarch
1 teaspoon ground cinnamon
1 teaspoon ground ginger
freshly grated nutmeg
¼ teaspoon salt

Preheat the oven to 350°F.

Place 1 cup of the granulated sugar and the water in a small saucepan, stirring until the sugar dissolves. Over high heat, cook until the sugar caramelizes. Gently swirl the pan from time to time, but do not stir. Watch carefully so that the caramel does not burn. Pour carefully into 8 six-ounce Pyrex custard cups or ovenproof ramekins and set aside.

In a medium bowl, whisk together the pumpkin, eggs and egg white, milk, and vanilla. In a small bowl, combine the remaining ¼ cup granulated sugar, brown sugar, cornstarch, cinnamon, ginger, several gratings of nutmeg, and salt. Add to the pumpkin mixture and whisk in until well blended.

Place the custard cups or ramekins in a shallow baking pan and fill them with the pumpkin mixture. Put the pan in the oven, then pull halfway out and fill carefully with enough hot water to come halfway up the sides of the cups. Cover the cups with a piece of aluminum foil. Bake for 45 to 50 minutes or until the custards are firm and a toothpick inserted in the center comes out clean. Remove the pan from the oven, transfer the cups to a wire rack, and let cool to room temperature. Chill for at least 2 hours. To serve, run a knife around the inside edge of each cup and turn the custards out onto dessert plates.

**Serves 8**

VARIATION:

*Pumpkin Custard:* Prepare as above but omit the caramel. Do not unmold to serve, but instead garnish with a dollop of Double Yoghurt Cream (page 261).

➤ *May be prepared a day ahead and stored, covered with plastic wrap, in the refrigerator. This recipe is easily doubled.*

| PER SERVING | |
| --- | --- |
| CALORIES | 243 |
| FAT | 3 GM |
| SATURATED FAT | 1 GM |
| CHOLESTEROL | 82 MG |
| SODIUM | 129 MG |
| PROTEIN | 5 GM |
| CARBOHYDRATE | 51 GM |

# Crustless Apple Pie à la Mode

*When I used to make standard apple pie, my flavor secret was a combination of apples: greenings, Cortlands, Macouns, McIntoshes — in other words, a combination of sweet and tart, crisp and soft. This special "pie" will still be delicious and amazingly satisfying if you use only one kind. You can indulge in the butter content because there is no pastry. Accompany with a scoop of nonfat vanilla frozen yoghurt or cinnamon ice cream.*

6 cups peeled and sliced apples (about 3 pounds)
1 tablespoon lemon juice
½ cup firmly packed light brown sugar
½ cup granulated sugar
2 tablespoons all-purpose flour

1 teaspoon ground cinnamon
pinch of salt
1 teaspoon pure vanilla extract
1 teaspoon grated lemon zest
⅓ cup golden raisins
2 tablespoons butter, cut into small pieces

Preheat the oven to 400°F. Butter a 9- or 10-inch pie plate.

In a large bowl, toss the apples with the lemon juice. In a small bowl, combine the brown sugar, granulated sugar, flour, cinnamon, and salt. Add to the apples and toss. Add the vanilla, lemon zest, and raisins and toss again.

Place the apple mixture in the prepared pie plate, dot with the butter, cover with aluminum foil, and bake until the apples are tender, about 50 minutes. Remove from the oven, uncover, and let cool for about 15 minutes. Serve warm, spooned onto dessert plates and moistened with the delicious juices.

Serves 6–8

➤ *Granny Smith, my favorite eating apple, does not do well in this pie, remaining so firm that it throws off the baking time.*

| PER SERVING PIE ONLY | |
|---|---|
| CALORIES | 234 |
| FAT | 4 GM |
| SATURATED FAT | 2 GM |
| CHOLESTEROL | 10 MG |
| SODIUM | 65 MG |
| PROTEIN | 64 GM |
| CARBOHYDRATE | 51 GM |

# Apple Crisp

*Everybody seems to like this apple dessert, which is fruitier, lighter, and lower in calories than a pie. The topping is made with much less butter than most crisps. Try it for Thanksgiving or other heavy holiday meals.*

vegetable cooking spray
5 medium Granny Smith apples,
    peeled, cored, and sliced ¼ inch
    thick (about 4 cups)
½ cup firmly packed light brown
    sugar
1 teaspoon ground cinnamon
freshly grated nutmeg
1 tablespoon lemon juice
2 tablespoons orange juice
grated zest of 1 medium orange

*Topping*

¾ cup firmly packed light brown
    sugar
½ cup rolled oats
⅔ cup sifted all-purpose flour
2 tablespoons unsalted butter
2 tablespoons apple juice

Preheat the oven to 375°F. Spray a shallow 2-quart baking dish or a 9-by-12-inch Pyrex baking dish with vegetable cooking spray.

Arrange the apples slices in the prepared baking dish. In a small bowl, combine the brown sugar, cinnamon, and several gratings of nutmeg and sprinkle over the apples. Add the lemon and orange juices and the orange zest.

To make the topping, in a large bowl combine the brown sugar, oats, and flour. Cut the butter into 5 or 6 pieces, and with a pastry cutter or your fingers blend it with the dry ingredients until the mixture is crumbly. Add the apple juice and stir with a fork until evenly moistened. Spread as evenly as possible over the apples.

Bake for 40 minutes or until the apples are tender and bubbling and the top has taken on some color. If you wish the top to be a little browner, place under the broiler for about 40 seconds, watching it constantly. Serve slightly warm or at room temperature.

**Serves 6**

➤ *This dessert can be made ahead and gently warmed in the oven before serving. Serve it with nonfat vanilla frozen yoghurt if desired.*

# Pear and Ricotta Pie

*The delicate flavor of pear is intensified in this handsome dessert by appearing in three guises: sliced on the bottom and top, diced in the filling, and reduced in the glaze. None of the steps is difficult, and the result will make you very proud!*

7 firm, ripe medium pears, preferably
    Bartlett
1½ cups water
1¼ cups sugar
juice of ½ medium lemon
¼ cup dark raisins
¼ cup golden raisins
cognac or brandy
1 six-ounce box zwieback biscuits

2 tablespoons canola oil
vegetable cooking spray
8 ounces reduced-fat ricotta cheese
2 large egg yolks, well beaten
½ teaspoon almond extract
grated zest of ½ lemon
1 tablespoon cornstarch
2 tablespoons cold water

Core the pears from the bottom and peel them. In a pot large enough to hold them, combine the 1½ cups water, 1 cup of the sugar, and lemon juice. Bring to a boil and simmer for 5 minutes. Add the pears, cover, and poach for 10 to 12 minutes or until they can be easily pierced with the tip of a sharp knife. Turn once or twice with a wooden spoon as they cook. Let cool in the pot, then remove and drain, reserving the poaching liquid.

While the pears are cooking, place the golden and dark raisins in a small bowl, add brandy or cognac to cover, and let soak for 20 minutes. Drain and set aside.

Process the zwieback in a food processor to create crumbs. Add the oil and mix with a fork until evenly moistened. Spray a 9-inch springform pan or glass pie plate with vegetable cooking spray and line with the crumbs, pushing them up the sides with your knuckle to form a 1-inch rim.

Preheat the oven to 375°F. Slice 3 pears and arrange on the bottom of the pan. In a medium bowl, whip the ricotta cheese with the remaining ¼ cup sugar, then stir in the egg yolks and almond extract. Fold in the raisins and lemon zest. Dice 2 pears and fold in. Fill the pan with the mixture. Bake in the center of the oven for 25 minutes. Cool on a wire rack, then chill in the refrigerator.

In a small pan, bring the poaching liquid to a boil and simmer until reduced by one-half. You should have about 1 cup. In a cup, mix the cornstarch with the 2 tablespoons cold water to dissolve. Add to the syrup and cook for a few minutes to thicken. Let cool slightly.

Slice the remaining pears into ¾-inch slices and arrange in a slightly overlapping pattern on top of the pie, leaving the center bare. Glaze with the syrup. Chill for at least 1 hour or until set.

**Serves 8**

➤ *Don't throw away the brandy or cognac you use to soak the raisins: Save it to sip after dinner!*

| PER SERVING | |
| --- | --- |
| CALORIES | 407 |
| FAT | 9 GM |
| SATURATED FAT | 2 GM |
| CHOLESTEROL | 64 MG |
| SODIUM | 78 MG |
| PROTEIN | 6 GM |
| CARBOHYDRATE | 79 GM |

# Blueberry-Peach Cobbler

*A classic American summer dessert that is uncomplicated, pretty as a picture, and low in fat and calories. You may substitute ripe nectarines for the peaches.*

6 medium ripe unpeeled peaches
    (about 1¾–2 pounds), sliced
1½ cups blueberries, rinsed and
    picked over
½ cup plus 1 tablespoon sugar
grated zest of 1 medium orange

⅔ cup all-purpose flour
⅓ cup yellow cornmeal
1 teaspoon baking powder
¼ teaspoon baking soda
2 tablespoons tub margarine or butter
⅔ cup low-fat buttermilk

Preheat the oven to 375°F.

In a large bowl, combine the peaches, blueberries, ½ cup sugar, and orange zest. Transfer to a 9-inch square or 8-by-12-inch glass baking dish.

In the same bowl, combine the flour, cornmeal, remaining 1 tablespoon sugar, baking powder, and baking soda. With a pastry blender or two knives, cut in the margarine or butter until the mixture resembles coarse meal. Add the buttermilk and stir with a rubber spatula until the dry ingredients are moistened.

Drop the batter in mounds (9 if you're using a square pan; 8 if you're using a rectangular baking dish) over the fruit. The batter will spread as it bakes. Bake for 30 minutes or until the top is golden. Serve warm.

**Serves 8 or 9**

| PER SERVING | |
| --- | --- |
| CALORIES | 200 |
| FAT | 3 GM |
| SATURATED FAT | 1 GM |
| CHOLESTEROL | 1 MG |
| SODIUM | 169 MG |
| PROTEIN | 3 GM |
| CARBOHYDRATE | 41 GM |

# Cranberry Crisp

*The play of tart and sweet here makes a nice, palate-cleansing end to any cold-weather meal that includes roast poultry or meat.*

2 sixteen-ounce bags fresh
    cranberries, rinsed and picked over
¾ cup sugar
grated zest of 1 medium lemon
1 tablespoon cornstarch
¾ cup orange juice (2 medium
    oranges)

**Topping**

¾ cup all-purpose flour
¾ cup rolled oats
¾ cup firmly packed light brown
    sugar
1 teaspoon ground cinnamon
2 tablespoons apple juice or cider
2 tablespoons unsalted butter

Preheat the oven to 400°F.

In a medium nonreactive saucepan, combine the cranberries, sugar, and lemon zest. Add the cornstarch to the orange juice, whisk until smooth, and add to the cranberries. Bring to a boil and stir. Pour into a 10-inch glass pie plate. Place a baking sheet or a piece of heavy-duty aluminum foil on the center rack of the oven, place the pie plate on top, and bake for 15 minutes.

Meanwhile, prepare the topping. Combine the flour, rolled oats, brown sugar, cinnamon, and apple juice in a bowl. Add the butter and cut in with a pastry blender until the mixture resembles coarse crumbs. (You also may use the food processor for this.)

Remove the cranberries from the oven, sprinkle the topping evenly over them, return to the oven, and bake for 20 minutes more. Let cool before serving.

**Serves 8**

➤ *Serve with nonfat vanilla frozen yoghurt or Double Yoghurt Cream (page 261).*

# Fruit Sorbet with
# Orange-Mango-Peach "Salsa"

*A delightful and refreshing dessert that is easy to prepare and extremely attractive. Discovering the flavor reprise in the sorbet beneath the fruit is an extra that delights guests. The fruit is prepared ahead, and the final assembly takes just minutes.*

1 large unblemished orange
1 cup sugar
½ cup cold water
2 tablespoons Grand Marnier
1 large ripe mango
3 medium ripe peaches

1 tablespoon lemon juice
1 pint mango sorbet
1 pint peach sorbet
fresh mint leaves for garnish
  (optional)

Using a swivel-bladed potato peeler, remove the zest of the orange in thin strips. Cut into long (approximately 2 inches) fine julienne and place in a small saucepan. Cover with cold water, bring to a boil, and simmer gently for 4 minutes. Strain and rinse with cold water. Set aside.

In the same saucepan, combine the sugar and water, bring to a boil, and cook, stirring, until the sugar dissolves and the syrup is clear. Add the zest to the syrup and simmer for 4 minutes. Remove from the heat, add the Grand Marnier, and let cool.

Peel the mango and cut into a rough dice, about ¾-inch dice. Place in a medium bowl. Peel and dice the peaches similarly, add to the bowl, and toss with the lemon juice. Pour the cooled syrup over the fruit and toss again. Refrigerate until serving time.

Place 1 small scoop of each sorbet in the bottom of a stemmed goblet or footed glass dish. Spoon the fruit and syrup over the sorbet and garnish each serving with a mint leaf if desired. Serve immediately.

**Serves 6–8**

➤ *Häagen-Dazs makes a mango and a peach sorbet, and they are splendid. If you can't find both, use just one kind or substitute orange and/or lemon sorbet. Serve this dessert with Thin Spice Cookies (page 247) or nut cookies.*

| PER SERVING | |
| --- | --- |
| CALORIES | 321 |
| FAT | 0 GM |
| SATURATED FAT | 0 GM |
| CHOLESTEROL | 0 MG |
| SODIUM | 2 MG |
| PROTEIN | 0 GM |
| CARBOHYDRATE | 80 GM |

# Blood Orange Sorbet

*When you ask for orange juice in Italy, you usually get the ruby-red juice of blood oranges, a sweet-tart variety that is instantly addictive. The good news is that blood oranges are now available in the United States. The imported ones have that unique acidic edge and more juice than their California cousins. Either way, this sorbet is a wonderful finish to any meal and a knockout when served together with bitter chocolate sorbet.*

8–12 blood oranges (4 cups juice)      2–4 tablespoons lemon juice
1½–1¾ cups sugar (see Note)              (optional)

Juice the oranges, removing any seeds and large pieces of membrane but allowing most of the juicy pulp to remain. You should have 4 cups of juice. Place in a medium bowl and stir in 1½ cups of sugar. Taste and add more sugar if needed. If a pleasant tartness is lacking, add some lemon juice in small increments until the taste balance is pleasant. Freeze in an ice cream maker according to the manufacturer's instructions.

**Makes about 1 quart, serving 4–6**

| PER SERVING | |
| --- | --- |
| CALORIES | 344 |
| FAT | 0 GM |
| SATURATED FAT | 0 GM |
| CHOLESTEROL | 0 MG |
| SODIUM | 5 MG |
| PROTEIN | 1 GM |
| CARBOHYDRATE | 86 GM |

Note: The amount of sugar needed for blood oranges depends on their acidity.

# Rosemary Lime Sorbet

*It is hard to imagine a more refreshing end to a meal of bold tastes than this intensely flavored sorbet. I frequently serve it after Italian meals, and my guests are always delighted with the clean, unusual combination.*

1 bunch fresh rosemary (about 4 good
    branches)
1½ cups sugar
2 cups water

juice of 10 limes (about 1⅓–1½ cups)
small sprigs fresh rosemary for
    garnish (optional)

Wash the rosemary and set aside.

Place the sugar and water in a medium saucepan and simmer until the sugar is dissolved and the syrup is clear. Cool slightly, then add the rosemary branches and let steep overnight in the refrigerator. Remove the rosemary or strain the syrup. Add the lime juice and freeze in an ice cream maker according to the manufacturer's instructions. Garnish each serving with a sprig of fresh rosemary if desired.

**Makes about 1 quart, serving 6**

➤ *This sorbet looks particularly beautiful when 2 or 3 small scoops are piled into a stemmed glass and garnished with a few raspberries and a sprig of fresh rosemary.*

# Grapefruit Sorbet

2 cups sugar

4 cups water

2 cups freshly squeezed grapefruit
   juice (2 medium to large
   grapefruits)

crème de cassis or vodka (optional)

Combine the sugar and water in a saucepan and simmer, while watching the pot, until the sugar is dissolved and the mixture is clear, about 5 minutes. Let cool to room temperature. Add the grapefruit juice, pour into an ice cream maker, and freeze according to the manufacturer's directions. Serve splashed with crème de cassis or vodka if desired.

**Serves 6**

PER SERVING

| | |
|---|---|
| CALORIES | 290 |
| FAT | 0 GM |
| SATURATED FAT | 0 GM |
| CHOLESTEROL | 0 MG |
| SODIUM | 1 MG |
| PROTEIN | 0 GM |
| CARBOHYDRATE | 75 GM |

# Espresso Granita

*An easy, nonfat way to have your coffee and dessert all in one, this granita also makes a nice treat on a hot summer afternoon.*

¾ cup finely ground regular or decaffeinated espresso coffee

2¼ cups boiling water

⅓ cup superfine sugar (or to taste)

2 tablespoons coffee liqueur, such as Tia Maria or Kahlúa

½ cup Double Yoghurt Cream (page 261) for garnish (optional)

Brew the coffee with the water, using your favorite method, preferably an electric or drip coffeemaker. Combine the sugar, hot coffee, and coffee liqueur and stir until sugar is dissolved. Let cool, then chill for 1 hour.

Pour into a shallow, nonreactive pan and freeze for about 5 hours, stirring every hour from the edges in to break up any ice crystals that form. When uniformly slushy, spoon into chilled parfait glasses or other stemmed or footed glasses, heaping the granita up on top, and freeze again. Garnish with a dollop of Double Yoghurt Cream if desired.

**Serves 6**

| PER SERVING | |
|---|---|
| CALORIES | 58 |
| FAT | 0 GM |
| SATURATED FAT | 0 GM |
| CHOLESTEROL | 0 MG |
| SODIUM | 2 MG |
| PROTEIN | 1 GM |
| CARBOHYDRATE | 13 GM |

# Thin Spice Cookies

*Don't be put off by the amount of butter in this recipe. It makes tons of cookies that last at least a month in a tin. Two cookies, which nicely satisfy one's need for a crunchy sweet with dessert, will not break your fat bank at all.*

2¼ cups sifted all-purpose flour
2 teaspoons ground ginger
1 teaspoon ground cinnamon
1 teaspoon ground cardamom
¼ teaspoon ground cloves
1 teaspoon salt
¼ cup (1 stick) unsalted butter

½ cup sugar
2 tablespoons nonfat yoghurt
½ cup dark corn syrup
1 tablespoon brandy
1 tablespoon lemon juice
1 tablespoon grated lemon zest
vegetable cooking spray (optional)

Sift together the flour, ginger, cinnamon, cardamom, cloves, and salt onto a sheet of waxed paper. With a handheld electric mixer, cream the butter and sugar together in a large bowl until fluffy. Beat in the yoghurt, corn syrup, brandy, lemon juice, and lemon zest. On low speed, beat in the flour mixture in 4 additions, blending well to make a soft, sticky dough. Wrap in plastic and chill well for several hours or overnight. (*May be prepared ahead up to this point and refrigerated for up to 3 days.*)

Place racks in the upper and lower third of the oven and preheat to 350°F. Line 2 baking sheets with parchment paper or spray with vegetable cooking spray.

Unwrap the dough and divide it in half. Keep one half refrigerated while you work with the other. Pinch off pieces of dough about 1 inch in diameter and place on the prepared baking sheet about 2 inches apart to allow for spreading. Repeat with the second baking sheet. Bake in the oven for 10 minutes or until pale golden brown. Rotate the sheets from top to bottom and front to back about halfway through the baking time. Remove from the oven. The cookies will appear soft but will harden. As they do, transfer them to a wire rack to cool. Repeat until all the dough is used.

It is essential to store these cookies in an airtight container, preferably a tin.

**Makes about 100 cookies**

➤ *You may bake half the dough, yielding about 50 cookies, and rewrap the balance in plastic or aluminum foil and freeze for up to 3 months.*

| PER 2 COOKIES | |
| --- | --- |
| CALORIES | 64 |
| FAT | 2 GM |
| SATURATED FAT | 1 GM |
| CHOLESTEROL | 6 MG |
| SODIUM | 60 MG |
| PROTEIN | 1 GM |
| CARBOHYDRATE | 10 GM |

# Chocolate Mousse Cake

*A one-inch wedge is all you need of this richly elegant cake, which manages to combine a nice chocolaty taste with a reasonable fat content. Serve it in a discreet puddle of raspberry coulis or with Double Yoghurt Cream (page 261). Very easy to make.*

vegetable cooking spray
3 large eggs plus 3 large egg whites
1½ cups sugar
1 teaspoon pure vanilla extract
⅓ cup all-purpose flour
⅔ cups Dutch-process cocoa powder
    (see Appendix)

½ cup evaporated skim milk
confectioners' sugar
1 recipe Raspberry Coulis (recipe
    follows) (optional)

Set an oven rack in the middle position; preheat the oven to 375°F. Spray an 8- or 9-inch springform pan with vegetable cooking spray and set aside.

With a handheld electric mixer, beat the eggs and egg whites until frothy and light in color, about 4 minutes. Add the sugar and vanilla and beat for 4 minutes more.

Mix together the flour and cocoa powder. Add to the egg mixture and beat for 2 minutes. Add the milk and blend in. Pour the mixture into the prepared pan and bake for 10 minutes. Lower the temperature to 325°F and bake for 35 minutes more. The center will not test clean but will firm up on cooling.

Cool for 1 hour on a wire rack, then chill for at least 3 hours without removing it from the pan. Release the sides and remove the cake. Do not cut until well chilled. The center will still be slightly soft and fudgy. Dust the top lightly with confectioners' sugar just before presenting. To serve, place 2 to 3 tablespoons Raspberry Coulis on a plate (if desired) and swirl decoratively, then place a wedge of cake in the center of the puddle.

**Serves 12**

| PER SERVING | |
| --- | --- |
| CALORIES | 160 |
| FAT | 2 GM |
| SATURATED FAT | 1 GM |
| CHOLESTEROL | 54 MG |
| SODIUM | 76 MG |
| PROTEIN | 4 GM |
| CARBOHYDRATE | 33 GM |

# RASPBERRY COULIS

*You will find this one of the most useful dessert sauces in the low-fat (or any other) repertoire. Spooned over sliced strawberries, poached peaches, or a mix of berries, it turns ordinary fruit into an elegant dessert. Use it as a drizzle for angel food cake, pound cake, or to contrast with a thin wedge of rich chocolate cake. It also freezes well.*

2 ten-ounce packages frozen
    raspberries, thawed
⅔ cup sugar

2 tablespoons Cointreau or Grand
    Marnier (optional)

Drain the raspberries, reserving the syrup for another use if desired. Puree the berries in a food processor or blender and push the puree through a sieve to remove the seeds. Return the puree to the blender or food processor, add the sugar, and process until the sugar has dissolved. Add the liqueur if desired and chill.

**Makes about 1 cup**

| PER 2 TABLESPOONS | |
| --- | --- |
| CALORIES | 137 |
| FAT | 0 GM |
| SATURATED FAT | 0 GM |
| CHOLESTEROL | 0 MG |
| SODIUM | 1 MG |
| PROTEIN | 0 GM |
| CARBOHYDRATE | 35 GM |

*Desserts*

# Cinnamon Streusel Coffee Cake

*This is one of the few low-fat cakes that behaves like one with much more butter or oil; it stays moist and flavorful for at least five days (if it lasts that long). My family loves having it around for snacking.*

vegetable cooking spray
2½ cups all-purpose flour
1½ teaspoons ground cinnamon
½ teaspoon salt
1 cup firmly packed light brown sugar

½ cup canola oil
1 teaspoon baking powder
1 teaspoon baking soda
1 large egg, lightly beaten
1 cup low-fat buttermilk

Position an oven rack in the bottom third position; preheat the oven to 350°F. Lightly spray a 9-by-13-inch baking pan with vegetable cooking spray and set aside.

Sift the flour, ½ teaspoon of the cinnamon, and the salt into a large bowl. Add the brown sugar and mix in with a rubber spatula. (If the sugar forms lumps, you may have to switch to a handheld electric mixer.) Stir in the oil, mixing well.

Remove ¾ cup of the mixture and place in a small bowl. To this add the remaining 1 teaspoon cinnamon and blend well with a fork. Set aside.

Stir the baking powder and baking soda into the remaining flour-sugar mixture. Add the egg and the buttermilk and blend until smooth. Pour into the baking pan and sprinkle the cinnamon mixture evenly over the batter. Bake for about 25 minutes or until the cake tests done in the center. Let cool in the pan on a wire rack and cut into 2-by-2-inch squares as needed.

**Serves 18**

➤ *This cake may be kept in a cool place — unrefrigerated and well covered with aluminum foil — for a day or so, but should be refrigerated after that.*

| PER SERVING | |
| --- | --- |
| CALORIES | 173 |
| FAT | 7 GM |
| SATURATED FAT | 1 GM |
| CHOLESTEROL | 12 MG |
| SODIUM | 181 MG |
| PROTEIN | 3 GM |
| CARBOHYDRATE | 26 GM |

# Shaker Lemon Nut Tea Bread

*Shaker housewives tended to make desserts that could be whipped up speedily while other food was being prepared. This low-fat version of their classic tea bread can be in the baking dish within about seven minutes once you have the ingredients lined up. Very nice with tea.*

vegetable cooking spray
1½ cups all-purpose flour
½ teaspoon baking soda
½ teaspoon baking powder
pinch of salt
½ cup low-fat buttermilk
2 large eggs, lightly beaten
¼ cup canola oil

1 cup sugar
⅓ cup chopped walnuts
grated zest of 1 large lemon

**Glaze:**

juice of 1 large lemon
⅓ cup sugar

Arrange an oven rack in center position; preheat the oven to 325°F. Spray an 8½-by-4½-inch loaf pan with vegetable cooking spray.

In a large bowl, sift together the flour, baking soda, baking powder, and salt. Add the buttermilk, eggs, oil, sugar, walnuts, and lemon zest and beat well with a wooden spoon for 2 minutes. Pour into the pan and bake for 45 minutes or until the cake tests clean in the middle.

While the bread is still hot, make the glaze by mixing together the lemon juice and sugar. Pour over the bread. Allow to cool completely, about 1 hour, before removing from the pan.

**Serves 12**

| PER SERVING | |
| --- | --- |
| CALORIES | 223 |
| FAT | 8 GM |
| SATURATED FAT | 1 GM |
| CHOLESTEROL | 36 MG |
| SODIUM | 100 MG |
| PROTEIN | 3 GM |
| CARBOHYDRATE | 36 GM |

# Fontina with Ripe Pears
# and Walnuts

*Fine cheese, like other high-fat foods, can fit into a low-fat diet as an occasional treat. Look for ways to eat it that maximize the pleasure of a relatively small amount. This is about the easiest dessert you can imagine and is a joyous play of tastes and textures. The idea is to eat a slice of peeled pear with a thin slice of cheese on a piece of whole wheat biscuit and a nibble of walnut. A sip of port heightens the delicate flavors.*

4–5 ounces Italian fontina, such as Val
    D'Aosta, at room temperature
4 ripe Comice or Bartlett pears
¼ cup walnut halves (about 12)

12 reduced-fat whole wheat biscuits,
    such as Carr's Wheatmeal Biscuits
port wine (optional)

Cut the cheese in half and then in half again. Place a piece on each of 4 dessert plates with a pear and a few walnut halves. Pass the biscuits and serve a small glass of port alongside if desired.

**Serves 4**

| PER SERVING | |
|---|---|
| CALORIES | 278 |
| FAT | 14 GM |
| SATURATED FAT | 6 GM |
| CHOLESTEROL | 33 MG |
| SODIUM | 283 MG |
| PROTEIN | 11 GM |
| CARBOHYDRATE | 31 GM |

# Chocolate-Dipped Strawberries

*I always make a beeline for these when they're offered. I love the combination of sweet and slightly tart, the sensuous yielding of the chocolate, and the soft berry flesh beneath. They are very easy to make and are a nice extra to pass with dessert.*

12 large, well-shaped strawberries
   with leaves attached
3 ounces high-quality semisweet
   chocolate, such as Ghirardelli or
   Lindt Excellence

Do not wash the berries; wipe gently with a damp paper towel and keep refrigerated until just before dipping. They should be cold and dry.

Melt the chocolate in the top of a double boiler over medium heat, stirring frequently, until smooth and shiny, about 3 minutes. Remove from the heat. (The chocolate also may be melted in a 2-cup measure in the microwave on high. Stir every 15 seconds for about 1½ minutes until melted and smooth.)

Lay a sheet of waxed paper on a small tray or flat plate. Grasp a berry by the stem or hull, dip halfway into the warm chocolate, twirl slightly to remove any excess, and place on the prepared tray. Repeat with the remaining berries. Refrigerate until the chocolate sets, about 15 minutes.

Makes 12

➤ *Dipped berries may be stored in a cool place for up to 1 day, but do not refrigerate for a long time after the initial setting. Berries for dipping should be ripe, of course, but not overripe and soft, or they will begin to weep.*

| PER SERVING | |
| --- | --- |
| CALORIES | 48 |
| FAT | 3 GM |
| SATURATED FAT | 2 GM |
| CHOLESTEROL | 3 MG |
| SODIUM | 0 MG |
| PROTEIN | 0 GM |
| CARBOHYDRATE | 5 GM |

# 16
# BASICS and EXTRAS

# Sandwiches

*Given the important role sandwiches play in our food life, it might seem odd to find them at the back of the book in a collection of miscellany. The placement indicates no lack of esteem on my part and has to do with the informal nature of sandwich making. Most sandwich "recipes" are really instructions and suggestions, and as such they are not consistent with the other sections of the book or even with each other. For the same reasons, no nutritional analyses are given here, except to tell you that none is excessively high in fat or saturated fat, as long as you keep the size reasonable.*

Remember the days when "cold cuts" were the answer to all food problems? You made a sandwich, and you had a meal. Today such foods often are regarded as unacceptably high in fat and saturated fat, especially since a high-fat cheese was frequently a component as well. Even a benign-sounding tuna on rye, made with half a cup of deli tuna salad and two tablespoons of mayo carries a walloping twenty-five grams of fat.

Nevertheless, this original "fast food" is still an indispensable part of our food life, and there is no reason to give up sandwiches just because you now find bologna impossibly salty and salami impossibly greasy. Identify some other quick sandwich fixings (plus lower-fat spreads and sources of moisture) you and your family enjoy and try to keep some on hand. Even half a sandwich is usually a much better and more nourishing snack than a bag of potato chips. And meat is not out of the question either; two or three ounces of fresh or smoked turkey breast, thinly sliced Black Forest ham, or lean roast beef can make a satisfying sandwich for the fat-conscious. The trick is to use just enough meat for flavor, go light on the mayo (if it's not the nonfat variety), or replace some or all of it with mustard and flesh it out with lettuce, tomato, red onion, cucumber, roasted peppers, cranberry sauce, chutney, or anything else that supplies nonfat moisture and bright flavor notes. Seek out interesting, flavorful fresh breads, another way to help keep mayo or butter to a minimum.

If you have a yen for a frankfurter, there are some good, reduced-fat ones to investigate. But read the nutritional labels very carefully when buying those made with turkey or chicken. They may sound nutritionally correct, but more often than not they contain dark meat and fatty skin, so that the fat count is only one or two grams less than an ordinary beef or pork sausage.

Turkey cold cuts are not automatically low in fat either. Often they are made from both dark and light meat and may contain fatty organ meats as well, plus lots of sodium and preservatives. Read the labels carefully and look for skinless turkey breast, smoked or regular, for your sandwiches. Lean turkey can be rather dry, however, so for that all-important moisture, rely on a smear of reduced-fat or nonfat mayo and tangy cranberry chutney and lettuce. Other ploys to enliven turkey breast sandwiches: puree regular chutney with a bit of nonfat or reduced-fat mayo or use ranch or creamy Italian salad dressing as a spread (these are thinner than mayo and come in reduced-fat or nonfat versions).

Hamburgers, which everyone seems to crave now and again, are between you and your conscience. In my opinion, they are relegated to the department of diminishing returns now that you must eat them lean and have them well-done to avoid worrying about food-borne pathogens. I'd rather have a tuna or salmon burger. Cheese, if you like it, can be used sparingly, along with some of the other fillers I've mentioned, so that you don't get walloped with a lot of saturated fat. A "melt" is a good way to get cheese on a toasted sandwich. If you use a shredded low-fat cheese, you can get away with less, and it will melt faster, too.

If you are a peanut butter junkie like me, it can be used judiciously in combination with other nonfat extenders to make a truly satisfying sandwich. Try peanut butter with mashed sweet potato or even mashed banana.

Vegetable sandwiches can be very satisfying, especially if you add a thin slice of meat such as smoked turkey for extra satisfaction. This is a perfect way to use savory leftovers such as roasted vegetables and my favorite, Turkish Beans (page 188).

Several of these sandwich strategies use other recipes found in this book. Those recipes can be made specifically for this purpose, especially if you wish to make several sandwiches, or you can create these and other sandwiches with leftovers. As an example, I found that leftovers of the delicious Ma Po's Tofu (page 191), when mashed lightly on whole grain bread and combined with arugula leaves, made a fabulous and healthy sandwich I might never have thought of. Similarly, leftover Chicken Chili (page 152) combined with some coleslaw makes a tasty sandwich on a bun. Some leftovers have made such extraordinarily good sandwiches that I now make the dish just for sandwiches. A case in point is Tuna Steak with Wasabi Mayonnaise (page 258).

A dozen of my favorite sandwiches follow, which I'm sure you will expand with healthy, low-fat additions of your own. For the most part, the directions are informal and the ingredient amounts, where given, are approximate to allow for variables such as the size of the bread or rolls you are using, the number of people to be fed, and your appetite. Each sandwich serves one person unless otherwise indicated.

## GRILLED ZUCCHINI WITH MINT, ROASTED PEPPERS, SMOKED MOZZARELLA, AND CHUTNEY MAYONNAISE ON A HERO

Prepare Grilled Zucchini with Mint (page 228) or use leftovers, and make Roasted Sweet Red Peppers (page 207) or buy them. Spread a split half of a small baguette or an Italian hero with Chutney Mayonnaise (page 275). Layer 3 or 4 slices of zucchini and half a pepper with a slice or two of smoked mozzarella. Top with the other bread half and compress the sandwich by pressing down firmly with both hands. Slice once on the diagonal for easier eating. Wrap tightly in plastic wrap if not using immediately. This sandwich travels well and is extremely satisfying.

## HUMMUS POCKET

Cut a warm pita bread pocket in two and gently open each half. Put a tablespoon of Hummus (page 50) into each half. Add shredded lettuce, thinly sliced red onion, chopped fresh tomato, and a sprinkling of chopped fresh mint or cilantro.

## BEAN POCKET

Cut a warm pita bread pocket in two and gently open each half. Stuff each with 2 to 3 tablespoons Turkish Beans (page 188) at room temperature and shredded lettuce.

# PHILLY VEGETARIAN HOAGIE

Known as a sub or a hero in other towns, these sandwiches never taste as good to me as those in Philadelphia. I think it's the onions. The givens are roasted vegetables, most importantly Roasted Sweet Red Peppers (page 207), paper-thin slices of red onion marinated in vinegar, a sprinkling of dried oregano and red pepper flakes, and a finishing dash of Garlic Vinaigrette (page 93). Italian-style cold cuts and provolone cheese are the classic hoagie components, but this vegetarian version beats them.

# TUNA STEAK WITH WASABI MAYONNAISE ON AN ONION ROLL

Split a ½-pound tuna steak through the middle so that you have 2 thin steaks. Spray a grill pan with vegetable cooking spray and heat. When very hot, grill the steaks for about 2 minutes per side. They should be nicely marked but rare in the center. Place each on the bottom half of a split onion roll, add a lettuce leaf, spread the top half with Wasabi Mayonnaise (page 276), and serve immediately.

**Serves 2**

# TUNA AND CARROT SALAD

Lightly spread 2 slices of whole wheat or seven-grain bread with 1 table-spoon (total) reduced-fat mayonnaise. Add ⅓ to ½ cup Tuna and Carrot Salad (page 82), a lettuce leaf, and some thin, unpeeled slices of Kirby cucumber.

# SLICED TURKEY BREAST WITH
# CRANBERRY GINGER COMPOTE

Spread 2 slices of bread with Cranberry Ginger Compote (page 266), place 2 or 3 slices of sliced turkey breast and lettuce or arugula leaves on one slice, and top with the other.

# PEANUT BUTTER AND
# HONEYED SWEET POTATO

Mash ¼ cooked sweet potato with 1 tablespoon honey. Spread 2 slices of whole wheat bread with 2 tablespoons unsalted peanut butter, then add the mashed sweet potato and a lettuce leaf if desired.

OTHER COMBINATIONS YOU MAY WANT TO TRY:

*Smoked Turkey Breast with Thin-Sliced Red Onion and Hot Mustard Mayonnaise*

*Grilled Sliced Turkey or Chicken Sausage with Caramelized Onions (page 267) and Lettuce on a Warm Bun*

*Grilled Salmon Burger (page 121), Red Onion, and Matthew Kenney's Tomato Jam (page 265) on a Toasted Bun*

*Sliced Vidalia Onion and Reduced-Fat Monterey Jack with Reduced-Fat Mayo on Rye Bread*

# Yoghurt Cheese

*Yoghurt "cheese," or double-thick yoghurt, which first appeared in* Low Fat & Loving It, *is such an easy and useful accessory for cutting fat that the recipe is worth repeating here, especially since it contains twenty-five to thirty-five grams of calcium in a tablespoon. Make sure the yoghurt you buy for this purpose does not contain gelatin, starches, or gums.*

16 ounces nonfat yoghurt

Line a strainer or sieve with rinsed double-thick cheesecloth and set it over a large bowl. (You can also use a Melita-type filter top lined with dampened filter paper.) Spoon the yoghurt into the strainer, cover with plastic wrap, and set in the refrigerator to drain for at least 8 hours or overnight. You can discard the liquid (whey) or drink it. The "cheese" will keep in a covered container for up to 1 week, refrigerated.

Makes about 1 cup, though yield depends on type of yoghurt used and time allowed for drainage.

➤ *Spread this "cheese" on a toasted bagel half and sprinkle with cinnamon sugar for a breakfast treat. Use as you would cream cheese or mix with chopped scallion, garlic, or parsley (or other herb), season to taste, and serve with crostini.*

| PER 2 TABLESPOONS | |
|---|---|
| CALORIES | 26 |
| FAT | 0 GM |
| SATURATED FAT | 0 GM |
| CHOLESTEROL | 1 MG |
| SODIUM | 31 MG |
| PROTEIN | 3 GM |
| CARBOHYDRATE | 3 GM |

# Double Yoghurt Cream

*Desserts slathered in whipped cream are a thing of the past, but this cream is a good substitute when a creamy finish is needed. I find this especially satisfying with Espresso Granita (page 246).*

1 cup Yoghurt Cheese (page 260)
¼ cup heavy cream
2 tablespoons sugar

Place the Yoghurt Cheese in a chilled bowl. In a separate chilled bowl, whip the cream with a handheld electric mixer until soft peaks form. Add the sugar and beat until the cream holds the peaks. Add 1 tablespoon whipped cream to the cheese and beat in with a whisk. Add the remaining cream and fold in gently with a rubber spatula.

**Makes 1¾ cups**

| PER 2 TABLESPOONS | |
|---|---|
| CALORIES | 36 |
| FAT | 2 GM |
| SATURATED FAT | 1 GM |
| CHOLESTEROL | 7 MG |
| SODIUM | 12 MG |
| PROTEIN | 2 GM |
| CARBOHYDRATE | 3 GM |

# Low-Fat Tartar Sauce

*I'm fond of tartar sauce with any kind of simple broiled or poached fish. I can't imagine eating crab cakes, one of my favorite foods, without it!*

1 cup nonfat mayonnaise

1½ tablespoons minced onion

2 teaspoons lemon juice

1½ tablespoons finely chopped dill
  pickle or gherkin

1 tablespoon finely chopped fresh
  parsley

1 tablespoon minced capers

½ teaspoon Dijon mustard

salt and freshly ground pepper to taste

Whip the mayonnaise lightly and add all the remaining ingredients. Refrigerate for 1 to 2 hours before serving to allow the flavor to develop.

**Makes about 1½ cups**

| PER ¼ CUP | |
|---|---|
| CALORIES | 29 |
| FAT | 0 GM |
| SATURATED FAT | 0 GM |
| CHOLESTEROL | 0 MG |
| SODIUM | 358 MG |
| PROTEIN | 0 GM |
| CARBOHYDRATE | 6 GM |

# Oven-Dried Tomatoes

*Intensely flavored oven-dried tomatoes are a wonderful way to extend the end-of-summer bounty, especially if your food life is heavily weighted with pasta, tomatoes, and tomato-based sauces. Once in the oven, they pretty much mind their own business. Make them plain or season with herbs or a flavored oil.*

24–28 medium plum tomatoes (about
  4 pounds), stem end cut off and
  halved lengthwise

2½ teaspoons extra-virgin olive oil

1 teaspoon kosher salt

freshly ground black pepper to taste

Preheat the oven to 200°F.

Using a pastry brush, coat the skin side of each tomato half lightly with olive oil. Place cut side up on one or two large rimmed baking sheets lined with foil or parchment. Sprinkle with salt and pepper. Bake until the tomatoes have shrunk and are almost flat and shriveled slightly but are still soft and juicy. This will take 4 to 6 hours, depending on size. Let cool on the baking sheet, then place in a container and refrigerate.

**Makes about 2 cups**

VARIATION:

Sprinkle with snipped fresh thyme (not dried) or brush with a favorite herb-flavored oil.

➤ *Keep these tomatoes on hand to chop up for quick, tasty sauces, as a foundation for soups, as a topping for sautéed fish, or layered with low-fat cheese on grilled bread for a quick snack. Oven-dried tomatoes are great in sandwiches.*

| PER 4-PIECE SERVING | |
| --- | --- |
| CALORIES | 34 |
| FAT | 1 GM |
| SATURATED FAT | 0 GM |
| CHOLESTEROL | 0 MG |
| SODIUM | 125 MG |
| PROTEIN | 1 GM |
| CARBOHYDRATE | 6 GM |

# Tomatoes Concassé

*This French classic, an intense reduction of ripe tomatoes enhanced with the flavor of shallots and herbs, makes any ordinary food elegant and adds color, flavor, and texture with little fat. Use it to dress up an omelet, a simple piece of broiled fish, or a chicken breast.*

1 tablespoon extra-virgin olive oil
4 shallots, finely chopped (about ½ cup)
2 cloves garlic, finely chopped
1 sprig fresh thyme, leaves stripped, or ¼ teaspoon dried pinch of rosemary

6 medium very ripe tomatoes, peeled, seeded, and diced, or 1 twenty-eight-ounce can Italian plum tomatoes, lightly seeded and chopped
1 bay leaf
¼ cup dry white wine
salt and freshly ground black pepper to taste

In a heavy, preferably nonstick skillet, heat the oil over medium-high heat. Add the shallot, garlic, and thyme or rosemary. Cook until the shallot is tender, about 3 minutes. Add the tomatoes and bay leaf and bring to a simmer. Cook over medium heat for 7 to 10 minutes, stirring frequently. Add the wine and simmer until reduced by one-half, about 10 minutes. Season with salt and pepper and let cool to room temperature. Discard the bay leaf before using.

**Makes about 2 cups, serving 4**

| PER SERVING | |
| --- | --- |
| CALORIES | 96 |
| FAT | 4 GM |
| SATURATED FAT | 0 GM |
| CHOLESTEROL | 0 MG |
| SODIUM | 20 MG |
| PROTEIN | 2 GM |
| CARBOHYDRATE | 13 GM |

# Matthew Kenney's Tomato Jam

*Matthew Kenney, one of my favorite chefs, serves this with grilled zucchini as a first course. I also like it on Grilled Salmon Burgers (page 121).*

8 medium tomatoes (about 2¾–3 pounds)

1 tablespoon plus 2 teaspoons olive oil

¼ cup minced fresh ginger (2-ounce piece)

2 cloves garlic, minced

¼ cup cider vinegar

2 cinnamon sticks

½ cup firmly packed light brown sugar

1 teaspoon ground cumin, toasted

pinch of ground cloves

¼ teaspoon cayenne pepper

½ teaspoon salt (or to taste)

freshly ground black pepper to taste

¼ cup honey

Peel, seed, and chop the tomatoes. You should have about 4 cups.

Heat the olive oil in a heavy nonreactive, preferably nonstick saucepan. Add the ginger and garlic and sauté until the garlic is translucent, about 1½ minutes. Add the vinegar and cinnamon sticks and cook to reduce the liquid by one-half. Add the tomatoes, brown sugar, cumin, cloves, and cayenne. Bring to a boil, turn down the heat to low, and cook slowly for 1 hour at a very gentle simmer or until all the tomato juices have evaporated. Add the salt and pepper. Add the honey and stir until the jam is shiny. Remove the cinnamon sticks, pour the jam into sterilized jars, and store at room temperature or keep refrigerated.

**Makes about 3 cups**

| PER 2 TABLESPOONS | |
| --- | --- |
| CALORIES | 49 |
| FAT | 1 GM |
| SATURATED FAT | 0 GM |
| CHOLESTEROL | 0 MG |
| SODIUM | 52 MG |
| PROTEIN | 0 GM |
| CARBOHYDRATE | 10 GM |

# Cranberry Ginger Compote

*My friend Carlie Feldman makes this superdelicious compote for Christmas gifts — a wonderful idea if you can bear to give it away!*

¾ cup dry white wine
¾ cup sugar
1 twelve-ounce bag cranberries, rinsed and picked over

grated zest of 1 navel orange
½ cup golden raisins
1-inch piece fresh ginger, grated
½ teaspoon ground cinnamon

In a 2½- to 3-quart nonreactive saucepan, mix the wine and sugar and stir together over medium heat until the sugar is dissolved. Bring to a boil, add the cranberries, cover, and simmer for about 5 minutes or until the berries begin to pop. Add the orange zest, raisins, ginger, and cinnamon. Simmer for 3 to 4 minutes more.

Remove from the heat and let cool. The mixture will thicken on standing. Spoon into a bowl or sterilized jars, cover, and refrigerate. The jam will keep for up to 1 month.

**Makes about 2¾ cups**

➤ *This is good not only as a condiment with poultry but as a breakfast spread on toasted French bread or as a topping for vanilla frozen yoghurt.*

| PER ¼ CUP | |
| --- | --- |
| CALORIES | 67 |
| FAT | 0 GM |
| SATURATED FAT | 0 GM |
| CHOLESTEROL | 0 MG |
| SODIUM | 150 MG |
| PROTEIN | 1 GM |
| CARBOHYDRATE | 17 GM |

# Caramelized Onions

*Caramelized onions have endless uses. Add a thin layer to sandwiches in place of mayonnaise for flavor and moisture, use as a bed for any grilled whitefish, or use as a topping for crostini or homemade pizza.*

3 medium red onions (about 1¼ pounds)
2 teaspoons olive oil

¼ teaspoon salt (or more to taste)
1 tablespoon balsamic vinegar
freshly ground black pepper to taste

Peel and quarter the onions and slice crosswise as thinly and evenly as possible. You should have about 3½ cups.

In a large, heavy nonstick skillet, heat the oil over medium-low heat. Add the onions and salt and cook slowly, stirring occasionally, until they are quite soft and lightly browned, about 15 to 20 minutes. Stir in the vinegar, adjust the salt, and season with pepper. Let cool. Can be refrigerated for up to 2 weeks.

Makes about 1 cup

➤ *You also can use Spanish, Vidalia, or yellow onions (or a combination) in this recipe.*

| PER ¼ CUP | |
| --- | --- |
| CALORIES | 309 |
| FAT | 10 GM |
| SATURATED FAT | 1 GM |
| CHOLESTEROL | 0 MG |
| SODIUM | 601 MG |
| PROTEIN | 9 GM |
| CARBOHYDRATE | 52 GM |

# Toasted Nuts and Seeds

## PINE NUTS

### On the Stove

Place the pine nuts in a large, dry skillet and cook, stirring, over medium heat for about 5 minutes or until lightly browned.

### In the Microwave:

Spread the nuts in a single layer in a microwave-safe dish and cook on high for 3 minutes or until lightly browned.

## WALNUTS AND PECANS

### In the Oven

Preheat the oven to 325°F. Spread the nuts in a single layer on an ungreased baking sheet and toast for 10 to 12 minutes.

### In the Microwave

Spread the nuts in a single layer in a microwave-safe dish and cook on high, stirring once. One cup nuts takes 3 to 5 minutes. Watch carefully.

## TOASTED SESAME SEEDS

Place required amount of sesame seeds in a small dry skillet, place over medium heat, and cook, shaking pan almost constantly, for about 1 minute or until seeds turn lightly golden and you hear one pop. Remove from heat immediately and shake pan one or twice.

# Jalapeño Corn Bread

*Corn bread goes well with almost any informal meal and is especially useful to give texture and substance to a vegetable dinner. This easy version has a sly bite of jalapeños for added interest.*

1½ cups yellow stone-ground
    cornmeal
½ teaspoon baking soda
1 tablespoon sugar
½ cup all-purpose flour
1 teaspoon salt
2 teaspoons baking powder
1 large egg plus 2 large egg whites, at
    room temperature

1 cup low-fat buttermilk
1 tablespoon vegetable oil
2 fresh jalapeño peppers, seeded and
    finely chopped, or 3 canned or
    pickled jalapeño peppers, drained,
    seeded, and chopped
vegetable cooking spray

Preheat the oven to 400°F.

In a medium bowl, combine the cornmeal, baking soda, sugar, flour, salt, and baking powder. Set aside.

In a separate bowl, combine the egg, egg whites, buttermilk, and oil. Stir until smooth. Add the jalapeños. Stir into the cornmeal mixture and blend with a spoon to form a smooth batter. Do not overmix.

Spray a heavy (preferably cast-iron) 9-inch skillet or 8-inch square baking pan with vegetable cooking spray and place in the oven to preheat. (If using a baking pan, heat for only 3 minutes, or the vegetable spray will burn.) Remove the hot pan from the oven and pour in the batter. Bake for 20 to 30 minutes or until a toothpick inserted in the center comes out clean. Cut and serve immediately.

**Makes 8 pieces**

| PER PIECE | |
| --- | --- |
| CALORIES | 176 |
| FAT | 3 GM |
| SATURATED FAT | 1 GM |
| CHOLESTEROL | 28 MG |
| SODIUM | 542 MG |
| PROTEIN | 6 GM |
| CARBOHYDRATE | 30 GM |

# Croutons

*Indispensable to add heft and crunch to soups and salads.*

1 medium French, Italian, or
   sourdough baguette

1 tablespoon plus 1 teaspoon olive oil
   (approximately)

Preheat the oven to 325°F.

Cut the bread in half. Trim the crust off each half and cut lengthwise into ½-inch-thick slices. Cut each slice into ½-inch strips and cube these. Toss with the olive oil, place on a rimmed baking sheet, and bake until lightly browned and crisp throughout, about 10 to 15 minutes.

**Makes about 100 croutons, serving 10**

VARIATION:

*Garlic Croutons:* Place the oil in a small bowl. Add 1 clove garlic through a press and a pinch of salt. Proceed as above. These are best used within 24 hours.

➤ *Croutons can be used immediately or stored in an airtight tin or jar for up to 5 days. Don't refrigerate. If you don't need this many croutons, halve the recipe.*

| PER SERVING | |
| --- | --- |
| CALORIES | 78 |
| FAT | 2 GM |
| SATURATED FAT | 0 GM |
| CHOLESTEROL | 0 MG |
| SODIUM | 138 MG |
| PROTEIN | 2 GM |
| CARBOHYDRATE | 12 GM |

# Bread Crumbs

1 loaf of leftover 2- to 3-day-old
    regular or sourdough French
    baguette (see Note)

Trim the crust from the bread. Cut the bread into slices, cube them, and whirl in a food processor until small, irregular, and coarse. Do not over-process, or the crumbs will be reduced to powder. You can also rub the bread against the largest hole of a box grater. Bread crumbs can be stored in an air-tight jar for several weeks.

➤ *Best when used fresh, these bread crumbs can be stored in the freezer in a tightly sealed plastic bag for up to a month. They are usable after that but lose their flavor.*

Note: You can use home-style white bread to make crumbs, but the added sweeteners in the bread give an off-flavor. These crumbs are usually satisfactory for meat or turkey loaf, however. If you need crumbs and have only fresh bread, dry it a bit by placing trimmed bread in a 250°F oven for 1 hour.

# Toasted Bread Crumbs

*Toasted bread crumbs can be used to enhance many vegetable dishes, such as cauliflower, that are either bland or lacking in color. They also give textural interest to steamed or poached fish or fish fillets baked in tomato sauce.*

1 cup fresh bread crumbs (see above)         pinch of salt
1½ tablespoons olive oil

Adjust oven rack to center-low position and preheat the oven to 325°F.
Mix the bread crumbs with the oil and salt and toss to coat evenly. Spread in a single layer on a small rimmed baking sheet and bake, stirring once after 5 minutes, until golden brown, about 10 to 12 minutes. Sprinkle over a finished dish, allowing 2 to 3 tablespoons per person.

**Makes about 1 cup**

## A NOTE ON STOCKS

When I make stock, I am always tempted to stew the vegetables in butter or oil or caramelize the onions before proceeding, as I love the way this strengthens the flavors. You *can* chill the stock and remove the fat, but ease of preparation usually wins out, and I omit this step.

When you don't know how a certain ingredient will work in a stock (especially vegetable stock), follow this suggestion from Deborah Madison, the founder of Greens Restaurant in San Francisco: cook the ingredient in question by itself and taste the water as it simmers. What happened? Did it turn grassy after ten minutes? Bitter after thirty? You can make vegetable stock out of almost anything; the key is to know your ingredients and understand what each contributes. Besides onions, which are basic to any stock, carrots add sweetness and celery adds body. Parsley "grounds" all the flavors, but I prefer to use the stems, which do not muddy the broth. Bay leaves add a strong, deep taste, and garlic also contributes depth. I don't use the brassicas (broccoli, cabbage, and the like), which add a sulfurous note.

Chicken stock can be made from bones, giblets, and wings (I save roasted carcasses, which contribute flavor) or from a whole chicken if you can use it. A butcher will give you or sell for a pittance the bones from boneless chicken breasts. Fish stock can be made with skeletons and heads begged from the fishmonger or as the natural result of poaching fish in court bouillon. Avoid oily fish for stock; the flavor may be unpleasant.

If you don't own a stockpot, you might consider buying one. A stockpot is tall in proportion to its diameter; it requires less liquid and keeps the liquid moving over the ingredients. A regular soup pot is useful if you want to reduce a weak stock.

# Basic Vegetable Stock

*Vegetable stock or broth is very useful to have on hand. It can be used to cook vegetables, in vegetable risotti, or to replace chicken stock when cooking for vegetarians. As the basis of other soups, it adds a rich, satisfying flavor.*

1 large leek

2 large unpeeled onions, quartered

3 carrots, scraped and coarsely
   chopped

2 stalks celery, coarsely chopped

1 handful celery leaves, chopped

1 whole head unpeeled garlic, cloves
   separated and crushed

2 large or 4 small bay leaves

2 quarts water (approximately)

12 black peppercorns

5 sprigs fresh parsley, preferably
   Italian flat-leaf parsley

3 sprigs fresh thyme (optional)

½ teaspoon salt (or to taste)

Trim off the roots and the top half of the green from the leek and discard. Slice in half lengthwise, fan out under running water, and rinse well to remove any sand. Slice crosswise into 1-inch pieces.

In a large stockpot or soup kettle, combine the leek with all the remaining ingredients, adding more water if necessary so that the vegetables are well covered with water. Bring slowly to a boil, then adjust the heat and simmer, partially covered, for 1 hour.

Strain the stock through a fine-meshed strainer, pressing on the vegetables with the back of a large wooden spoon to extract the last drops of flavor. Discard the vegetables. If you're not using the stock immediately, let cool, cover, and refrigerate. Can be refrigerated for up to 4 days or frozen for up to 2 weeks.

**Makes about 8 cups**

➤ *You can vary the vegetables according to what is fresh and abundant. Two fresh tomatoes are a nice addition, adding color and an acidic note. Four ears of sweet corn, cut into pieces, or a few mushrooms also are suitable.*

| PER 1 CUP | |
| --- | --- |
| CALORIES | 16 |
| FAT | 0 GM |
| SATURATED FAT | 0 GM |
| CHOLESTEROL | 0 MG |
| SODIUM | 144 MG |
| PROTEIN | 0 GM |
| CARBOHYDRATE | 4 GM |

# Basic Chicken Stock

*My freezer is never without homemade chicken stock. It is an indispensable element of my cooking life, enriching any grain dish, de rigueur for risotto, and a good base for other soups.*

3 pounds chicken necks, backs, wings, and giblets plus cut-up carcasses
3 quarts water (or enough to cover by 2 inches)
salt to taste
1 medium onion, unpeeled
3 cloves garlic, unpeeled

1 carrot, scrubbed
1 stalk celery and/or leafy tops of 2 stalks celery
several sprigs fresh parsley
2 bay leaves
1 teaspoon black peppercorns

Wash chicken parts and bones well. Place in a large, heavy soup pot or stockpot, add the water and salt, and bring to a simmer. Cook for 5 to 7 minutes, skimming off any scum that rises to the top.

Add all the remaining ingredients, partly cover the pot, lower the heat so that the liquid is just barely boiling, and simmer gently for 1 hour. Stir from time to time.

Strain the liquid, discarding the solids after pressing down on them with a wooden spoon to extract the last essence. To remove the fat, either chill until the fat has hardened and can be removed from the top, strain again through a cheesecloth-lined sieve, or use a fat-removing ladle or Gravy-Skimmer (see Appendix). Let cool, cover, and refrigerate. Can be stored, tightly covered, for 4 to 5 days in the refrigerator or up to 1 year in the freezer.

**Makes about 12 cups**

➤ *Don't let the stock boil again after the initial boiling. The more you skim the stock, the clearer it will be.*

| PER 1 CUP | |
| --- | --- |
| CALORIES | 32 |
| FAT | 0 GM |
| SATURATED FAT | 0 GM |
| CHOLESTEROL | 0 MG |
| SODIUM | 64 MG |
| PROTEIN | 7 GM |
| CARBOHYDRATE | 1 GM |

# Three Flavored Mayonnaise Spreads

*These spreads can turn ordinary ingredients into very special sandwiches. Each can be stored in the refrigerator, tightly covered for up to a week.*

## CHIPOTLE MAYONNAISE

3 tablespoons reduced-fat mayonnaise

2 tablespoons nonfat plain yoghurt

1 to 2 teaspoons puree of chipotle
   chili in adobo (see pages 68–69)

pinch salt

½ teaspoon lime juice (optional)

In a small bowl stir together the mayonnaise and yoghurt and chili puree. Taste for seasoning and add the salt and lime juice if desired.

**Makes about ⅓ cup, enough for 3 sandwiches**

| PER TABLESPOON | |
| --- | --- |
| CALORIES | 29 |
| FAT | 2 GM |
| SATURATED FAT | 0 GM |
| CHOLESTEROL | 0 MG |
| SODIUM | 117 MG |
| PROTEIN | 0 GM |
| CARBOHYDRATE | 2 GM |

## CHUTNEY MAYONNAISE

1 tablespoon Major Grey's chutney or
   more to taste

3 tablespoons reduced-fat mayonnaise

freshly ground black pepper

Push the chutney through a sieve or chop finely. Combine with the mayonnaise and black pepper in a small bowl.

**Makes about ⅓ cup**

| PER TABLESPOON | |
| --- | --- |
| CALORIES | 63 |
| FAT | 2 GM |
| SATURATED FAT | 0 GM |
| CHOLESTEROL | 0 MG |
| SODIUM | 84 MG |
| PROTEIN | 0 GM |
| CARBOHYDRATE | 2 GM |

# WASABI MAYONNAISE

2 tablespoons reduced-fat mayonnaise
2 tablespoons nonfat sour cream

1 teaspoon lime juice
2 teaspoons wasabi paste (see Note)

Stir together the mayonnaise, sour cream, lime juice, and wasabi paste, and add enough wasabi paste to yield the degree of heat you like, starting with 1 teaspoon.

## Makes about ⅓ cup

Note: Wasabi is a parsnip-like root grown in Japan. It has both heat and flavor and is highly addictive. Outside Japan, where it is freshly grated as needed, it is available in powdered form. *To reconstitute dried wasabi*: make a paste by blending ½ teaspoon warm water with one heaping teaspoon wasabi powder. Let paste stand 10 to 15 minutes to develop flavor. Makes about 2 teaspoons paste.

| PER TABLESPOON | |
| --- | --- |
| CALORIES | 24 |
| FAT | 1 GM |
| SATURATED FAT | 0 GM |
| CHOLESTEROL | 0 MG |
| SODIUM | 53 MG |
| PROTEIN | 0 GM |
| CARBOHYDRATE | 2 GM |

# Simple Syrup

*This light syrup is very useful to have on hand. It is the base of many fruit sorbets, which means a special dessert can be made virtually at the last minute, and it is far superior to plain sugar for sweetening homemade iced tea without graininess. It takes only a few minutes to make and has an endless life in the refrigerator.*

4 cups water                                      4 cups sugar

Combine the water and sugar in a saucepan and simmer, watching the pan, until the sugar is dissolved and the mixture is clear, about 5 minutes. Let cool and refrigerate in a covered jar.

**Makes about 4 cups**

| PER TABLESPOON | |
| --- | --- |
| CALORIES | 48 |
| FAT | 0 GM |
| SATURATED FAT | 0 GM |
| CHOLESTEROL | 0 MG |
| SODIUM | 0 MG |
| PROTEIN | 0 GM |
| CARBOHYDRATE | 12 GM |

# Minted Iced Tea with Lemon

*It may seem silly to give a recipe for iced tea, something anyone can make with a tea bag and some ice cubes, but so many people have asked how I make my particular iced tea that I added this for them. The amounts of everything can be varied according to your taste. Make the tea at least an hour before you plan to serve it.*

6 tea bags, preferably Twinings Prince
    of Wales, English Breakfast, or a
    mixture of both
2 quarts cold water
3 or 4 sprigs fresh mint
juice of ½ lemon (or more to taste)

⅓–½ cup Simple Syrup (page 277)
2 or 3 orange slices, halved
lemon slices, halved, for garnish
    (optional)
additional fresh mint for garnishing

Have a large glass or ceramic pitcher ready, with a large metal spoon in it to conduct heat. Place the teabags in the pitcher. Bring the water to a boil and pour over the tea bags. Let steep for 5 to 10 minutes, stirring occasionally. Remove the tea bags, squeezing the last drop of tea out with two spoons, and discard the bags.

Add the mint, stir, and let steep for about 15 minutes more. Add the lemon juice and sweeten with sugar syrup to taste. When cooled sufficiently, refrigerate.

To serve, place 1 or 2 half slices of orange in a tall glass, add ice cubes, fill with tea, and garnish with mint and a half slice of lemon, cut halfway through so it can sit on the rim of the glass, if desired. This tea will keep refrigerated without changing flavor for up to 1 week.

Serves 8

➤ *The secret of this tea lies in the strength and flavor of the basic brew (which allows it to stand up to ice cubes), steeping the mint, and sweetening it with simple syrup instead of plain sugar, which doesn't dissolve properly and feels gritty in the mouth.*

PER SERVING

| | |
|---|---|
| CALORIES | 46 |
| FAT | 0 GM |
| SATURATED FAT | 0 GM |
| CHOLESTEROL | 0 MG |
| SODIUM | 7 MG |
| PROTEIN | 0 GM |
| CARBOHYDRATE | 12 GM |

# California Sunset

*When you need a thirst quencher that tastes and feels really good in the mouth (the kind of yen that would have sent you out for a rich milk shake or an ice cream soda in earlier days), try this. It's deliciously refreshing and very satisfying.*

½ cup good-quality vanilla frozen yoghurt, such as Häagen-Dazs
2 tablespoons raspberry sorbet
½ cup orange juice, chilled

½ cup mandarin orange–flavored seltzer, chilled (approximately)
Fresh mint leaves for garnish (optional)

Combine frozen yoghurt, sorbet, orange juice, and seltzer in a blender until thick and frothy. Use more or less seltzer according to how thick you like your drink. Serve in a tall glass garnished with mint if desired.

Serves 1

PER SERVING

| | |
|---|---|
| CALORIES | 173 |
| FAT | 2 GM |
| SATURATED FAT | 1 GM |
| CHOLESTEROL | 5 MG |
| SODIUM | 64 MG |
| PROTEIN | 4 GM |
| CARBOHYDRATE | 37 GM |

# Fruit Smoothie

*Smoothies are easy to make and are an excellent way to add calcium to your diet. Teenagers on the run love them because they are filling and tasty and can be made in minutes. Besides calcium, the drink also supplies fiber and nutrients from the fruit.*

1 medium banana; 10 medium strawberries, hulled; 1 ripe medium peach; or any combination thereof

1 cup 1 percent or skim milk
1 teaspoon pure vanilla extract
pinch of sugar (or to taste)

Cut up the fruit and place in a blender. Add the milk, vanilla, and sugar and whirl.

**Makes approximately 12 ounces, serving one**

VARIATION:

*Soy Smoothie High-Protein Fat-Free Shake*: Add 2 tablespoons soy protein isolate powder (see Note) and 1 or 2 ice cubes or crushed ice to approximately 8 ounces of any smoothie mixture. Whirl in a blender until very cold.

**Serves 1**

| PER SERVING | |
| --- | --- |
| CALORIES | 223 |
| FAT | 3 GM |
| SATURATED FAT | 2 GM |
| CHOLESTEROL | 10 MG |
| SODIUM | 123 MG |
| PROTEIN | 9 GM |
| CARBOHYDRATE | 40 GM |

Note: Soy protein isolate powder can be bought in any health food store.

# *Appendix*

## About the Nutritional Analyses

Each recipe in this book has been analyzed by a registered dietitian. Following each is a nutritional breakdown per serving or portion for you to keep in mind when putting together meals for a day or week.

All the ingredients in a given recipe have been included in the analysis. Excluded are suggested accompaniments, optional ingredients, and those that say "to taste." If a marinade is used and discarded, it is assumed that about one-quarter of it remains in the food. When a substitute ingredient is suggested in the introductory material or in a page note, it is not included in the analysis.

**Calories** are a measure of energy.

**Fat** is the number of fat grams in a serving, as specified in the recipe. One gram of fat contains 9 calories. No more than 30 percent of total calories consumed in a day should derive from fat, preferably less.

**Saturated fat** is hard at room temperature, is derived from animal products and some tropical oils, and has been found to raise cholesterol levels in the blood to a greater degree than actually eating cholesterol. It should represent no more than 10 percent of calories.

**Cholesterol** is present in foods of animal origin. Experts recommend no more than 300 milligrams in your daily diet.

**Sodium** is derived from salt and is present naturally in many foods. One teaspoon of salt equals 2,200 milligrams of sodium. One teaspoon of sea salt or coarse or kosher salt contains 1,800 milligrams of sodium. Black pepper does not add nutrient value.

**Protein** is a nutrient. One gram contains 4 calories. A healthy diet derives about 15 percent of calories from protein.

**Carbohydrates** are classified as either simple (sugars) or complex (starches). One gram of carbohydrate contains 4 calories.

**A Note on Percentages:** Since May 1994, all food manufacturers have been required to carry a standardized food label that includes, in addition to vitamin content and information such as that above, the "percent daily value." This is based on an arbitrary daily intake of 2,000 calories, considered average, which may be higher or lower than your actual calorie needs. Further, the fat percentages are based on a fat intake of 30 percent of calories, which is the *maximum* you should consume but may not be your average.

While the percentage can give you an idea of whether a packaged food is high or low in fat, my feeling is that you can figure this out yourself. Since most people interested enough to count fat grams have a fat budget or fat gram allowance in mind, I consider the percentage superfluous, though it can serve as a red flag for a food you might want to pass up. Further, it is the overall intake that counts, and I believe that you are smart enough to trade off and balance out where you have to. There are already enough figures to contend with!

## Notes on Ingredients

**Broccoli Rabe:** The leafy green *Brassica napus* or rape (also raab, brocoletti di rape, and rapini) is a non-heading variety of broccoli, has long, thin stems, small leaves, and scattered clusters of tiny, open yellow buds, and is related to both the cabbage and turnip family. All of it is edible. The green, which has become the designer vegetable of the '90s, has a pungent bitter flavor, which is an acquired taste. Italians are particularly fond of rape. Rapeseed oil, expressed from the seeds, is known as canola oil.

**Buttermilk:** Despite its name, buttermilk is a type of skim milk. It is the liquid that remains in the churn after butter is made. The buttermilk one buys in supermarkets, however, is a cultured product in which a lactic acid bacterial culture is added to skim or partially skim milk. Salt may be added to extend the shelf life. If fresh buttermilk is not available for a recipe, add 1 tablespoon white vinegar to 1 cup skim or 1 percent milk and let stand for 1 hour. You might not want to drink this, though.

**Capers:** Capers add a special flavor to many foods that might otherwise be considered bland, especially important in a low-fat diet. This bud of a Mediterranean plant pairs wonderfully with fish, with cauliflower, in tomato sauces like Puttanesca, and carries special punch when used in tandem with olives or anchovies. Capers are found in two sizes: nonpariel and Spanish, the latter being very large. Use nonpareils in cooking, the Spanish type in salads.

**Cocoa:** Cocoa, an unsweetened powder made from the cocoa bean after some of the cocoa fat has been pressed out, has less fat than regular chocolate and thus can frequently be used for a lower-fat dessert. This is especially important because so many people love chocolate desserts. I have found high-quality cocoa marvelous in making bitter chocolate sorbet and cakes. In reworking a recipe, you might try a combination of cocoa and chocolate, using proportionately less of the latter. Remember that when substituting cocoa for bittersweet chocolate, you must add sugar, which will vary anywhere from 25 to 100 percent of the volume of the cocoa. You'll have to experiment a bit. Always use Dutch-process cocoa powder, preferably imported. Flavors vary from brand to brand; the one I like most for its deep, rich chocolate flavor is Pernigotti, imported from Italy and available through Williams-Sonoma. Lindt and Valrhona are other good brands available in specialty shops. Droste, available in supermarkets, also is acceptable.

**Chile Powder/Powdered Chili:** Finely powdered chili peppers, made from one type of dried, roasted red chilies, is not to be confused with chili powder, which is a blend of ground red chili peppers and other spices. Also packaged as "pure chili powder."

**Couscous:** This staple, to North African cuisine what pasta is to the Italians, is a granular form of semolina, the coarsely ground durum wheat from which most good pasta is made. Packaged "instant" or precooked couscous is available in Middle Eastern markets and large supermarkets. It can be served as a meal accompaniment, mixed with milk as a porridge, or sweetened and mixed with fruit for a dessert. The name *couscous* also refers to the famous Maghrebian dish in which semolina or cracked wheat is steamed in the top part of a pot called a couscousier, while chunks of meat, vegetables, chickpeas, and raisins simmer in the bottom part.

**Ginger:** Look for ginger that is hard, with a smooth, unshriveled skin and no mold on the ends. When cut, the inside should be juicy and pale yellow with a clear, fresh scent and a hot, spicy taste. Young ginger, sometimes called spring ginger, has a milder flavor and a pale, thin skin that requires no peeling. It is found in oriental markets in the spring.

The best way to store ginger is in the refrigerator, in a small brown paper bag placed inside an airtight plastic container. The paper bag retards rotting but still holds enough moisture so that the root does not dry out. To prolong storage life, replace the bag when it becomes damp. For long-term storage, peel the ginger, place in a glass jar, cover with sherry, and keep in the refrigerator.

Ground ginger, while good in baking, has a completely different flavor and is not an appropriate substitute for fresh ginger.

**Miso:** A salty paste, with the consistency of peanut butter, made from fermented soybeans. It is a Japanese culinary mainstay. Available in the traditional red aged form and in white and yellow. The lighter colors are used in delicate soups and sauces and the darker in heavier dishes. It is also excellent stirred into soups. Miso can be found in oriental markets and health food stores. It should be refrigerated in an airtight container (see Chapter 2).

**Nuoc mam:** Bottled fish sauce used in Vietnam under this name or nuoc nam and in Thailand under nam pla. The strong smell disappears when cooked. Can be found in supermarkets and oriental markets. If unavailable, a less authentic substitute can be made with 1 mashed anchovy fillet mixed with 2 teaspoons light soy sauce and 1 teaspoon water.

**Soy Sauce:** A salty condiment made from fermented soybeans, salt, water, and sometimes wheat. Both Chinese- and Japanese-style sauces are increasingly used in non-Asian dishes. Japanese sauces are not quite as salty as Chinese. *Shoyu* is a Japanese-style sauce made with a wheat and soybean starter. *Tamari* is made with soybean starter only and is preferred by many Western cooks for its clean, tangy flavor.

Chinese-style sauces come in several intensities. Sodium watchers should note that "thin" or "light" on the label refers to the consistency, not the amount of sodium. Chinese thin or light sauces, used both as a condiment and in cooking, are actually saltier than dark sauces, which are used in cooking and sweetened with molasses. For reduced-sodium sauces, look for those labeled "low-sodium" or "lite." They contain 100 milligrams of sodium per one-half teaspoon, compared with 160 milligrams for regular soy sauce. (For comparison, table salt has about 1,000 milligrams of sodium in half a teaspoon.) Tamari also is available in a "lite" version.

Moderately salty Kikkoman brand is my favorite for its mellow, complex flavor and moderate salt. I also like San-J Tamari.

**Tofu:** Also known as bean curd, tofu is made from fresh soybeans soaked, ground, and cooked with water to make soy milk, which some people drink instead of regular milk. The soy milk is then separated into curds and whey through the use of a natural coagulant, and the curds are strained and pressed into small cakes. There are many types of tofu in Asia but only four basic types in the United States: extra-firm, firm, soft, and silken. The first two are for grilling, stir-frying, or any preparation in which the bean curd has to retain its shape. Soft tofu, which is creamy, can be used for cheesecakes, and silken tofu may be added to salad dressings.

Tofu is relatively high in fat (10 grams per 8-ounce serving), so there is no fat saving in using it instead of dairy products, although the fat is not saturated. The point of adding a small amount of it to your diet is its health benefits, discussed in Chapter 2.

**Tomatoes, canned:** I try to use the best canned tomatoes available, since tomato-based sauces are such an important part of low-fat eating. I usually use the Progresso brand. For special sauces, I use one or another brand of real San Marzano tomatoes, imported from Italy, which produce a sauce so superior in color and flavor that they are worth the extra cost. These plum tomatoes are grown on the San Marzano plain near Salerno, where the sun, soil, and weather conditions combine to produce a unique tomato with fewer seeds and less water than other kinds. Their pulp creates a thicker, more vibrantly colored, more flavorful sauce, which is both sweet and tart at the same time. Read the label carefully; labels that say "San Marzano style" or "imported Italian style" tomatoes may be from Chile or Turkey and are not the same thing at all. San Marzano tomatoes are usually found in gourmet markets specializing in Italian products.

**Tomatoes, sun-dried:** Available packed dried or in olive oil, sun-dried tomatoes add a concentrated flavor to pasta dishes and salads, particularly where tomatoes are already used. Those packed in olive oil are more pliable and frequently have garlic and herbs added. They are ready to be used as is, diced, or sliced. If you do not want the extra oil (though it is delicious on a piece of peasant bread), simply rinse it off with boiling water. Or save it to use as part of the oil in salad dressing.

The dry-packed kind require rehydrating in hot water to cover for about 30 minutes. (Save the liquid to use in soup or salad dressing; it's delicious.) Oven-Dried Tomatoes (page 262) are a good substitute.

About 5 sun-dried tomatoes, reconstituted or oil-packed, will give you about ¼ cup chopped tomatoes. About 18 yield 1 cup and weigh about 1½ ounces. Commercial sun-dried tomatoes are available in Italian groceries, gourmet food stores, and some supermarkets. Look for the kind sold in bulk; air-dried tomatoes sold in plastic bags are usually short on flesh and do not reconstitute well.

## Equipment

**Fat-removing ladle:** Skims away unwanted fat from stocks, soups, and stews. Lower the ladle into the liquid until the fat on top flows through the slots around the edge and collects in the bowl. When the ladle is full, discard the fat by pouring it off from the opposite, nonslotted side. Made of stainless steel. Available from Williams-Sonoma.

**Food mill:** An indispensable kitchen accessory for pureeing foods, especially vegetables and fruits. You can make applesauce simply by quartering the apples and cooking them with some lemon juice, instead of peeling and coring the fruit, because the mill will hold back skins, cores, seeds, and stems. Similarly, you can make a smooth sauce from fresh tomatoes without peeling and seeding them. I also use the mill to puree potatoes for mashed potatoes and butternut squash for squash puree and making baby food.

**Gravy-Skimmer:** Permits the removal of fat from liquids such as chicken stock if you don't have time to chill it and lift the fat off the top. It resembles a measuring cup with a long spout. Clear liquid can be poured off via the spout while the fat collects in the bottom of the cup. Available at good house-wares and kitchenware shops, or call or write to East Hampton Industries, P.O. Box 5069, East Hampton, NY 11937 (1-800-645-1188).

**Nonstick pans:** When a recipe in this book specifies a nonstick skillet, it means it was tested in one. If you do not have a nonstick pan or do not have the appropriate size, use regular heavy-gauge cookware, but you may have to increase the amount of oil used. Since low-fat cooking is a way of life, it makes sense to invest in nonstick cookware of as good a quality as you can afford.

## The Bottom Line: Q&A

From time to time, I am invited to lecture on food, nutrition, or health. The following issues are among those frequently raised during the question-and-answer periods that follow.

Q. *I'm confused by cholesterol. What is a healthy ratio of total cholesterol to HDLs?*
   Low-density lipoproteins (LDLs), or "bad" cholesterol, and high-density lipoproteins (HDLs), or "good" cholesterol, are viewed as separate risk factors for heart disease. The National Cholesterol Education Program has set up the following guidelines:

### LDL Levels (mg/dl)

| | |
|---|---|
| Below 130 | Desirable |
| 130–159 | Borderline–high risk |
| 160 or greater | High risk |

In addition, an HDL level below 35 mg/dl is considered a risk factor for heart disease.

   Should you be given your ratio of total cholesterol to HDL, a simple way to think about it is this: your total cholesterol should be no more than about four times higher than your HDL. According to Dr. William Castelli of the Framingham Heart Study, the "ideal" ratio is under 3.5. A ratio lower than about 4.5 suggests that your risk for heart disease is below average; a ratio higher than that suggests a higher than average risk.

Q. *I understand that a low-fat diet tends to lower "good" (HDL) cholesterol along with the "bad" (LDL). Is there any way to boost HDLs while eating low fat?*
The most effective nondrug measure, say the experts, is aerobic exercise. Losing weight and quitting smoking help, too.

Q. *I just can't do without mayonnaise; I really miss the flavor. What kind do you recommend?*
I'm with you; the only one that works for me is the "light" variety. Regular mayo contains about 11 to 12 grams of fat per tablespoon. "Light" contains about 5, and it tastes fine to me. "Reduced-fat" has about 3 grams of fat, and "fat-free" contains less than 0.5 gram. Neither satisfies me. You can, of course, extend reduced-fat mayo with yoghurt or mustard, depending on how you are using it.

Q *When my husband was diagnosed with very high cholesterol, his doctor told him to watch his saturated fat intake and use margarine and foods made with safflower oil. Now I have heard that polyunsaturates are "out" and only olive and canola oils are "in." Were we wrong to follow his advice?*
As more studies emerged, it became apparent that not only does unsaturated fat lower serum cholesterol but also the kind of unsaturated fat eaten can influence the kind of cholesterol you reduce. Monounsaturates and polyunsaturates can both lower total cholesterol levels to the same degree. But whereas polyunsaturates lower *both* HDLs and LDLs, monounsaturates tend to lower LDLs and spare HDLs, which we now know to be protective. Many researchers believe that the low incidence of heart disease in southern Italy and Greece is a reflection of the LDL-reducing capacity of olive oil. (For more on this, see Chapter 2.)

Q. *I'm confused by the fact that canola oil, which I understand to be a polyunsaturated oil, contains saturated fat. I thought it was a totally okay oil.*
I think the confusion lies in the fact that *all* oils are composed of saturated, polyunsaturated, and monounsaturated fats. The difference, and what gives oils their classification, is the ratio of saturated to unsaturated fats they contain. (Even our darling olive oil is 14 percent saturated, which is acceptable, especially when you compare it to lard, which is 41 percent saturated, or butterfat, at 66 percent!) Of the cook-

ing oils, canola oil, which comes from a variety of rapeseed in the mustard family, is 6 percent saturated, making it lowest in saturated fat and second only to olive oil in monounsaturates. But keep in mind that all fat, saturated or not, contains the same number of fat grams, 13.6, the equivalent of 120 calories.

Q. *Isn't it healthier to eat raw vegetables than cooked ones?*
There's a nutritional paradox here: some nutrients are lost from cooking, but others are actually increased. Although cooking does destroy some heat-sensitive vitamins, it also frees others, such as beta-carotene, actually making them more available to the body than they are from raw foods. In raw foods, beta-carotenes don't always get released from inside the fibrous walls of plants. That's what stays in your intestines and acts as bulk. Lycopene, the potent beta-carotene found in tomato skins, is *only* released when cooked.

# References

## Chapter 1

Jacobson, Michael, and Bruce Maxwell. "The Obesity Epidemic." In *What Are We Feeding Our Kids?* New York: Workman Publishing, 1994.

## Chapter 2

Brody, Jane E. "After 4,000 Years Medical Science Takes a Serious Look at Garlic." *New York Times,* September 4, 1990.

Chase, Marilyn. "Food Specialists Seek . . . Right Recipe for Cancer-Smart Diet." *Wall Street Journal,* May 8, 1995.

Claflin, Edward, ed. "Phytochemicals: Cancer-Fighting Foods." In *Healing Yourself with Food.* Emmaus, PA: Rodale Press, 1995.

Levine, Barbara. "Phytochemicals: Cancer-Fighting Foods." *Newsweek Health Supplement,* October 16, 1995.

Winawer, Sidney J., and Moshe Shike. *Cancer Free.* New York: Simon & Schuster, 1995.

## Chapter 3

Anderson, J. W., et al. "Meta-Analysis of the Effects of Soy Protein Intake on Serum Lipids." *New England Journal of Medicine* 333:5 (August 3, 1995).

Angier, Natalie. "Benefits of Broccoli Confirmed as Chemical Blocks Tumors." *New York Times,* April 12, 1994.

"Antioxidants." *Tufts University Diet and Nutrition Letter.* Vol 13, no. 8 (October 1995).

Brody, Jane E. "Clarifying Studies on Cholesterol and Fat." *New York Times,* March 24, 1993.

Centers for Disease Control and Prevention, National Center for Health Statistics. *Overweight in America*. 1994.

Claflin, Edward, ed. "Antioxidants: Beta-carotenes." In *Healing Yourself with Food*. Emmaus, PA: Rodale Press, 1995.

"Fat and Breast Cancer." *New England Journal of Medicine*. February 7, 1996.

Healy, Bernadette. "Calcium." In *A New Prescription for Women's Health*. New York: Viking, 1995.

Hudnal, Marsha. "Optimal Health Goals of Revolutionary New RDA's." In *Environmental Nutrition*. Vol. 20, no. 10 (October 1997).

Liebman, Bonnie. Letter. *Washington Post,* January 14, 1997.

Nebeling, Linda C., et al. "The Impact of Lifestyle Characteristics on Carotenoid Intake in the United States: The 1987 National Health Interview Survey." *American Journal of Public Health*. Vol. 87, no. 2 (February 1997).

Proulx, Lawrence. "Beta-carotene Pills Yield No Benefit." *Washington Post,* May 14, 1996.

"Salt and Hypertension." 1991. *Tufts University Diet & Nutrition Letter,* 8, no. 12 (February).

Saltman, Paul, Joel Gurin, and Ira Motherer. *California Nutrition Book*. Boston: Little, Brown, 1987.

## Chapter 4

"Heart Disease Rates among Greeks and Japanese." 1994. *Science* 264:536.

## Chapter 5

Narisettei, Raju. "Anatomy of a Food Fight." *Wall Street Journal*. July 31, 1996.

*University of California at Berkeley Wellness Letter*. Vol. 12, no. 5 (February 1996).

# Bibliography

Andrews, Jean. *Red Hot Peppers.* New York: Macmillan, 1993.

Goldstein, Joyce. *Back to Square One.* New York: Morrow, 1992.

Herbst, Sharon Tyler. *Food Lover's Companion.* New York: Barron's, 1990.

Madison, Deborah. *The Greens Cookbook.* New York: Bantam, 1987.

Passmore, Jackie. *Encyclopedia of Asian Food and Cooking.* New York: Hearst Books, Morrow, 1991.

Raichlin, Steve. *High-Flavor, Low-Fat Vegetarian Cooking.* New York: Viking, 1995.

Sahni, Julie. *Savoring Spices and Herbs.* New York: Morrow, 1996.

# Index

Dandelion greens, 11
De-Shalit, Erna, 84
Desserts, 229–253
    Apple Crisp, 237–238
    Apple Pie à la Mode, Crustless, 236
    Blood Orange Sorbet, 243–244
    Blueberry-Peach Cobbler, 240
    Chocolate-Dipped Strawberries, 253
    Chocolate Mousse Cake, 248–249
    Cinnamon Streusel Coffee Cake, 250
    Compote Andalouse, 232–233
    Cranberry Crisp, 241–242
    Double Yoghurt Cream, 261
    Espresso Granita, 246
    Fontina with Ripe Pears and Walnuts, 252
    Fruit Sorbet with Orange-Mango-Peach
      "Salsa," 242–243
    Grapefruit Sorbet, 245
    Lemon Nut Tea Bread, Shaker, 251
    Lemon Rice Pudding, 234
    Pear and Ricotta Pie, 238–239
    Pumpkin Custard, 235
    Pumpkin Flan, 234–235
    Raspberry Coulis, 249
    Rice Pudding, Low-Fat, 233–234
    Rosemary Lime Sorbet, 244–245
    Spice Cookies, Thin, 247–248
    Strawberries in Red Wine Syrup, 231–232
Diane's Zucchini Soup, 73–74
Dieting, 34–36
Dinner, in Five-a-Day Program, 32
Dips:
    Babagannoush, 43–44
    Black Bean, No-Fat, 51–52
    Coriander-Mint, 53–54
    Eggplant Caponata, 48–49
    Hummus, 50–51
    Watercress, 52–53
Double Yoghurt Cream, 261
Dressings, 77–78, 92–94
    Garlic, Rosa's, 92–93
    Lemon Mustard Vinaigrette, 93–94
    Miso, 94
    Sesame Rice Vinegar, 92

Eggplant:
    Babagannoush, 43–44
    Caponata, 48–49
    Mixed Roasted Vegetables, 224–225
    Spiced Potatoes and, 212–213
    and Tomato Sauce, Spaghetti with, 101–102
Eggs, 5, 11, 26–28
    serving of, 31
    Sweet Pepper, Ham, and Onion Omelet,
      209–210

Equipment, 285–286
Espresso Granita, 246
Essential fatty acids, 5
Exercise, 28, 287

Far Eastern diet, 15, 28–29
Fat, 4–8, 18, 33, 287–288
    calories and, 6–7, 8, 35
    hydrogenated, 7–8
    need for, 4–5
    in nutritional analyses, 281
Fat allowance, 33, 34
Fat-removing ladles, 285
Fava beans, cooking times for, 184
Fennel:
    Braised, 206
    Seared Salmon on a Bed of, 120–121
Fettuccine with Shrimp and Spicy Tomato
    Sauce, 109–110
Fiber, 4, 7, 35–36, 21
Figs, Crostini of, 47
Finch, Christi, 103
First courses:
    Beet, Potato, White Bean, Arugula, and Red
      Onion Salad, 78–79
    Broccoli Soup, Cold, 74–75
    "Israeli" Salad, 84
    Mussels, Greek-Style Cold Stuffed, 133–134
    Peppers, Roasted Sweet, Marinated with Ca-
      pers and Anchovies, 208
    Peppers, Roasted Sweet Red, 207
    Potato Watercress Soup, 70–71
    Risotto of Wild Mushrooms, 173–174
    Risotto with Asparagus, 174–175
    Scallion Pancakes, Korean, 193–194
    Scallops, Seviche of, 135–136
    Tomato Soup, Fresh Roasted, 72–73
    Zucchini Soup, Diane's, 73–74
    see also Hors d'oeuvres and appetizers; Pasta
Fish, 14, 26–28, 29, 111–126
    Bluefish, Broiled, 113–114
    Bluefish with Red Pepper Relish, 114–115
    Catfish, Cornmeal-Crusted, on Mixed
      Greens, 116–117
    Poached, and Red Onion Sauce, 157
    Potato Vinaigrette as sauce for, 124–125
    Salmon, Cold Poached, 123–124
    Salmon, Seared, on a Bed of Fennel, 120–121
    Salmon Burgers, Grilled, 121–122
    Salmon Steaks, Teriyaki, 119–120
    serving of, 31
    Sole, Pan-Grilled, 117–118
    Sole Fillets, Oriental, 118–119
    Tuna, Seared, in a Black Pepper Crust,
      125–126

*Index*